Helion & Company Limited
Unit 8 Amherst Business Centre
Budbrooke Road
Warwick
CV34 5WE
England
Tel. 01926 499 619
Email: info@helion.co.uk
Website: www.helion.co.uk
Twitter: @helionbooks
https://helionbooks.wordpress.com/

Cover image: A Saracen APC captured by the LTTE during operation Unceasing Waves 3 in 1999. (LTTE)

Designed and typeset by Mach 3 Solutions (www.mach3solutions.co.uk)
Cover design Paul Hewitt, Battlefield Design (www.battlefield-design.co.uk)

ISBN: 978-1-804510-16-2

British Library Cataloguing-in-Publication Data
A catalogue record for this book is available from the British Library

We always welcome receiving book proposals from prospective authors.

CONTENTS

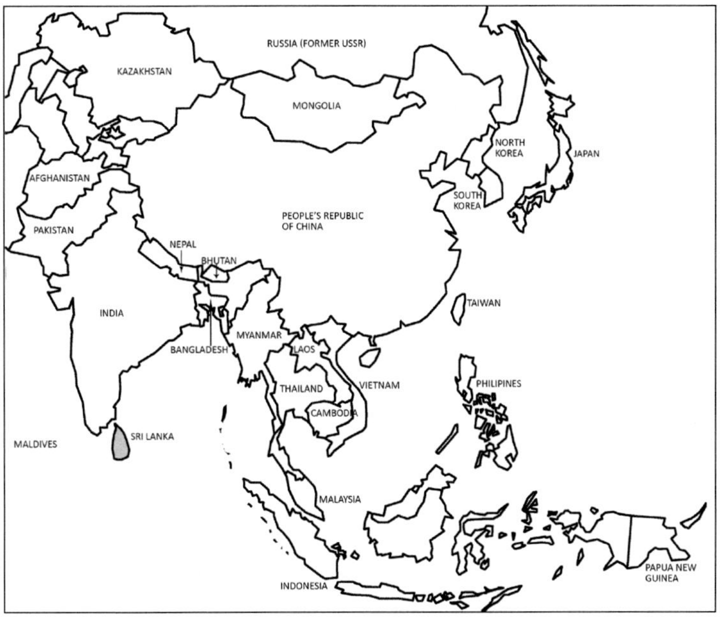

Note: In order to simplify the use of this book, all names, locations and geographic designations are as provided in *The Times World Atlas*, or other traditionally accepted major sources of reference, as of the time of described events.

NOTE

In order to simplify the use of this book, all names, locations and geographic designations are as provided in *The Times World Atlas*, or other traditionally accepted major sources of reference, as of the time of the events described. For reasons of simplicity, genuine designations for Soviet/Russian-made weapons used in this book are mentioned once, and then their ASCC (or 'NATO') codes are used instead.

ABBREVIATIONS AND ACRONYMNS

AB	Air Base
AK	Russian for Automat Kalashnikova; general designation for a class of Soviet-or former East Bloc-manufactured class of assault rifles calibre 7.62mm
AN	Antonov (the design bureau led by Oleg Antonov)
APC	Armoured Personal Carrier
ATGM	Anti-Tank Guided Missile
BAI	Battlefield interdiction
CAS	Close Air Support
CASEVAC	Casualty evacuation
CO	Commanding officer
COIN	Counterinsurgency
CRPF	Central Police Reserve Force
CVF	Citizen Volunteer Force
ENDLF	Eelam National Democratic Liberation Front, group created by the merger of TELO and PLOTE breakaway factions
EPRLF	Eelam People's Revolutionary Liberation Front
EROS	Eelam Revolutionary Organisation
FAC	Fast Attack Craft
FAO	Forward Artillery Observer
FGB	Fast Gun Boat
GPMG	General Purpose Machine Gun, mostly 7.62mm calibre machine-guns
GR	Gajaba Regiment
GW	Gemunu Watch
HMG	Heavy Machine Gun, 12.7 to 14.5mm calibre machine-guns
HU	Helicopter Unit
IAF	Indian Air Force
IAP	International Airport
ICRC	International Committee of the Red Cross
IN	Indian Navy
INAS	Indian Navy Air Squadron
IPC	Inshore Patrol Craft
IPKF	Indian Peacekeeping Force
JVP	Janatha Vimukthi Peramuna (People's Liberation Front)
KIA	Killed in Action
Km	kilometre
LCM	Landing Craft Medium
LKR	Sri Lankan Rupee
LTTE	Liberation Tigers of Tamil Eelam
LZ	Landing Zone
MANPAD(S)	Man-portable air defence system(s) – light surface-to-air missile system that can be carried and deployed in combat by a single soldier.
MIA	Missing in Action (In the Sri Lankan Army context, this meant that the soldiers had been killed, but classified as missing as long their bodies had not been retrieved and formally identified)
MV	Motor Vessel
OBM	Outboard motor
PFLT	People's Front of Liberation Tigers; the LTTE's political party
PLOTE	People's Liberation Organization of Tamil Eelam
POW	Prisoner of War
RAW	Research and Analysis Wing (Indian intelligence agency)
Sqn	Squadron
SLA	Sri Lanka Army
SLAC	Sri Lanka Armoured Corps
SLAF	Sri Lanka Air Force
SLLI	Sri Lanka Light Infantry (Regiment)
SLFP	Sri Lanka Freedom Party
SLN	Sri Lanka Navy
STF	Special Task Force, the Sri Lanka Police dedicated counterinsurgency unit
SVBIED	Suicide Vehicle Borne Improvised Explosive Devices)
UAV	Unmanned Aerial Vehicle
UDT	Underwater Demolition Team
UNP	United National Party, main Sri Lankan political party.
WIA	Wounded in Action

PREFACE

This volume is the fourth of this mini-series and covers the so-called Eelam War III, which lasted between 1995 and 2002. For a series of reasons including the necessity to not overburden an already lengthy manuscript, the focus on the present volume lies on military operations in the Northern Theatre of the War. The war in the East is mentioned but the related operations not described in detail. Suffice to say that this was a 'classical' protracted guerilla warfare, where the insurgents based in camps well hidden in the dense jungles of the area launched countless ambushes and small-scale attacks against the security forces, whilst keeping the local Tamil population under their aegis and frequently targeting Sinhalese and Muslim communities with deadly attacks. From time to time, the Tigers launched large-scale assaults against Army or Special Task Force garrisons. In turn, the Security Forces launched periodic large-scale sweeps, more often than not forcing the insurgents to evacuate their camps but failing to encircle and destroy them. Still, the war in the East was vicious, and merciless, with both sides committing horrendous exactions against civilian populations. This leads us to forewarn the reader again that this volume does not cover in detail either the atrocities or human rights violations which marked the conflict. These are however well covered by easily accessible reports published by NGOs such as Amnesty International. Similarly, the - often complex - political aspects of the war are not explored in any length because these were already synthesized in the first three volumes of this mini-series and are in any case already covered by a wealth of specialized literature. Indeed, one cannot emphasize enough the fact that the Sri Lankan conflict was both politically extremely complex, and vicious.

As with previous issues, this volume aims to provide a balanced narrative of the conflict's military operations. This proved particularly ambitious, as while there is a wealth of publications related to the experiences of the security forces, the same is not true for the Liberation Tigers of Tamil Eelam (LTTE). Indeed, numerous official and semi-official publications covering Sri Lankan armed forces operations during the decades-long war have appeared over time, ranging from senior officers' autobiographies, such as those of Maj. Gen. Kamal Gunaratne and Maj. Gen. Sarath Munasinghe, to institutional semi-official histories from the Sri Lanka Army (SLA) and Sri Lanka Air Force (SLAF). Local historians and journalists, such as Channa Wickremesekera, L.M.H. Mendis, and C.A. Chandraprema, have also published extensive works. Post-war studies, including the 2011 Ministry of Defence report and JSK Colombage's comprehensive study on naval warfare, have further contributed valuable data. Conversely, there are relatively few English-language publications originating from the LTTE. However, the autobiographies of Adèle-Anne Balasingham and Thamizini offer insider perspectives on the inner workings of the Tamil Tigers. The movement was significantly more prolific in Tamil and published numerous books on specific operations, military units, and commanders. Fortunately, several online articles in English provide excerpts from these works or draw exclusively on this corpus. Additionally, archives of wartime LTTE communications, accessible via websites such as TamilNet, have proved immensely helpful in reconstructing the chronology of specific operations.

Equally crucial were a series of interviews conducted with researcher and consultant Kagusthan Ariaratnam between 2019 and 2020, during which he shared his experience as a former LTTE Imran Pandian Padai Ani soldier, later an officer, and subsequently an intelligence officer within the LTTE's military intelligence wing. The author also expresses gratitude to 'Johnny', a former LTTE infantryman and instructor, who generously provided detailed information on the movement's infantry organization, training, and tactics during the latter stages of the war. Altogether, this body of work has made it possible to achieve at least a reasonable coverage of the 'other side of the hill'.

The author would also like to thank Albert Grandolini for allowing the use of his collection of pictures, Tom Cooper, for all support provided with the time, David Bocquelet, for his meticulous reconstruction of the equally elusive SLN ships and Sea Tiger crafts and to Duncan Rogers and all of the Helion and Company team for their proof checking and editing of this manuscript.

INTRODUCTION

The so-called Eelam War II, which lasted from 1990 to 1994, saw the Sri Lankan Armed Forces and the Liberation Tigers of Tamil Eelam (LTTE) fight each other to a standstill, with both sides winning major victories and suffering crushing defeats. During this period, the war evolved into a semi-conventional conflict, at least in the North, while it remained an insurgency in the East. By the end of 1994, the LTTE had managed to establish a makeshift navy, the Sea Tigers, and had gradually honed its ground units into a highly capable professional force, capable of executing sophisticated operations. However, the movement—comprising roughly 10,000 full-time fighters—suffered extensive losses and struggled to expand its forces due to the limited demographic pool available for recruitment. Furthermore, it was severely shaken by the Mathaya affair—a large-scale infiltration of the LTTE by India's Research & Analysis Wing (RAW)—which forced the group to restructure its entire command apparatus.

Government forces, particularly the Sri Lanka Army (SLA), managed to hold their ground despite facing an array of almost intractable challenges. Chief among these was the difficulty of simultaneously conducting a brutal counterinsurgency campaign in the East while launching operations against enemy strongholds in the North. As a direct consequence, the SLA could not sustain more than one major offensive at a time, while a large-scale expansion of the military was unfeasible due to inadequate funding and high attrition rates, driven by both combat casualties and endemic desertion.

After four years of war, the strategic situation remained largely unchanged from when it began, with most of Northern Sri Lanka still under LTTE control. However, government forces maintained footholds in the Jaffna Peninsula (the Palali complex, the chain of islands facing the peninsula, and Elephant Pass), as well as in the Vanni (Pooneryn and Mullaitivu). In the East, the LTTE continued

A pro-LTTE demonstration. The movement could rely on widespread support among the Sri Lankan Tamil communities around the world, and these were crucial for providing the Tigers with the funds they needed to sustain their war effort. (Albert Grandolini Collection)

Chandrika Kamaratunga, seen here with Secretary of State Colin Powell in 2005, was the heir of a powerful political family, with both her father and mother having been Prime Ministers, and was herself President of Sri Lanka between 1994 and 2005. (US government)

to wage a deadly guerrilla campaign that tied down large numbers of security forces. Nevertheless, the government gradually gained the upper hand—if only because the insurgents had transferred a significant number of local militants to support their conventional operations in the North.

By mid-1994, war weariness had become widespread among the Sri Lankan population, leading to the election of Chandrika Kumaratunga as President on 12 November 1994. She had campaigned on a political platform advocating peace through negotiations. Simultaneously, the People's Alliance—a coalition of several left-wing political parties, including her own Sri Lanka Freedom Party—secured a majority in Parliament. As a result, both sides entered negotiations, culminating in a ceasefire formally concluded on 5 January 1995, which took effect three days later. However, the ceasefire was short-lived, as both sides pursued irreconcilable agendas. As Chandrika Kumaratunga later explained:

> I wanted to end the war as fast as possible. My point was that, even if Prabhakaran was not willing to accept anything other than separate state - which we were not willing to give at all - by constantly knocking at their doors we would convince increasing number of Tamil people of our bona fide intentions, that we really wanted to do something for them. Thy didn't want awards but only their rights, not a separate state. Once they knew that we were willing to give them their rights and this man was not willing, then they would move away from him.[1]

During the peace talks, Colombo gradually made several major concessions to the LTTE, including lifting the economic embargo that had isolated LTTE-held areas and partially easing fishing restrictions in those regions. However, the government firmly rejected key LTTE demands, which included dismantling the Pooneryn army and navy base and granting freedom of movement to LTTE militants in the East. By mid-March 1995, the Tigers issued a veiled ultimatum, and on 18 April, the die was cast. A letter from the LTTE leader to the President declared: "We are left with no choice other than to take a painful decision to discontinue our participation in the negotiating process and withdraw from the cessation of hostilities."[2]

The war was on again, and as subsequent events were to show, the LTTE had got the time it needed to reorganise and reinforce itself and plan for its next operations.

April disasters

The first LTTE attack occurred during the night of 18–19 April 1995. At least four Sea Black Tigers—two women from the Angaiyarkanni unit and two men from the Sulojan unit, the two Sea Tigers Underwater Demolition Teams—successfully infiltrated the Trincomalee Naval Base. Their approach was significantly aided by the Sri Lanka Navy's (SLN) relaxation of security measures during the ceasefire. As a result, the Navy had ceased its practice of randomly dropping grenades and gelignite sticks into the waters surrounding its moored ships. Taking advantage of this lapse in security, the divers reached the pier undetected, where Shanghai-class Fast Gun Boats (FGB) *Ranasaru*, *Ranaviru*, *Sooraya*, and *Jagatha* were moored. They then planted a series of four containers, each loaded with 100 kg of C-4 explosives, on the seabed beneath the vessels. The resulting colossal detonations instantly sank *Ranasaru* and *Sooraya*, while *Ranaviru* and *Jagatha* sustained light damage. The attack killed 11 sailors and wounded another 21. The four Sea Black Tigers also perished in the explosion, and their bodies were later recovered.[3]

It was not long before a second—and even worse—disaster struck the Sri Lankan Armed Forces. On 28 April, CR-835, one of the five HS.748 aircraft operated by the No. 201 Heavy Transport Squadron, crashed shortly after takeoff from Palali Air Base, killing all 48 crew members and passengers aboard—most of them severely wounded soldiers being transported to Colombo for treatment. Also among the casualties was Wing Commander Roger Weerasinghe, who had just completed an inspection tour of the air base. While the aircraft crashed within the Palali complex's defensive perimeter, the cause of the accident was not immediately determined. That night, another HS.748 landed at Palali, loaded the bodies, and departed again without incident. At dawn on 29

Velupillai Prabhakaran, posing with Santha (alias of Vijayathevi Sivasubramaniam), one of the four Sea Black Tigers killed in the 19 April 1995 Trincomalee attack. Taking a picture of Black Tigers posing with the LTTE leader before their last mission was a standard practise – at least for operations that would be claimed by the movement. (LTTE)

SLNS *Ranasaru,* seen here capsized after the 19 April 1994 attack by the Sea Tigers combat divers. Whilst utterly obsolete by 1995, this class of FGB proved invaluable during the war, foremost because of their heavy armament. (Collection Adrien Fontanellaz)

April, CR-834, another HS.748, took off from Ratmalana Air Base carrying 52 people—mostly soldiers returning from leave, along with three members of the Sri Lanka Air Force (SLAF) Board of Inquiry, including its president, Wing Commander Shirantha Gunatilake, who had been tasked with investigating the crash of CR-835. This time, however, witnesses on the ground saw the transport aircraft struck by a surface-to-air missile as it approached Palali Air Base. The aircraft crashed outside the Sri Lanka Army (SLA) defensive perimeter, killing everyone on board. In response, the SLAF was forced to suspend its air bridge to Palali. With nearly all supplies for the garrisons in the Jaffna Peninsula now dependent on shipments by sea, troops soon began to experience shortages, including a lack of fresh vegetables.

Roughly two weeks later, on 17 May, 9 Brigade—comprising the 6th and 8th Sri Lanka Light Infantry (SLLI) and the 3rd Gajaba Regiment (GR)—launched an operation heavily supported by tanks, engineers, and at least two airstrikes conducted by pairs of F-7s from the No. 5 Jet Squadron, each carrying a pair of 500 lb bombs. Additional fire support was provided by several Sri Lanka Navy (SLN) Fast Gun Boats (FGBs) and Fast Attack Craft (FACs). The brigade advanced from the defensive perimeter towards the Thondamannar Lagoon, capturing a 10-square-kilometer area to secure the airbase's landing approaches. The LTTE did not offer significant resistance beyond heavy mortar shelling, and only 25 soldiers were wounded during the two-day operation, aptly codenamed "Safe Passage." This success enabled the resumption of the air bridge on 25 May.[4]

A Sri Lankan Army soldier in Palali, Jaffna, 1995. He is carrying a Type 56 LMG, the Chinese version of the Soviet designed RPD. (SLA)

LTTE's Special Commander Balraj whilst he was leading the operation Tiger Leap in Jaffna on 14 July 1995 (LTTE)

Tigers' victories... and defeat

The LTTE wasted no time in launching a series of offensives across Northern and Eastern Sri Lanka. In the East, it had used the ceasefire to infiltrate an estimated 1,000 fighters from the North into the districts of Trincomalee, Ampara, and Batticaloa. As early as 21 April, the insurgents launched a large-scale attack against an army camp at Kattumurippukulam in the Batticaloa district, overrunning it before withdrawing. 45 soldiers from the 2nd (Volunteer) Sri Lanka Light Infantry (SLLI) and the 1st Commando Regiment were killed, while another 80 were reported Missing in Action (MIA). On 8 May, 19 Special Task Force (STF) policemen were killed when their patrol was ambushed in Ampara district. Later, on 23 May, 27 soldiers from the 7th Vijayabahu Infantry Regiment (VIR) were killed in another ambush at Panichchankeni in Batticaloa district. The Tigers continued launching hit-and-run attacks from their well-hidden jungle and coastal camps, striking at Sinhalese villages, particularly in Trincomalee district. In response, government forces withdrew from their most exposed positions before launching repeated cordon-and-search operations and large-scale sweeps against LTTE strongholds. While these offensives often succeeded in capturing insurgent camps, the LTTE fighters themselves typically escaped with minimal casualties. Despite increasing its pressure in the East, the LTTE was unable to establish 'liberated' areas comparable to those in the North. At most, it could tie down large numbers of government troops while maintaining control over the local Tamil population—extracting both funds and manpower to sustain its forces in the East and reinforce the Northern Theatre.[5]

Something much more ambitious was to take place in the North. The LTTE gathered around 1,000 fighters from the Sea Tigers, the Jaffna regional command and the Charles Anthony Padai Ani, in order to launch an all-out assault against the Island of Mandaithivu, facing Jaffna itself. The operation was led by Soosai, head of the Sea Tigers, and Special Commander Sornam, head of the Jaffna regional command. Both Mandaitivu and Kayts Islands were held by a single Brigade Headquarters, located in Velanai on Kayts, under Brigadier Sarath Fonseka. The Brigade controlled the 10th (V) GW, which was based in Mandaitivu, and the 6th and 10th GR both deployed on Kayts Island. The latter unit had already found itself on the receiving end of a deadly attack on 28 April, which had killed 27 soldiers.

The Tigers launched their onslaught at 2 AM on 28 June, when three distinct groups of fighters disembarked from dozens of boats and infiltrated the positions of the 10th (Volunteer) Gemunu Watch (GW). The battalion was ill-prepared to face the attack, as it was a newly raised volunteer unit composed of inexperienced soldiers, and to make matters worse, nearly half of its personnel were on leave. Unsurprisingly, the insurgents broke through the battalion's defences, surrounded its headquarters, and overran it within a few hours. However, several Sri Lankan subunits continued to hold their positions, putting up determined resistance. Meanwhile, the 6th Gajaba Regiment (GR) was ordered to launch a rescue operation. The battalion advanced on foot, as the access roads were expected to be mined at the onset of the operation, making them impassable for vehicles. Upon crossing the causeway linking the two islands, the unit engaged in a fierce firefight with an LTTE blocking force, which had been deployed precisely to counter such an intervention. At dawn, the bulk of the insurgents withdrew, taking with them a significant cache of weapons, including two 12.7mm heavy machine guns (HMGs), several mortars, and 150,000 rounds of ammunition. By mid-afternoon, the 6th GR had cleared the entire island. However, the 10th (V) GW had been decimated, suffering the loss of four officers, including its commanding officer, Captain Keerthi Dharmawardene, along with 86 soldiers killed in action (KIA) and at least 100 others wounded.[6]

On 9 July, the Sri Lanka Army (SLA) initiated Operation Leap Forward, a two-pronged offensive launched from Palali with the intent of drawing the insurgents into a head-on battle and inflicting maximum casualties. To achieve this, the Army mobilised 11 infantry battalions, supported by the largest concentration of armour assembled so far in the war. This included two squadrons of T-55s and one squadron each of BMPs, T-85s, and T-86s, totalling 50 armoured vehicles contributed by the 3rd, 4th, and 5th Sri Lanka Armoured Corps (SLAC). The first column advanced towards Alaveddy and Sandipilay, while the second moved along the coast towards Vaddukoddai, penetrating deep into LTTE-held territory. However, the insurgents did not mount a determined resistance beyond frequent mortar harassment and delaying actions, allowing the Army to achieve its objectives within four days. On 14 July at 01:30 AM, the LTTE launched a massive counterattack, codenamed Operation Tiger Leap. Hundreds of its fighters executed a sudden onslaught, exploiting the undefended gap between the two SLA columns to employ their signature "Battle of Infiltration" tactics. Facing heavy casualties, both SLA columns were forced to withdraw towards the Palali complex. 64 soldiers and five officers were killed during Leap Forward, while another officer and 15 soldiers were reported missing in action. The Sri Lanka Air Force (SLAF), whose F-7s, SM.260s, and Pucarás flew a total of 43 airstrike sorties in support of the operation, lost one Pucará, which was shot down by a surface-to-air missile (SAM). While the Army claimed to have killed a staggering 665 insurgents, Leap Forward was ultimately acknowledged as a failure—notably due to poor coordination between armour and infantry, inadequate inter-battalion communication, and a lack of effective flank protection. For its part, the LTTE assessed that the true goal of the operation was not just to inflict casualties but also to probe their defences and mislead them regarding future SLA axes of advance.[7]

The LTTE did not have much time to celebrate the success of its counterattack. Its leadership was already preparing a large-scale operation of its own, targeting the Manal Aru region (known as Welioya to the Sinhalese). This area was strategically crucial, as it connected the North and the East, and controlling it would have allowed the Tigers to move forces freely between the two theatres. The area was under the responsibility of SLA 6 Brigade, commanded by Brigadier Janaka Perera, with its headquarters in Parakarampura. The brigade oversaw a network of bases and fortified camps, many of which were positioned to protect local Sinhalese settlements. The Tigers planned to strike five of these camps, including the Brigade HQ, while concentrating their main effort on the Jayasinhapura and Kokkuthudwai camps, both held by the 4th Gemunu Watch (GW). The Jayasinhapura camp was to be taken by a ground assault, while Kokkuthudwai would be attacked via an amphibious operation. The bulk of the ground assault force was to be contributed by the Chiruthaigal (Leopard) Padai Ani, which had by then evolved into an elite unit, supported by several Kutti Sri Padai Ani mortar batteries. Several Black Tiger teams were also assigned to the operation, including one tasked with attacking 6 Brigade HQ and another targeting an artillery half-battery located in the Mullaitivu camp, which was held by 25 Brigade.

However, Army Military Intelligence was tipped off about the forthcoming onslaught on the evening of 28 July. In response, garrisons in Welioya, along with the Sri Lanka Navy (SLN) and Sri Lanka Air Force (SLAF), were placed on high alert, and ambush parties were deployed outside the camp perimeters. Artillery units within range were also placed on full readiness, prepared to engage the enemy using pre-registered fire coordinates. Unsurprisingly, the LTTE attack, which began at 2:00 AM on 29 July, turned into a disaster. Two Black Tiger teams, each consisting of three operatives, were neutralised before reaching their targets, while the militants assaulting the 4th Gemunu Watch (GW) positions were decimated by withering defensive fire. As the attack commenced, the defenders swiftly withdrew to their second line of defence, luring the militants into open fields of fire. Even worse, the Sea Tiger flotilla sailing towards Kokkuthudwai was intercepted by SLN Fast Attack Craft (FACs), resulting in the loss of several LTTE boats. At dawn, SLAF aircraft conducted multiple airstrikes, further crippling the insurgents. By mid-morning, the battle had ended. The military suffered only two soldiers killed in action (KIA) and one wounded in action (WIA), while claiming to have counted the bodies of 182 LTTE militants. Additionally, they captured 75 assault rifles, 12 light machine guns (LMGs), six mortars, and five RPG launchers. The Navy reported sinking 10 enemy boats, including four waterjets that had been captured by the insurgents in Pooneryn in 1993.[8] This was indeed a heavy defeat for the Tigers, as recalled by Thamizhimi, a cadre of the movement's Women Political Wing:

> The attack did not go through as the Movement had hoped. On the contrary, it brought massive losses to us. The Leopard Brigade, the Leader's dream brigade, had met with destruction. More than 200 male and female combatants lost their lives, and their shattered bodies were delivered by the Sri Lankan government to the Tigers, through the ICRC.[9]

The war for peace gamble

Whilst the LTTE leadership's resumption of the war demonstrated its confidence in achieving its ultimate goal—an independent state—through military means, the administration of Chandrika Kumaratunga initially found itself wrong-footed. However, this setback did not last. Colombo's war strategy, dubbed 'war for peace', aimed to weaken the LTTE militarily until the group could be coerced into negotiating on acceptable terms. At the operational level, the Sri Lankan government pursued this objective by focusing its efforts on the Northern theatre, making the crucial decision to withdraw several units from the Eastern Province. This shift resulted in only a bare minimum force being left in the East—just enough to maintain nominal control over the region. Consequently, this opened the way for the Tigers to further expand their influence across the three Eastern districts. Meanwhile, the government invested vast sums of money to enhance the firepower of the armed forces, strengthening their capability to sustain the conflict.

Both the government and the military opted to concentrate virtually all available assets to launch an unprecedented offensive aimed at recapturing the entire Jaffna Peninsula. This operation was intended to deliver an almost unbearable blow to the LTTE. Jaffna was not only the birthplace of Tamil separatism and the LTTE's de facto capital, making it a crucial symbolic stronghold, but it also housed a significant portion of the organisation's infrastructure. The peninsula's population was a key source of tax revenue and recruitment, while its proximity to southern India was instrumental in facilitating large-scale smuggling operations. At the very least, the loss of Jaffna and the peninsula was expected to shatter the morale of LTTE militants and serve as a powerful demonstration of the government's strength. This, in turn, was seen as a step towards forcing the Tigers into negotiations, aligning with Colombo's overall objective of compelling the LTTE to the bargaining table.[10]

1
TIGERS AND LIONS

Once the war resumed, it became evident that the LTTE had used the ceasefire effectively to strengthen its military branches. Despite suffering heavy losses in the following years—the movement later acknowledged the loss of a staggering 11,107 killed in action (KIA) between 1995 and 2002—it still managed to expand its combat strength from approximately 10,000 fighters in 1994 to around 15,000 between 1998 and 2000. This expansion, however, was only possible by drawing even more heavily from the local Tamil population, which was relatively small. Unsurprisingly, forced recruitment became endemic, and households were expected to contribute at least one fighter to the struggle. During this period, the LTTE also became notorious for its use of underage fighters. Despite this, the LTTE maintained its emphasis on professionalism, ensuring that new recruits underwent a six-month-long basic and specialised training programme, usually conducted in batches of around 150 men or women in various training camps. Alongside its regular forces, the LTTE continued to deploy part-time militias, who received only two weeks of basic training before being assigned to support roles, such as transport, fortification building, or guarding quieter areas, thereby allowing frontline combat troops to focus on active engagements. Following an intensive recruitment drive in 1997–1998, the total number of these militia forces reached approximately 15,000.

The contribution of the female population increased significantly, as evidenced by the expansion of the LTTE's Women's Military Wing. During Eelam War III, this wing gave rise to three major infantry units. The 2nd Lt. Malathi Padai Ani[1]came into being at the end of 1995. It was followed mid-1996 by another similar outfit, the Maj. Sothiya Padai Ani[2]. The third such unit, the Capt. Anparasi Padai Ani[3], followed between 1996 and 1997, and its combatants were exclusively drawn from the three Eastern districts. These units were led by three female Special Commanders—Vithusha, Thurka, and Mathana, respectively. Like their male counterparts, these formations were not tactical units but operated similarly to the British Army or Sri Lanka Army (SLA) regimental system. However, instead of battalions, they controlled a variable number of autonomous infantry companies, which could be attached to tactical and operational formations or Task Forces as required. The Chiruthaigal (Leopard) Padai Ani also evolved over time, transitioning from a support force into a commando unit, with its soldiers primarily drawn from orphanages. This unit included both male and female companies. These new infantry units reinforced those originally raised during Eelam War II—namely, the Charles Anthony, Imran-Pandian, and Jeyanthan Padai Ani—which also saw their strength increase significantly during the conflict. As before, the LTTE could also rely on infantry companies that were organically integrated into its five regional commands: Jaffna, Vanni, Mannar, Trincomalee, and Batticaloa.

The LTTE also reorganised its infantry companies during Eelam War III, reducing their size while increasing their firepower. The section was downsized from 12 combatants to nine, divided into three teams of three fighters, armed with AKM, Type 56, or Type 81 assault rifles, along with one RPD light machine gun (LMG) and one RPG-7. Three sections formed a platoon, which was led by a command and support team consisting of two or three combatants. This team not only carried a PKM general-purpose machine gun (GPMG) but was also trained as forward artillery observers, capable of calling for and guiding indirect fire support. In turn, a company comprised a command element and three infantry platoons, for a total of approximately 100 fighters. Despite the reduction in manpower, these restructured companies maintained roughly the same number of support weapons as the previous 150-strong formations. With this reform, LTTE infantry companies became almost identical in structure to their SLA counterparts.

The LTTE raised two dedicated fire-support outfits between 1994 and 1996. A specialized mortar unit, the Kutti Sri Padai Ani[4], operated an increasing number of captured or imported mortars of 81, 82 and 120mm calibre. By late 1996, the LTTE had acquired at least six Chinese-made Type 86 120mm mortars, captured from the Sri Lanka Army (SLA), along with several dozen 81mm and 82mm mortars, which were organised into batteries of four tubes. It is also certain that the Kutti Sri Padai received heavy mortars that were directly acquired and smuggled into the country by the LTTE, although their exact quantities and types remain unknown. This unit functioned as a flexible artillery pool, from which batteries—manned by either female or male crews—could be deployed to specific areas or operations as needed. By 1998, its significance had grown to the extent that the majority of SLA casualties were caused by mortar fire. A dedicated artillery unit, the Col. Kittu Padai Ani[5] was raised in the aftermath of the seizure in July 1996 in Mullaitivu of two Type 83 122mm guns as well as single Type 56 85mm divisional gun captured latter during the same year in the Batticaloa district. The Kittu Padai Ani expanded significantly in 2000 with the induction of two Type 83 and three Type 66 152mm artillery pieces, all captured at Elephant Pass. Furthermore, it remains uncertain whether the unit acquired additional artillery guns that were directly smuggled into the island by the LTTE.[6]

Other specialised support units emerged around 1995. The Victor Padai Ani was responsible for overseeing the movement's various anti-tank teams. These teams operated in sections of six to eight fighters, armed with RPG-7s and anti-tank mines, and were attached to infantry formations whenever enemy armour was expected. In addition to its anti-tank teams, the Victor Padai Ani operated several 106mm M40A1 and 73mm SPG-9 recoilless rifles, as well as a small number of armoured vehicles captured from the Sri Lanka Army, including a single T-55 tank. The unit also reportedly operated a very limited number of anti-tank guided missiles (ATGMs). On 24 September 1999, one such system was allegedly used to destroy a Type 63 armoured personnel carrier (APC) in Paranthan. Meanwhile, the Sri Lanka Navy (SLN) reported that several Fast Attack Craft (FACs) had been sunk by unspecified long-range weapons fired from the shore. While this could have referred to the T-55 tank known to have been employed by the Victor Padai Ani for such purposes, it may also suggest the use of additional ATGMs.

Similarly, the Mayuran and the Ponamman Padai Ani were specialised in sniping and mine warfare, respectively. Mine warfare, in particular, was a crucial component of the LTTE's tactical portfolio, and the movement's sappers gained a reputation for being extremely meticulous and inventive in their approach. Almost every piece of cover in a field of fire was either mined or booby-trapped, while their mine-laying patterns were invariably tight and carefully executed.[7] The Capt. Miller Unit was composed of the infamous Black Tigers—highly trained commandos dedicated to one-way missions against critical targets.[8]

Table 1: Known LTTE Ground combat formations or commands active during Eelam War III

Jaffna regional command	
Vanni regional command	
Mannar regional command	
Trincomalee regional command	
Batticaloa regional command	Regional command covers the Ampara and Batticaloa districts. Because of its isolation and thus autonomy, it was known as an 'LTTE within the LTTE'. Led by Karuna Amman.
Charles Anthony Padai Ani	Raised 1991. Infantry formation, at least 1,500 men.
Imran Pandian Padai Ani	Raised 1992. Infantry formation.
Jeyanthan Padai Ani	Raised 1993. Infantry formation, at least 1,500 men recruited in the Eastern districts.
2nd Lt. Malathi Padai Ani	Exclusively female infantry unit. Raised at the end of 1995 in the aftermath of Operation Riviresa. CO Special commander Vithusha.
Maj. Sothiya Padai Ani	Raised in 1996. Female infantry unit. CO Special Commander Thurka.
Capt. Anparasi Padai Ani	Raised in 1996 or 1997. Female fighters, recruited in the Eastern districts.
Chiruthaigal (Leopard) Padai Ani	Dubbed the 'Baby Brigade' by the SLA. Several male and female companies, drawn partly from the LTTE-run orphanages. At first dedicated to support functions but gradually evolved into a commando force.
Lt. Col. Kutti Sri Padai Ani	The LTTE dedicated mortar unit, pooling all the available mortars of 81, 82 and 120mm calibre, usually deployed in batteries of four.
Col. Kittu Padai Ani	The LTTE dedicated artillery unit, operating all the available guns and howitzers. Built up from 1996 onward.
Victor Padai Ani	Specialized in anti-tank warfare and the use of RPG's, SPG-9 recoilless rifles and AT mines. Also operated the armoured vehicles captured by the movement.
Ponamman Padai Ani	Specialized in mine warfare.
Mayuran sniper unit	Dedicated sniper unit, 150 men strong in 1993.
Capt. Miller unit	Commando force exclusively composed of Black Tigers, that is highly trained militants who have volunteered for one-way missions. Often used for launching suicidal assaults against high value targets such as headquarters or artillery positions.

Teenage combatants of the LTTE during the mid-90's, wearing the typical LTTE tiger-striped camouflaged uniform. Considering their age, they are most probably part of the Chiruthaigal Padai Ani, which was decimated in the Manal Aru area in October 1995. (Albert Grandolini Collection)

Top: A 120mm mortar of the Kutti Sri Padai Ani preparing to fire. (LTTE)

Centre: Special Commander Balraj with Thurka, the CO of the Maj. Sothiya Padai Ani and Vithusha (right), the CO of 2nd Lt. Malathi Padai Ani. (LTTE)

Bottom: Fighters of the Victor Padai Ani, also known as the 'RPG Division' manning a SPG-9 recoiless gun – the LTTE's most potent anti-tank weapon during Eelam War III. (LTTE)

Top: A female demining team of the Ponamman Padai Ani securing a road. The LTTE also excelled in laying extremely deadly and well-designated minefields. (LTTE)

Centre: The Kittu Padai Ani in action, firing the two Type 83 guns of 122mm calibre captured in Mulaitivu in July 1996. (LTTE)

Bottom: A fighter of the Charles Anthony Padai Ani firing his Type 56 assault rifle from a defensive position in the Vanni. (LTTE)

Tiger fangs

By the mid-1990s, the LTTE had evolved into a well-honed, battle-experienced light infantry force that compensated for its lack of numbers and firepower with an almost fanatical emphasis on training and indoctrination, continuous tactical refinement, thorough planning, and intelligence gathering. As before, the Tigers excelled in coordinating their forces, supported by a dense and well-equipped communication infrastructure. Great care was taken to provide troops with ample radio and walkie-talkies, down to the platoon and even section level.

Before launching an offensive, the Tigers spent weeks infiltrating specially trained operatives, known as Spy Tigers, behind enemy lines to gather detailed intelligence. They meticulously mapped enemy positions, including those in rear areas, and identified safe access routes through minefields. Each operation was planned with the precision of a modern business project, with LTTE leadership assigning an experienced Special Commander to lead the mission. This commander would be allocated a variable number of subunits, drawn from the movement's main formations, along with a designated supply of ammunition, to be used for both training and execution. Once the necessary intelligence had been gathered, the Tigers carefully rehearsed their operations on sand tables, followed by full-scale exercises integrating infantry, support, and specialised units before launching the actual attack. In this regard, it is telling that one of Special Commander Balraj's mottos was "10 bullets in training, one in battle."

To illustrate with a hypothetical example, a Special Commander tasked with seizing a small army base might be assigned two companies from the Charles Anthony Padai Ani, another three from the 2nd Lt. Malathy Padai Ani, and several mortar batteries from the Kutti Sri Padai Ani. If necessary, a Black Tiger team from the Capt. Miller Unit could be deployed, while anti-tank sections from the Victor Padai Ani might be allocated if enemy armoured units were present nearby. If the target was near the sea, Sea Tiger elements could conduct a simultaneous amphibious assault.

It took years and immense casualties for the LTTE to perfect these sophisticated assault tactics against fortified enemy positions. However, these tactics matured with the successful capture of the Pooneryn base in 1993. Despite often being described by their foes as 'human wave attacks', the LTTE's assault doctrine was anything but. Instead, it closely resembled the German *Stosstruppen* infiltration tactics of World War I. The LTTE leadership always recognised that its limited recruitment pool meant it could not afford to waste manpower. As a result, its tactics were designed to minimise its own casualties. This philosophy also explains why LTTE training emphasised night operations, with large-scale assaults almost invariably conducted during moonless nights. The movement also avoided concentrating its forces within range of enemy support weapons whenever possible. Even the deployment of Black Tigers in suicide operations was seen as a means to reduce broader losses, ensuring that fewer fighters would be sacrificed than if conventional tactics were used.

Defensive warfare ... the LTTE way

On the operational level, the Tigers remained firm adherents of what they called the 'Battle of Infiltration', a tactic that involved allowing the enemy to advance, only to encircle them and launch a series of flank attacks. On the tactical level, this approach meant that the LTTE rarely attempted to hold positions at all costs. Instead, they focused on inflicting maximum casualties on the advancing enemy before withdrawing and repeating the process. By 1996, the standard LTTE defensive tactic—once the enemy's main axis of advance had been identified—was to construct well-camouflaged bunkers and firing positions at ground level, often reinforced with logs and sandbags and connected by narrow, deep, zigzag-patterned shallow trenches positioned in front of open fields of fire. At times, in imitation of SLA defensive practices, these positions were further reinforced with earthen or sand berms. The defences typically consisted of three successive lines, with the bulk of the militants stationed in the second and third lines, ready to reinforce any part of the first line that came under heavy pressure. The approaches and available cover were densely mined and rigged with booby traps and improvised explosive devices (IEDs) to disrupt enemy movement. The LTTE fighters typically waited for the enemy to advance within 150 to 200 metres of their firing positions. At such close quarters, the SLA was often reluctant to call in artillery or air support, fearing friendly fire. In contrast, LTTE mortar crews and forward artillery observers (FAOs) had no such restrictions, allowing them to maintain accurate and effective fire support throughout the engagement.[9] The Tigers also constantly patrolled the areas in front of their entrenchments, or even launched spoiling pre-emptive attacks to confuse the enemy planning, as recalled by a female fighter:

> At night, we also needed to send our small teams beyond our vanguard defence to position themselves beside the army defence and spy on the army's nocturnal movements. If we saw the army edging forward at night, we needed to launch a counter strike immediately. Our vanguard defence had to be ready in an instant to attack and quash their progress.[10]

Altogether, these defensive systems allowed the LTTE to slow down and wear down large SLA formations while engaging only a minimal number of militants and limiting their own casualties as much as possible. As soon as the army was on the verge of overwhelming or outflanking a position, the defenders simply withdrew, ready to repeat the process elsewhere. These tactics proved highly effective, turning the Vanni into a brutal war of attrition from the SLA's perspective. As veteran SLA officer Kamal Gunaratna later described, the Tiger defences posed immense challenges to government forces, making each advance a grinding and costly endeavour:

> They would study the ground configuration and would employ the bare minimum needed to cause maximum damage to us or complete a given task. They adhered to basics in strategies and tactics of fieldcraft, gaining ground advantage. [...] Their defensive positions were small but well-constructed and strong, to withstand our artillery and mortar attacks. They were also well camouflaged, blending in with the terrain and making it difficult for us to identify at a distance. Even when we did, it was difficult for us to target them due to its low height. [...] They also used these defensive positions to observe our movements and identify effective fields of fire. Sometimes, in order to counter the advance movement of a battalion they used only about 10 people. In the small group, they always employed 2 people as "Forward Observation Officers" who were trained in acquiring targets, directing and correcting artillery and mortar fire at the correct time, to the correct place. [...] They employed the other 7 or 8 people with machine guns, to cover the open areas we had to cross during our advance. They waited patiently until we approached their effective range of fire, to spray us with bullets in this open space, in which we were sitting ducks. [...] When our troops

> tried to avoid the open areas and use whatever limited cover to advance, they were decimated by landmines, IEDs and booby traps which had been cleverly laid out. All the while, they would cover the area with artillery and mortar fire, which caused further damage to us. This entire exercise was carried out by about ten terrorists, whilst we were using an entire battalion.[11]

Thus, in a nutshell, Eelam War III saw the LTTE ground forces continue to evolve into an increasingly potent semi-conventional army, expanding both their manpower and firepower. However, what made them truly lethal was not just their strength in numbers or weaponry, but the combination of unwavering commitment and a relentless emphasis on professionalism, training, planning, reconnaissance, coordination, discipline, and systematic after-action reviews to continuously refine their tactics.

Of guns and armour

The changing nature of the war, shifting from counterinsurgency to a semi-conventional conflict, at least in the North, compelled the Sri Lanka Army (SLA) to increase its firepower as much as possible throughout the 1990s. However, due to chronic funding shortages and the reluctance of Western countries to supply adequate weaponry, Colombo continued to rely on suppliers that could provide heavy equipment at affordable costs and without political conditions. Chief among these were the People's Republic of China, Israel, and several former Warsaw Pact countries.

The artillery branch, in particular, underwent massive expansion between 1990 and 2002, not only growing in size but also replacing its inventory of outdated guns, such as the 25-pounders, with far more powerful weaponry. Throughout the 1990s, China remained the most significant supplier of artillery to Sri Lanka. The Sri Lanka Artillery received 12 Type 59-I 130mm guns from China in 1991 and, from 1995 onwards, acquired at least 60 Type 66 152mm and Type 83 122mm guns, significantly enhancing its firepower.[12] In the aftermath of the Elephant Pass disaster in 2000, the Army rushed to reinforce its artillery by an order of magnitude by adopting MRLS. Six KRL-122 were ordered from Pakistan, together with 24 RM-70 in Czechia (16) and Slovakia (8). These were pressed into service in the 14th Rocket Regiment of Sri Lanka Artillery which was raised on 13 September 2001.

Sri Lanka Artillery regiments were organised into multiple batteries, each consisting of six guns. However, the SLA rarely employed large-scale artillery concentrations; instead, batteries typically operated individually or in pairs, providing fire support for specific units or operations. To protect against LTTE commando raids, artillery units were usually positioned within fortified firebases. On some occasions, half-batteries—comprising two or three guns—were deployed to support specific units, as seen in the Mullaitivu battle in 1996. The artillery branch continued to rely on Forward Artillery Observers (FAOs)—or Forward Observation Officers (FOOs) in SLA terminology—as well as pre-planned fire missions based on grid coordinates, a practice that had been in place since Operation Liberation in 1988.[13]

Table 2 Sri Lanka Artillery

Unit	Activation	Notes
4th Field Regiment of Sri Lanka Artillery	26 April 1963	Type 56 85mm divisional gun, reequipped with Type 59 130mm and Type 83 122mm guns during Eelam War III.
5th Volunteer Regiment of Sri Lanka Artillery	1980	N/A, might have been used as infantry unit, if at all.
6th Field Regiment of Sri Lanka Artillery	1 September 1985	Converted from 25 Pounders to Type 83 122mm guns during Eelam War III.
7th Light Regiment of Sri Lanka Artillery	10 November 1988	Type 86 120mm mortars.
8th Medium Regiment of Sri Lanka Artillery	1 January 1994	Served as an infantry unit, until it converted to Type 59-I 130mm guns in March 1996.
9th Field Regiment of Sri Lanka Artillery	23 January 1997	Four batteries, all equipped with Type 83 122mm guns
10th Medium Regiment of Sri Lanka Artillery	10 January 1997	Served as an infantry unit the following year when it converted to Type 66 152mm guns.
12th Volunteer Regiment of Sri Lanka Artillery	September 1998	N/A
14th Rocket Regiment of Sri Lanka Artillery	13 September 1998	One battery with six KRL-122, four batteries with six RM-70 each.

Decommissioned Sri Lanka Army Type 59-I displayed at the Orr's Hill Army Museum, Trincomalee. These 130mm guns were the Chinese variant of the infamous M-46 gun, notorious for its 27 kilometre range. (Adrien Fontanellaz Collection)

Decommissioned Sri Lanka Army Type 83 displayed at the Orr's Hill Army Museum. The Type 83 was one of the first artillery pieces entirely designed in the People's Republic of China and had a 15 kilometres range. It did not enter in service in large quantities in the People's Liberation Army and was seldom exported. Its conventional carriage system made it much more adequate to South Asian countries compared to the otherwise similar Soviet-designed D-30. (Adrien Fontanellaz Collection)

A decommissioned Sri Lanka Army KRL-122, with KRL standing for Kahuta Research Laboratories. The Sri Lanka ordered six of these systems to Pakistan in the aftermath of the fall of Elephant Pass in April 2000 and these were rushed into service as soon as they arrived. (Adrien Fontanellaz Collection)

The Sri Lanka Armoured Corps (SLAC) was significantly reinforced during Eelam Wars II and III. The 3 SLAC was re-equipped with a total of 21 Type 85 vehicles—including 18 Infantry Fighting Vehicles (IFVs), two Armoured Recovery Vehicles (ARVs), and one command variant—along with 12 Type 86 vehicles, comprising six Armoured Personnel Carriers (APCs) and six command variants, between August 1991 and September 1992. As a result, its previous inventory of Saracen and Saladin armoured vehicles was reassigned to the 1 SLAC. From 1992 onwards, 1 SLAC operated the entire fleet of remaining British-designed wheeled armoured vehicles until their withdrawal in 2001. However, to compensate for its losses, the unit received a batch of BTR-80 and BTR-80A vehicles in 1998.

The 4 SLAC continued to operate its fleet of 25 T-55 tanks and two VT-55A armoured recovery vehicles, which had been acquired from Czechoslovakia in 1991. However, it was reinforced in November 1995 with a small number of T-55 AVLBs (Armoured Vehicle-Launched Bridges) and, more significantly, with 18 T-55AM2 tanks, which arrived on 7 January 1998. These Czech modernised T-55s represented a major improvement for the SLAC, offering enhanced armour protection and a superior fire-control system. Despite these upgrades, the unit suffered significant losses, with several T-55s either destroyed or captured by the LTTE. Additionally, the SLAC faced chronic shortages of spare parts, making it difficult to repair battle-damaged vehicles in a timely manner. Between January and April 2001, the 4 SLAC received an additional batch of 36 T-55AM2 tanks, along with a badly needed consignment of spare parts. This allowed the regiment to transfer 11 of its surviving T-55s to the 3 SLAC, which subsequently became a mixed unit, with its A and B squadrons equipped with Infantry Fighting Vehicles (IFVs) and its C squadron operating tanks. Although the T-55s were outdated, they were well-regarded within the SLAC. The Corps had to adapt their use to the unique conditions of the Sri Lankan battlefield, as recalled by a former officer of the regiment:

> Despite the machine's bulk, the interior of a T-55 is very cramped. The crew of four (Commander, gunner, loader and driver) must remain seated for hours (only the loader can stand up) in a vehicle that was designed with scant regard for human ergonomics. The interior is mostly metal with little cushioning. Steel blocks, columns and plates protrude everywhere, and the crew gets slammed into them as the giant beast lumbers on its multiple axles. The noise from the crude 12-cylinder diesel engine and the rattle of the tank tracks are deafeningly amplified when the main gun is fired. Combined with the stench of fuel and explosive, the heat and claustrophobia conspire to make a closed T-55 fighting in the tropics something that many brave men could not deal with. [...] Driving the beast needs both muscle and a delicate touch, to be able to 'play the piano with a five-kilogram hammer' as our instructors put it. [...] When the main gun is fired with the hatches closed, the noise is unbelievably loud and is accompanied by a compression 'shock wave' which reverberates around the interior. The recoil of the main gun is enough to demolish a concrete wall; the heavy gun, chamber and the entire cradle moves back about 30cm at lightning speed. If the loader has not moved away from the path of recoil, he will be badly injured. [...]
>
> Despite the obsolete gear, the T-55A proved to be a fearsome weapon that adapted well to tropical conditions, albeit with some crew discomfort. Though rather crude and unsophisticated, the beast was simple enough to maintain so that we could operate in tough conditions with minimal tools and equipment.
>
> In the heat of battle, the intensity of the action is unbelievable. The tank would be lurching across uneven ground, the engine roaring and producing clouds of smoke. Huge plumes of dust raised by incoming fire exploding all around us produces more haze. The interior is like a cauldron with the temperature over 40°C. Machine guns chatter in both directions, with hot lead filling the air and impacting on the armour plating. [...] Other than aiming and shooting, the key to fighting in the T-55 was for the tank commander to be a good judge of terrain. The beast weighs 42,000 kg (think 55 Toyota Land Cruisers) and was designed to fight on the plains of Europe. Using it in the scrub jungles of Asia required a different skill set. Damp ground, ditches, or soft sand would mean it would get bogged down very easily. Extricating a stuck tank requires use of the log that was carried on every tank. [...] For a typical operation the battle planners would study the terrain and identify 'mobility corridors' that could take the weight of the T-55s. One, two, or even three Troops would be allocated for the operation, depending on how many tanks the terrain could support. When learning tank warfare with other (foreign) armies, we were taught the classic 'combined arms' formations with field artillery, mobile infantry, combat engineers and close air support. But given the terrain and limited resources, our operations were mostly Troop- or Squadron-sized in support of infantry.[14]

The 5 SLAC, raised on 6 January 1994, continued its build-up, which had begun in July of the same year, with the induction of 16 BMP-1 and BMP-2 vehicles delivered from Ukraine. These were followed by the arrival of 30 Chinese Type 63-II Armoured Personnel Carriers (APCs) on 29 September 1995, allowing the unit to form its A and C squadrons, while the B Squadron was equipped with BMPs. The unit was further reinforced with the delivery of a small batch of Type 86 vehicles—the Chinese variant of the BMP-1—on 9 September 1997. However, the Type 63-II quickly proved to be a disappointment—to say the least—as later recalled by Kamal Gunaratne:

Decommissioned 4 SLAC T-55 displayed at the Orr's Hill Army Museum, with its typical Sri Lanka anti-RPG rubber protections removed. By early and mid-90s standards these were already obsolete tanks, but in the Sri Lankan context, they did the job, and were appreciated for their ruggedness despite their poor ergonomics. This tank survived the detonation of at least a single AT mine. (Adrien Fontanellaz Collection)

> The T-63-2 model APC looked like toys and when used in the operational area, one got caught to a landmine and was totalled. [...] The body was so thin and weak, even a bullet from a T56 could penetrate it, despite having an 'armoured' protection. [...] The troopers of the Armoured Corps named them "Ice Cream Vans" and upon realizing its inability to perform, the APCs were used only for casualty evacuation and to transport ammunition etc.[15]

The Sri Lanka Armoured Corps (SLAC) continued its expansion with the activation of the 6 SLAC on 29 January 1997. Initially, it functioned as an infantry unit until June 1998, when it received a batch of 22 BTR-80 and BTR-80A armoured personnel carriers. The unit was further reinforced in 2002 with the addition of 20 BMP-2 Infantry Fighting Vehicles (IFVs). Two additional regiments, the 7 (Volunteer) SLAC, raised on 30 July 1999, and the 8 SLAC, raised on 30 July 1998, were also formed during Eelam War III. However, both remained infantry units and were primarily deployed for security duties in the Jaffna Peninsula until the end of the war.[16]

The Sri Lanka Army (SLA) established a mechanised brigade at the onset of Eelam War II. This formation, formally designated as the 533 Armoured Brigade on 30 September 1995, was responsible for overseeing the 3, 4, and 5 SLAC. However, despite this structural development, the SLA continued to primarily employ its armour as fire support vehicles, rather than as an independent manoeuvre force. As a result, tanks, APCs, and IFVs were mostly deployed in squadron-sized formations, providing support to various infantry formations. Tank squadrons were typically organised into three troops, each consisting of three vehicles, plus an additional tank operated by the squadron commander. Nevertheless, there is no doubt that the expansion of the SLAC and the induction of new combat vehicles—particularly tanks, BMP-2s, and BTR-80As, both armed with highly effective 30mm rapid-fire cannons—allowed the SLA to exert increasing influence on the battlefields of Northern Sri Lanka. These assets played a crucial role in enabling infantry forces to break through otherwise impregnable LTTE defensive positions.

Table 3 Sri Lanka Armoured Corps 1990-2002

Unit	Notes
1 SLAC	Concentrates the Armoured Corps entire park of British-made armoured vehicles from 1992 on. Received a first shipment of 11 BTR-80 and BTR-80A in 1998, allowing it to reequip one of its squadrons. A second batch of 24 BTR-80 and BTR-80A delivered in August 2002 allows it to withdraw from service its antiquated Saladin and Saracen.
3 SLAC	Transfer its remaining Saladin and Saracen on 1 SLAC in 1992 after the induction of Chinese-made Type 85 and 86. One squadron reequipped with 14 T-55 transferred from 4 SLAC in 2001.
4 SLAC	Raised in 1991 and equipped with a total of 25 Czech T-55 and two VT-55A, as well as several T-55 AVLB delivered in 1995. Reinforced with a batch of 18 Czech T-55AM2 in January 1998 and another of 36 T-55AM2 in early 2001.
5 SLAC	Raised 1994, when it inducted a batch of 16 BMP-1 and BMP-2. Received 30 Type 63-II APC in September 1995 and an unknown number of Type 86 IFV two years later.
6 SLAC	Formed early 1997, acted as infantry until mid-1998 when it received a batch of 22 BTR-80 and BTR-80A. Further reinforced with a batch of 20 BMP-2 in 2002.
7 (V) SLAC	Formerly 7th SLNG transferred to the Armoured Corps on 30 July 1999. Acted as an infantry unit.
8 SLAC	Raised 30 July 1998. Acted as an infantry unit.

Queen of the Battlefield

Whilst the SLA made significant efforts to reinforce its armour and artillery branches, the war remained above all an infantryman's conflict from beginning to end. At the onset of Eelam War II in mid-1990, the Sri Lanka Army maintained 30 infantry battalions, both regular and volunteer, with six battalions in each of its five infantry regiments. Over the next four years, an additional 19 battalions were raised, bringing the total to 50 by the end of 1994. These forces were supplemented by 16 battalions of the Sri Lanka National Guard (SLNG), which had been activated between 1989 and 1992. However, the SLNG units were primarily fit for rear-area security duties and lacked the capability for frontline combat. Despite these reinforcements, the SLA struggled to sustain both the semi-conventional war in the North and the manpower-intensive counter-insurgency campaign in the East. Unsurprisingly, the army sought to further expand its infantry branch during Eelam War III. Between 1995 and 2002, another 16 regular and volunteer battalions were formed, alongside at least four additional SLNG battalions, numbered 17 to 20.

The Sri Lanka Army could also rely on its Commando Brigade, which oversaw the 1st Commando Regiment, raised in 1986 from the pre-existing Commando Squadron, and the 2nd Commando Regiment, established on 1 March 1993. However, it was the Special Forces that saw the most significant expansion. The 1st Special Forces Regiment (1 SF Regiment) was activated on 10 December 1988, followed by the 2nd Special Forces Regiment, raised on 18 February 1994, and the 3rd Special Forces Regiment, established in August 1996. That same year, a Special Forces Brigade headquarters was activated to oversee all three regiments. Both Commando and Special Forces units provided the SLA with a wide range of tactical capabilities, including amphibious operations, VIP protection, and Long-Range Reconnaissance Patrols (LRRP) behind enemy lines. However, these elite formations were frequently misused, often being deployed in battalion-strength formations as shock troops on the frontlines rather than as highly specialised units. As a result, they suffered heavy casualties, undermining their intended role in the conflict.

The growing number of combat units compelled the Sri Lanka Army (SLA) to reactivate field division headquarters, each overseeing a variable number of brigades, which typically controlled two to three battalions each. The first three divisions—51, 52, and 53 Divisions—were established in 1995 in preparation for Operation Riviresa. These were followed by 54 Division in the summer of 1996, 55 Division in October of the same year, 56 Division on 1 October 1997, and 21 Division in 1998. The infantry brigades assigned to these divisions were numbered accordingly; for example, 51 Division controlled the 511, 512, and 513 Brigades, while 56 Division commanded the 561, 562, and 563 Brigades. However, at times, some divisions had only one or two organic infantry brigades, while others had as many as seven. Additionally, specialist formations, such as the Armoured Brigade or the Air Mobile Brigade, could be attached to any division for specific operations as required, as could artillery regiments. In essence, the SLA's operational structure remained highly flexible, allowing adaptability in the deployment of forces based on battlefield requirements.

Poor Bloody Infantry

Altogether, the Sri Lanka Army expanded from 59,567 personnel—including both volunteers and regulars—in 1990 to 90,572 by 1994 and 125,616 by 1998. Military expenditures increased accordingly, with the Army's budget rising from 2.73% of the national budget in 1990 to 4.73% in 1995, and reaching 7.13% in 1998. By that year, the Army's budget amounted to approximately USD 353 million.

However, while this military expansion might have appeared impressive at first glance, it concealed a number of critical weaknesses. The first major flaw was that, in relative terms, the LTTE ground forces were expanding at a similar rate to the SLA. As a result, the force ratio between the army and the insurgents remained largely unchanged—or, in some cases, may even have shifted in favour of the LTTE. Secondly, despite the scale of the conflict, the Sri Lankan state never initiated full-scale mobilisation. Among other constraints, it refused to introduce conscription and failed to allocate sufficient funding, forcing the armed forces to fight the war on a shoestring budget. Due to these financial limitations—compounded by endemic corruption—troops frequently faced shortages of essential supplies, including food and crucial protective equipment such as flak jackets. The SLA was constantly searching for cheaper sources of military equipment, sometimes with dire consequences. One notable example occurred in early 1997, when the SLA acquired a shipment of 100mm shells from China for the 4 SLAC's T-55 tanks. However, these shells differed slightly from their Soviet or Czech-produced counterparts, a discrepancy that had been overlooked. The entire stock had to be discarded after three tank guns were fatally damaged upon firing their first Chinese shells.

The paucity of funds and lack of full political support for the war had another, far worse consequence. Recruitment remained entirely voluntary, while pay and benefits for the rank and file remained meagre. Initially, this did not pose a significant problem at the beginning of Eelam War II, as thousands of young men enthusiastically enlisted out of patriotism and the belief that the war would end quickly. However, this initial enthusiasm gradually faded as the conflict dragged on, turning into a prolonged and seemingly unwinnable struggle, marked by several devastating defeats. Casualties continued to mount, further dampening morale. The SLA officially acknowledged the loss of 3,531 soldiers by the end of 1994 and another 6,180 between 19 April 1995 and 1 July 1999. However, the actual death toll was almost certainly higher. Official records only classified soldiers as 'killed in action' (KIA) if their bodies were recovered and identified. As a result, hundreds, if not thousands, of fallen soldiers remained classified as 'missing in action' (MIA), leaving their families in uncertainty about their fate. A soldier classified as MIA for one year was then officially declared KIA, only after which his family would receive the due compensation and pension. Unsurprisingly, as the war continued, the majority of new recruits came from the poorest strata of Sri Lankan society, particularly rural communities, where an army salary and pension still provided a significant financial incentive.

Thus, the SLA's struggle to secure the manpower necessary to both replace its losses and sustain its expansion only worsened as the war progressed. In 1996, a recruitment drive aimed at enlisting 10,000 new soldiers yielded only 1,800 recruits. Similarly, between February and March 2000, just 1,500 men volunteered out of an expected 15,000. To compensate for these shortfalls, the SLA resorted to short-term measures that ultimately exacerbated the problem in the long run. Recruits who had volunteered for less exposed regiments, such as the armoured corps, artillery, or military police, were forcibly reassigned to infantry regiments. Additionally, soldiers who had completed their 12-year service term—and were legally entitled to leave the army—were forced to extend their service on a year-to-year basis. To address the shortage of officers in the Volunteer Corps, the SLA commissioned officer cadets from the Education Department—middle-aged, barely trained teachers—into the Volunteer Force. This measure significantly weakened the effectiveness of the volunteer infantry battalions, further undermining the army's overall combat capability.

But even worse was the rampant desertion that plagued the SLA. By mid-1997, at least 10,000 soldiers had deserted, and by May 1998, the number had skyrocketed to 25,000. In October 1998, the army acknowledged that 5,000 men had deserted in the previous three months alone. In response, the government regularly declared General Amnesties, allowing deserters to return without punishment. By mid-1998, approximately 14,500 deserters had surrendered themselves and volunteered to rejoin the army. However, these soldiers were often unmotivated and, in many cases, distrusted by their officers. As a result, they were mostly assigned to secondary duties whenever possible. This further weakened unit cohesion, but for an army critically short of manpower, there was little alternative. The SLA found itself trapped in a vicious cycle, as noted by Lt. Gen. Gerry H. De Silva, who had served as Commander of the Army from 1 January 1994 to 30 April 1996, when he reflected on the issue in 1998:

> Troop strength are never enough. Field commanders always request for more. Despite this premise the Sri Lanka Army had been, over a period of time, 'managing' with inadequate strengths. Developing countries cannot afford to sustain large military structures over prolonged periods and politicians always suspect large armies. […] The capture and holding of ground is essential and absorbs a large manpower resources denuding 'bayonet' strengths for fighting. […] Incidentally, a 110,000 strong Army costs the government exchequer Rupees One Billion a month to maintain, without firing a shot. […] Inadequacy in fighting strengths are also caused by the large number of casualties taken by a prolonged war, especially the wounded in action and permanently disabled. Notwithstanding this factor, sustained military action over 14 years have taken a heavy toll on absentees and deserters. The Sri Lanka Army is the only army in the world where its entire bayonet strength has been deployed continuously since the Northern conflict began. Imagine the trauma of a fighting force that has not had time to rest, recuperate, relax and retrain in a normal cycle of military life enjoyed by most armies in the world. It is enough to drive most soldiers 'nuts'.[17]

Hence, it is hardly surprising that SLA units were constantly undermanned. By 1998, the authorised strength of the entire army, including both regular and volunteer forces, was 7,282 officers and 175,195 other ranks. However, the actual strength recorded on its musters was only 5,743 officers and 119,873 other ranks, leaving a significant shortfall. As a result, in the aftermath of severe defeats, the SLA had no choice but to disband three infantry battalions between 1997 and 2000 due to insufficient manpower.[18] The training system was heavily strained, though the length of basic training for soldiers remained at 13 weeks. However, most combat units were constantly deployed on the frontlines, leaving them little opportunity to provide their troops with refresher courses. This continuous frontline deployment was also one of the key factors contributing to high desertion rates. A stark example of the decline in training standards was observed by Maj. Gen. Sarath Munasinghe when he assumed command of 54 Division in July 1998. He discovered that marksmanship had deteriorated to such an extent that more than a third of his soldiers were unable to hit a target at 100 metres on the firing range.[19]

Table 4 Infantry battalions raised 1995-2002

Unit	Unit Activation	Abbreviation/Motto
Sri Lanka Light Infantry Regiment	**"I Serve"**	
11th Battalion of Sri Lanka Light Infantry	15 June 1996	11th SLLI
12th Battalion of Sri Lanka Light Infantry	1 July 1997	12th SLLI
14th (Volunteer) Battalion of Sri Lanka Light Infantry	31 December 1996	14th (V) SLLI
15th Battalion of Sri Lanka Light Infantry	4 February 1997	15th SLLI
Sri Lanka Sinha Regiment	**"Swift and Bold"**	
12th Battalion of Sri Lanka Sinha Regiment	September 1996	12th SLSR
14th Battalion of Sri Lanka Sinha Regiment	13 December 1996	14th SLSR
15th (Volunteer) Battalion of Sri Lanka Sinha Regiment	1 January 1997	15h (V) SLSR
16th Battalion of Sri Lanka Sinha Regiment	16 January 1997	16th SLSR
Gemunu Watch Regiment	**"Tarry not Forward"**	
11th Battalion the Gemunu Watch	4 September 1996	11th GW
14th (Volunteer) Battalion the Gemunu Watch	7 January 1997	14th (V) GW
Vijayabahu Infantry Regiment	**"Nothing is beyond endurance for the one who excels"**	
9th Battalion the Vijayabahu Infantry Regiment	6 September 1996	9th VIR
11th Battalion the Vijayabahu Infantry Regiment	10 January 1997	11th VIR
12th (Volunteer) Battalion the Vijayabahu Infantry Regiment	10 January 1997	12th (V) VIR
Gajaba Regiment	**"Unity is strength"**	
14th Battalion the Gajaba Regiment	27 December 1997	14th GR
15th (Volunteer) Battalion the Gajaba Regiment	23 January 1997	15th (V) GR

2
DANGEROUS SKIES

To say that the loss of two transport aircraft within two days came as a shock to the Sri Lanka Air Force (SLAF) would be an understatement. While it was quickly determined that the aircraft had been downed by MANPADS (Man-Portable Air Defence Systems), the exact type of weapon used remained uncertain. However, the primary suspect was the Soviet-designed Strela-2 (NATO designation: SA-7), an older but still effective infrared-guided surface-to-air missile.

As it turned out, the LTTE had managed to acquire a small batch of 9K34 Strela-3 (NATO designation: SA-14) in 1994 or early 1995 from an unknown supplier. Unsurprisingly, these Strela-3 missiles were assigned to the Radha Padai Ani, the LTTE's dedicated air defence unit, which had previously been equipped only with heavy machine guns (HMGs) of 12.7mm and 14.5mm calibre. The introduction of MANPADS significantly enhanced the unit's effectiveness, increasing its air defence capability by an order of magnitude.[1] Indeed, at least eight SLAF transport aircraft and helicopters were shot down by MANPADS during Eelam War III.

The LTTE had already attempted to develop its own air branch as early as the 1980s. In 1984, several militants were reportedly trained at private flying schools in France and the United Kingdom. Additionally, in early 1987, the Tigers attempted to assemble a small two-seater aircraft in one of their workshops in the Jaffna Peninsula. However, these early efforts failed to yield any operational results, as no recorded insurgent aerial activities took place at the time. The Sky Tigers (*Vaan Pulikal*) were officially established in 1995, and in October of that year, the Sri Lanka Army (SLA) captured a partially assembled aircraft in the Jaffna Peninsula. Little is known about the development of the Sky Tigers during Eelam War III, apart from the fact that they were led by Col. Shankar (Vaithilingam Sornalingam), a former engineer, and were part of the Radha Padai Ani. By this period, the unit had acquired a small number of Ultra-Light Motorised (ULM) aircraft and one or possibly two Robin R-22 or R-44 micro-helicopters, the existence of which was revealed by the LTTE on 27 November 1998. This tiny air fleet was primarily used for reconnaissance missions, flying mostly at night. However, on at least one occasion, a ULM aircraft was used to shoot down a Sri Lanka Air Force (SLAF) Super Scout UAV. The LTTE never publicised this victory, likely in an effort to keep the enemy unaware of the capabilities of its fledgling air component.[2]

DEADLY GREMLIN

Whilst often described as a mere evolution of the Strela-2, which was developed and introduced into the Soviet Army during the 1970s, the Strela-3 proved to be a far more potent weapon than commonly assumed.

The development of the Strela-3 began on 2 September 1968 at the Arsenal Plant in Kyiv and was introduced into the Soviet Army in 1974. It featured several major improvements over its predecessors, the Strela-2 and Strela-2M, with the most significant being its new 9E45 cryogenically cooled seeker. This high-resolution seeker was far superior to the electrically cooled 9E46 seeker of the Strela-2M and even more so to the uncooled 9E42 seeker of the Strela-2, significantly enhancing its target acquisition and tracking capabilities. Additionally, the Strela-3 was equipped with an improved battery pack, which extended the operator's engagement time, making it easier to acquire and lock onto targets. Once identified by NATO, it was designated SA-14 'Gremlin'. The Strela-3 system weighed 17 kg and had an effective engagement range of up to 4,500 metres and a maximum altitude of 3,000 metres. Its 9M36 missile weighed 10.3 kg, carried a 1.1 kg warhead, and travelled at a speed of 1,440 km/h. Overall, the Strela-3's performance was roughly comparable to the US FIM-43C Redeye in terms of range and capability.

Unlike its predecessors, the Strela-3 was not widely exported until the end of the Cold War, despite approximately 56,000 missiles being produced by 1988. One major exception was Iraq, which received a batch of Strela-3 systems and deployed them in combat against Allied forces during Operation Desert Storm. In this conflict, the Strela-3 proved relatively effective, with one of its most notable successes occurring on 31 January 1991, during the Battle of Khafji, when it was responsible for shooting down a US AC-130H Spectre gunship.[3] Thus, at the time of its induction into the LTTE in 1995, the Strela-3 remained both a highly capable yet relatively unknown system. This lack of familiarity proved to be a major challenge for the Sri Lanka Air Force (SLAF) throughout Eelam War III, significantly complicating air operations and posing a persistent threat to Sri Lankan aircraft.

A rare picture issued by the LTTE during the mid-90s showing Velupillai Prabhakaran together with the crew of one of the few ULM acquired by the elusive Sky Tigers. Those light aircraft were used for reconnaissance purpose but might have shot down two SLAF UAVs. (Adrien Fontanellaz Collection)

An operator from the Radha Padai Ani showing his Strela 3 MANPADS, better known under its ASCC designation SA-14 Gremlin. This system proved devastating in the hands of the LTTE. (Adrien Fontanellaz Collection)

The Pucara CA-604, which crashed in the Polonnaruwa district after suffering from a mid-air explosion on 15 March 1997. The pilot ejected successfully. (Albert Grandolini Collection)

The F-7BS CF-707 during taking off. Two of these fighters were engaged in a high-risk 'show the flag' mission over the Jaffna Peninsula in the aftermath of the LTTE's induction of surface to air missiles. (Albert Grandolini Collection)

The Y-8 CR-871, shot down just before landing at Palali AB on 18 November 1995 by a missile fired from a Sea Tiger boat. Only one out of the crew of six survived the crash. (Albert Grandolini Collection)

The MANPADS effect

The Sri Lanka Air Force (SLAF) rushed to acquire countermeasures to address the new MANPADS threat, but it took months to procure and install a limited number of Israeli-produced Missile Approach Warning Systems (MAWS), which were interfaced with automatic flare dispensers. The first system was tested on a Bell 212 over Negombo Lagoon on 19 September 1995. However, between 1995 and 1996, only nine systems were delivered, which were installed on Bell 212 and Mi-17 helicopters, as well as on the newly acquired An-32B transport aircraft. As a result, the majority of the SLAF fleet remained highly vulnerable to the MANPADS threat until much later, when a sufficient number of countermeasure systems had finally been delivered and deployed.

In the meantime, the SLAF had no choice but to temporarily halt its airbridge to Palali Air Base (AB) from 30 April 1995 onwards, as a direct response to the MANPADS threat. Additionally, fixed-wing aircraft were forced to fly above 6,000 metres when overflying LTTE-held areas to stay beyond the effective range of enemy surface-to-air missiles. Helicopter operations, however, continued but were conducted at extremely low altitudes, minimising the time available for LTTE MANPADS operators to aim and fire their missiles or heavy machine guns (HMGs). After a few weeks, the SLAF resumed its airbridge to Palali, but only after adopting a completely revised flight pattern, inspired by the Indian Air Force (IAF) procedures during Operation Pawan. SLAF transport aircraft departed from Colombo, maintaining an altitude of 7,000 metres, flying well off the coast towards India. They followed a route through four designated waypoints, named MIKE 1 to 4, before reaching waypoint NAVY, where they turned inland and descended to approximately 100 metres for the final approach to Palali, flying straight in before landing.

Take-offs were also conducted exclusively towards the sea, with aircraft flying at low altitude for a period before ascending at waypoint NAVY. Additionally, An-32B transport aircraft systematically deployed flares during landing and take-off, even though the new flight pattern ensured they remained outside the firing range of MANPADS positioned around the Palali complex perimeter. However, disaster struck on 18 November 1995, when Sea Tiger boats managed to position themselves directly in the flight path of a Y-8 transport aircraft (C-871) as it was landing. The insurgents fired a missile, bringing down the aircraft, leaving only one survivor. Mi-24 attack helicopters, based in Palali, were immediately scrambled and intercepted the Sea Tiger boats as they attempted to land on the coastline. The helicopters claimed to have destroyed several enemy boats, though one Hind sustained a direct hit to its windscreen from a heavy machine gun (HMG). Only a few days later, on 22 November 1995, another tragedy occurred when An-32B CR-862 crashed while approaching Palali, killing all crew members on board. The most likely cause of the disaster was a repeat of the LTTE's attack on 18 November. These back-to-back incidents finally prompted the Sri Lanka Navy (SLN) to intensify patrols around Palali, ensuring the approaches were closely monitored to prevent further Sea Tiger infiltrations. This enhanced security posture remained in place until the Jaffna Peninsula was fully recaptured by the SLA, significantly reducing the LTTE's ability to operate in the area.

The cessation of the airbridge had a devastating effect on troop morale among SLA forces stationed in the Jaffna Peninsula. In response, Squadron Leader Harsha Abeywickrema, the Commanding Officer of No. 5 Jet Squadron, decided to conduct a two-ship "show the flag" strike mission over Jaffna to boost morale. He and Flight Officer Janaka Wijetilleke took off from China Bay Air Base aboard their F-7 fighter jets:

> I briefed FO Wijetilleke of the mission and instructed him to just hang to my wing and to follow. Some of those based at China Bay felt that it could be our last mission. As we got into the cockpits, some personnel waved at us as at least one of us could end up as the latest missile victim. We took two bombs each and 30mm cannon. We dived north of SLA's forward defence line (FDL) north of Elephant Pass (EP) base and directed bombs at LTTE fortifications and manoeuvred towards the eastern FDL of the EP base, while firing cannon at the enemy. We continued at tree-top level over Velvetiturai and Thondamannar and pulled up over the sea. We flew over the peninsula regardless of the consequences, as we felt nothing could have boosted the morale of those under siege in the Jaffna peninsula. Later, I was told how troops at Elephant Pass and Palaly cheered seeing jets flying low over LTTE-held territory. Although they fired anti-aircraft guns at us, we were too fast. Our mission infused confidence in the pilots. Gradually, we developed strategies to counter threat posed by missiles. Although the LTTE brought down several other aircraft with heat seeking missiles, the SLAF didn't lose a single jet fighter to a missile attack or anti-aircraft fire.[4]

Despite these morale-boosting efforts, the SLAF suffered another major loss on 14 July 1995, when Pucará CA-601 was shot down by a MANPADS while conducting an airstrike over the Jaffna Peninsula in support of Operation Leap Forward. The aircraft's pilot, Flight Lieutenant Dilhan Perera, was killed in action, dealing a severe blow to the SLAF's ability to support ground troops. Following this incident, the two remaining Pucarás and the F-7 fighter jets were forced to drop their bombs from medium or high altitude, resulting in a significant loss of accuracy. Meanwhile, the SF.260 aircraft became effectively irrelevant as strike platforms due to their limited capabilities and vulnerability to enemy fire. Compounding the issue, the Pucarás became increasingly difficult to maintain, as spare parts grew harder to procure, and their airframes suffered from severe corrosion issues. A second Pucará (CA-604) was lost on 15 March 1997 during a night flight from Trincomalee to Batticaloa, though the pilot successfully ejected. By 1999, the last two Pucarás were withdrawn from service, marking the end of their operational use in Sri Lanka. Lastly, the F-7BS fighters remained hampered by their limited payload capacity, typically restricted to two 250kg bombs, and by their lack of an adequate targeting system, further reducing their effectiveness in strike missions.[5]

Return of the Alligators

The SLAF swiftly responded to the loss of CA-601, recognising the urgent need to restore its ability to conduct close air support (CAS) missions. To address this, a team was dispatched to Ukraine to procure Mi-24 attack helicopters. The first batch of three Mi-24V helicopters, numbered CH-610, CH-611, and CH-612, arrived in Sri Lanka on 4 November 1995. Shortly after, on 15 November, two Russian instructors, nicknamed 'Slava' and 'Vova', were brought in to train SLAF pilots on the new aircraft. The first combat airstrike using the Mi-24s took place in the Eastern Province on 17 November 1995, with each helicopter crewed by a Russian instructor and a Sri Lankan co-pilot. On the same day, the helicopters were flown to Palali, where they were eagerly awaited to support the ongoing Operation Riviresa. Still operated by mixed Russian-Sri Lankan crews, the Hinds were rushed into combat operations, as later recalled by Senaka Dharmawardena, one of Sri Lanka's early Mi-24 pilots:

> It was a flying tank with a lot of armour plating. Getting in and out of the cockpits was very difficult and familiarizing myself with the gunship's Russian control system was mind boggling. Flying in a tandem cockpit configuration where I could not see my Captain who could not utter a word in English was a challenge which was further aggravated due to his use of a throat mike which garbled out communications.[6]

The three Mi-24V helicopters became the nucleus of No. 9 Attack Helicopter Squadron, which was formally activated on 24 November 1995. The squadron initially comprised six pilots and 26 mechanics, with Wing Commander Jagath Rodrigo serving as its first commanding officer. By mid-February 1996, nine SLAF officers, mostly experienced Bell 212 pilots, had converted to the Mi-24 after completing 15 to 20 flight hours on their new aircraft. Thereafter, the Russian instructors ceased flying combat missions but remained with the squadron as advisors until 2000.

The three Mi-24Vs proved highly effective during Operation Riviresa, flying 72 combat missions, primarily using S-8 rockets and their onboard cannons. Pleased with these results, the SLAF invested heavily in expanding No. 9 Attack Helicopter Squadron, acquiring an additional 23 Mi-24 and Mi-35 helicopters between 1996 and 2001. The new acquisitions included:

- Four Mi-24s in 1996
- Three Mi-35s in 1998
- Two Mi-24s and two Mi-35s in 1999
- Six Mi-35s in 2000

By 1999, the squadron operated six Mi-24V/Ps and four Mi-35s, making it an essential fire support asset for both the Sri Lanka Army (SLA) and Sri Lanka Navy (SLN). The unit flew 127 combat missions in 1997 and 174 in 1999. By 1998, the SLAF enhanced the Hind's versatility by equipping them with locally produced SIG-24 bombs.

The Mi-24s and Mi-35s continued to operate at low altitudes to minimise exposure to enemy flak and MANPADS. However, their lack of advanced countermeasures made them highly vulnerable. Their only defensive system, infrared jammers, proved almost useless, as the SLAF lacked the necessary technical knowledge to calibrate them against the Strela-3 heat-seeking frequencies. It was only in mid-2001 that the Hinds were finally equipped with Israeli Elta EL/M-2160 missile approach warning systems and flare dispensers. Due to their vulnerability and heavy combat deployment, a total of six Mi-24/35 helicopters were shot down by the LTTE before 2001.[7]

A pair of Mi-24 of the No 9 Squadron flying over central Sri Lanka. The introduction of the Hind increased the SLAF firepower by an order of magnitude. Whilst these helicopters were highly appreciated for their ruggedness and ability to sustain heavy damages, six were shot down during Eelam War III. (Albert Grandolini Collection)

The Mi-24V CH611 was one of the first three delivered to Sri Lanka and was heavily engaged in the Jaffna Peninsula days after its introduction, in support of Operation Riviresa. (Albert Grandolini Collection)

Mock-up of the locally-manufactured SIG series of bombs, as shown in the SLAF Museum in 2017. The SIG 24 was also used to arm the Mi-24s. (Adrien Fontanellaz Collection)

CF-710 was the only Kfir TC.2 ordered by the SLAF, which arrived in-country on 10 January 1996, allowing for the conversion of the six first Sri Lankan pilots to the new type by Israeli instructors. (Albert Grandolini Collection)

A nice view of Kfir CF-716 shortly after its delivery in 1996. (Albert Grandolini Collection)

A trio of No 10 Squadron Kfir C.2 in the early 2000s. These Israeli fighters remain the most versatile type in service with the Air Force since their induction, especially so with the arrival of the C.7 variant in 2000. (Albert Grandolini Collection)

In the land of the Lion Cub

While the induction of the Mi-24 provided a solution to the SLAF's lack of close air support (CAS) capabilities, another issue remained: the need to deliver heavier bomb payloads with greater precision than before. The existing jet fleet, particularly the F-7, was severely limited in both payload capacity and targeting accuracy, as noted by Commander Ranasinghe, who highlighted the frustrating constraints of the only combat jet then in service:

> They dropped the bombs from altitude of 5-8,000 feet, which did not make for pinpoint accuracy. We had several problems to overcome to maintain bombing accuracy. The F-7 could not carry more than two 250 kg bombs per mission. In actual fact the punitive capabilities of the SLAF were constrained due to the lack of more sophisticated ground attack aircraft.[8]

Thus, the SLAF began to look for a new attack aircraft, investigating several options such as the acquisitions of the Sukhoi Su-25 or the Nanchang A-5, until Tel-Aviv proposed the Kfir, which was being phased out of the Israeli Air Force and available for sale at very competitive prices, as explained by O.D.N.L Perera, the than SLAF Director Aeronautical Engineering; "The Israelis were offering us completely overhauled Kfirs at an extremely reasonable price of USD 3.5 million apiece. The time frame for delivery of the jets was also short. At the time, it was a very attractive package for the Air Force."[9]

In 1994, the SLAF dispatched a small delegation to Israel, led by then-Director of Operations, Air Commodore Jayalath Weerakkody, to assess Israeli aircraft designs. During the visit, the delegation toured the Israeli Aircraft Industry (IAI) facilities in Tel Aviv. Additionally, Squadron Leader Harsha Abeywickrema, who was part of the team, was given the opportunity to fly several sorties aboard a TC.2, the dual-seat variant of the fighter:

> I flew a couple of missions in Israel with their test pilots who proudly displayed the capability of Kfir flying to its limits. I was impressed and recommended it instantly. The main highlights that impressed me was its J-79 engine made in the USA and the WDNS (weapon delivery and Navigational system). I was there for 10 days studying various systems and flying. Israel is the only country one can fly below sea-level and I was privileged to fly six times over the Dead Sea. The Dead Sea is a large place in the middle of the country some 1300 ft below sea level and we flew just over water and that was an unbelievable experience.[10]

To say that SLAF pilots were impressed by the Kfir would be an understatement. The aircraft was vastly superior to virtually any other option the SLAF could have realistically afforded, particularly when compared to the Su-25 and A-5. While based on the Dassault Mirage 5 design, the Kfir C.2 was significantly enhanced. It was powered by a General Electric J-79-J1E engine, equipped with an Elta 2001B ranging radar, and featured an Elbit S-8600 multi-mode navigation and weapon delivery system, along with a head-up display (HUD). These upgrades provided the Kfir with exceptional bombing accuracy, capable of hitting targets within eight meters under favourable conditions. In addition to its precision strike capability, the Kfir C.2 had a substantially greater flight range than the F-7BS. It could reach 768 kilometres while flying a high-low-high ground attack mission profile, carrying a typical loadout of seven 225 kg bombs, two air-to-air missiles, and two 1,300-litre drop tanks.

Before long, Colombo placed an order for six Kfirs—five C.2s (CF-711, 712, 713, 714, and 716) and one TC.2 (CFT-710). To operate them, a new unit, No. 10 Squadron, was formed on 5 January 1996, under the command of Squadron Leader Priyantha Gunasinghe. The TC.2 and the first two C.2s arrived by ship in Colombo on 10 January 1996, accompanied by two Israeli flight instructors. These instructors trained six SLAF pilots, and the squadron was officially declared operational on 7 March 1996, with its first combat mission taking place four days later. The remaining three C.2s arrived roughly a month later. The Kfirs were soon heavily involved in combat, flying 232 missions in 1997. However, on 21 January 1997, CF-712 crashed during a training sortie over Negombo Lagoon, though the pilot ejected successfully. Perhaps due to persistent delays in the supply of spare parts for the J-79 engines, which were subject to US State Department approval, the number of combat sorties fell to 111 in 1999. Nonetheless, due to their ability to carry heavy weapon loads, including 250 kg, 500 kg, and 1,000 kg bombs, with high precision and virtual immunity to LTTE air defences, the Kfirs remained a central pillar of SLAF firepower. In 1997, the SLAF experimented with deploying Griffin laser-guided bombs, using a Kfir paired with an An-32B fitted with a Cockpit Laser Designator. However, this system proved unreliable when tested on a training range on 4 August 1997 and was ultimately abandoned. Despite these setbacks, the SLAF remained highly satisfied with its Kfirs and placed an additional order with Israel for four more C.2s and four C.7s, all of which were delivered in 2000.

Spies in the skies

The Israeli connection also enabled the SLAF to enter the field of Unmanned Aerial Vehicles (UAVs). In 1995, a team of Israel Aerospace Industries (IAI) representatives visited Sri Lanka to promote the Super Scout UAV. As part of their demonstration, they brought one of the drones with them. SLAF airmen, recognising the critical shortage of reconnaissance assets, were highly enthusiastic about the capability the UAV offered. They successfully convinced the Israeli delegation to leave their demonstration drone in Sri Lanka, while the SLAF placed an order for a full system, consisting of four UAVs and one Ground Control Station. These drones entered service with the newly established No. 11 UAV Flight, under the command of Squadron Leader Dushan Thalagala. The unit was based in Vavuniya, allowing it to conduct reconnaissance missions deep into LTTE-held areas in the Vanni.

While the Super Scout UAVs were nominally the SLAF's only real-time intelligence source, they ultimately proved disappointing, largely due to the Air Force's own bureaucratic inefficiencies. Captured mission footage had to be copied onto VHS cassettes, which were then sent to Air Force Headquarters in Colombo for analysis before being forwarded to a combat squadron. This entire process took 48 hours—far too long for actionable intelligence—allowing any mobile target ample time to disappear. This issue persisted despite No. 11 UAV Flight being paired with the Service Air Intelligence Unit, while LTTE fixed infrastructure remained both well-hidden and well-defended. To make matters worse, the SLAF suffered the loss of two Super Scouts in quick succession in 1997—one on 17 January and another on 1 May, both likely shot down by Sky Tiger ULM aircraft. A third UAV was lost in 1998, followed by the fourth and final Super Scout in 1999. It was only in 2001 that the SLAF compensated for these losses, acquiring a batch of Searcher Mk II UAVs, which offered significantly superior performance and capabilities.[11]

The body of one the 14 Black Tigers killed during the 24 July 2001 Katunayake AB attack. (Albert Grandolini Collection)

Mi-17's CH589 and 599 in flight. Operated by No 6 Squadron, the type proved a true workhorse for the SLAF with its ability to carry sometimes more than 30 passengers. (Albert Grandolini Collection)

One of the SLAF MiG-27Ms displayed in the SLAF museum, showing the array of weapons it could carry, from S-8 rockets to FAB-500 bombs. (Adrien Fontanellaz Collection)

Expansion & Reorganisation

The second half of the 1990s marked a period of unprecedented growth for the Sri Lanka Air Force (SLAF). In addition to the activation of No. 9 and No. 10 Squadrons and the No. 11 UAV Flight, the SLAF also significantly expanded its transport capabilities by acquiring new aircraft. The loss of two Avro aircraft and the obvious vulnerability of the Y-8 prompted the SLAF to procure three An-32B transport aircraft from Russia, which were delivered in July 1995. These were followed by four additional An-32Bs in August and September 1996, further strengthening the SLAF's airlift capacity. In 1998, the SLAF sent six pilots to Pakistan for conversion training on C-130 Hercules aircraft. This was followed by the acquisition of two second-hand C-130E aircraft (CR-880 and CR-881) from the Royal Air Force in 1999, which were delivered in 2000. The SLAF also expanded its transport helicopter fleet, acquiring six new Mi-17 helicopters in December 1995. This doubled the fleet of these highly valued aircraft, which were renowned for their ruggedness and reliability. As expected, the significant expansion of the SLAF led to a notable increase in personnel. By the end of 1994, the SLAF had 591 officers and 11,005 airmen. By the end of 1999, this had risen to 883 officers and 12,171 airmen. However, pilots remained in short supply, despite efforts to rapidly increase their numbers. The SLAF nonetheless more than doubled its pilot strength in just a few years, as explained by Air Marshal Oliver Ranasinghe, who served as Commander of the SLAF from February 1994 to March 1998:

> When I took command, I had 65 pilots to fly 100 aircraft. I really needed 250-300 pilots. When my command period ended, I had 150 pilots. How? I got them recruited and then trained in Bangladesh, India, Pakistan and Malaysia.[12]

The expansion of the fleet and the intensified operational tempo prompted the SLAF to reorganise its structure, leading to the creation of new specialised squadrons and the renumbering of existing ones. As part of this restructuring, Squadrons 201, 202, 401, and 402 were disbanded, while No. 2, No. 4, No. 7, No. 8, No. 9, and No. 10 Squadrons were either newly established or reinstated. This new organisational framework was finalised in November 1995 and implemented in the following months. Once in place, it remained virtually unchanged for the remainder of the war.[13]

Table 5 SLAF Order of Battle as of 1999

Unit	Location	Comment
No 1 Flying Training Wing	Anuradhapura AB (AHP)	5 SF-260TP, 8 SF-260W, 6 Cessna 150. Last Pucara withdrawn from service that year.
No 2 Heavy Transport Squadron	Ratmalana AB (RMA)	3 HS.748, 4 An-32B, 1 Y-8 and 1 Cessna 421C
No 3 Maritime Squadron	China Bay AB	Dormant
No 4 Helicopter Squadron	Katunayake AB (KAT)	4 Bell 412, 1 Bell 206. Tasked mainly with VIP and liaison duties.
No 5 Jet Squadron	China Bay AB	4 F-7BS, 1 FT-7, 2 FT-5
No 6 Helicopter Squadron	Vavuniya AB (VNA)	10 Mi-17
No 7 Helicopter Squadron	Hingurakgoda AB (MIN)	11 Bell 212, 5 Bell 206
No 8 Light Transport Squadron	Ratmalana AB (RMA)	7 Y-12, 1 Beech King Air B 200T
No 9 Attack Helicopter Squadron	Hingurakgoda AB (MIN)	6 Mi-24, 4 Mi-35
No 10 Jet Squadron	Katunayake AB (KAT)	4 Kfir C.2, 1 Kfir TC.2

Costly war

The expansion of the SLAF from the mid-1990s onward led to a significant increase in operational activity, making the air force an increasingly critical component in the conduct of the war. In 1995, SLAF aircraft flew a total of 14,832 hours. In addition to combat missions, they transported 185,065 passengers across the island. One of the most crucial roles of the SLAF was CASEVAC (Casualty Evacuation) missions, which were often conducted under dangerous conditions. In 1995 alone, the SLAF evacuated 3,455 wounded soldiers and transported 949 bodies of fallen troops. The tempo of operations intensified in 1996, with SLAF aircraft logging 22,084.40 flight hours—an almost 50% increase compared to the previous year. During this time, the SLAF claimed to have interdicted 620 enemy targets. This was followed by 21,895 flight hours in 1997 and 18,281 hours in 1998, despite the challenges of sustaining a high operational tempo. In this period, the SLAF transported roughly 320,000 passengers and over 4,500 tons of supplies, playing a vital logistical role in moving personnel and equipment across the island. This capability was made possible in part by the increased capacity provided by the newly inducted transport aircraft and helicopters, which greatly enhanced the SLAF's strategic mobility.[14]

The small and close-knit Sri Lankan airmen community paid a staggering price for these achievements—both in blood and equipment. During Eelam War III, the SLAF lost a total of 38 aircraft and helicopters. Of these, 23 were downed by LTTE action, while another 15 were lost due to accidents or unknown causes. Certain years proved particularly devastating for the SLAF:

- 1995: Six aircraft lost
- 1997: Nine aircraft lost
- 2001: Ten aircraft lost

More often than not, entire crews and passengers perished along with their aircraft, dealing crippling losses to an already small community where everyone knew each other. These casualties placed an immense burden on the SLAF, both in terms of human loss and operational capacity, making every mission an increasingly high-risk endeavour.

Table 6: Known SLAF losses during Eelam War III (1995-2002)

Date	Aircraft	Unit	Comment
28 April 1995	HS.748 CR-835	No 201 Heavy Transport Squadron	Shot down by LTTE MANPADS whilst landing at Palali AB. All crew and passengers died.
29 April 1995	HS.748 CR-834	No 201 Heavy Transport Squadron	Shot down by LTTE MANPADS whilst landing at Palali AB. All crew and passengers died.
14 July 1995	IA-58 Pucara CA-601	No 1 Flying Training Wing	Shot down by LTTE MANPADS. Pilot Flt Lt D.F.D.S Perera KIA.
13 September 1995	An-32B CR-861	No 201 Heavy Transport Squadron	Crashed due to technical failure in the sea a few minutes after take-off from Ratmalana AB. All 81 crew and passengers onboard died.
18 November 1995	Y-8 CR-871	No 201 Heavy Transport Squadron	Shot down by MANPAD fired by Sea Tiger boats whilst approaching Palali AB at low altitude. Only one survivor out of the crew of six.
22 November 1995	An-32B CR-862	No 201 Heavy Transport Squadron	Shot down by suspected LTTE MANPAD whilst approaching Palali AB. All three crew and 60 passengers died.

Date	Aircraft	Unit	Comment
22 January 1996	Mi-17 CH-587	No 6 Squadron	Crashed off Point Pedro whilst flying at low altitude as a result of a suspected LTTE attack. All 39 crew and passengers on board died.
23 September 1996	SF-260W CT-160	No 1 Flying Training Wing	Crashed during a training accident.
7 December 1996	Bell-212 CH-546	No 7 Squadron	Force landed in LTTE held areas because of a fuel shortage. Aircraft destroyed whilst all crew and passengers reached friendly-held areas.
17 January 1997	Super Scout	No 11 UAV flight	Unknown reason but probably shot down by a Sky Tiger ULM.
20 January 1997	Y-12 CR-831	No 8 Squadron	Disappeared on a reconnaissance mission at sea.
21 January 1997	Kfir C.2 CF-712	No 10 Squadron	Crashed during a training sortie over the Negambo lagoon. Pilot ejected successfully.
21 February 1997	An-32B CR-865	No 2 Squadron	Crashed whilst taking off from Ratmalana AB.
5 March 1997	Y-12 CR-856	No 8 Squadron	Destroyed on the ground by LTTE assault against China Bay AB.
15 March 1997	IA-58 Pucara CA-604	No 1 Flying Training Wing	Crashed in the Polonnaruwa district after suffering from a mid-air explosion, pilot ejected successfully.
19 March 1997	Mi-24 CH-614	No 9 Squadron	First loss of Mi-24. Disappeared whilst flying low off Mulltaitivu. Suspected Sea Tiger action.
1 May 1997	Super Scout	No 11 UAV flight	Unknown reason but probably shot down by a Sky Tiger ULM.
14 June 1997	SF-260TP CT-122	No 1 Flying Training Wing	Crash-landed during a training sortie near Anuradhapura.
10 November 1997	Mi-24 CH-561	No 9 Squadron	Shot down by MANPADS over the Kilali lagoon whilst escorting three Mi-17 carrying troops to Elephant Pass. Crew KIA.
25 November 1997	Bell-212 CH-561	No 7 Squadron	Crashed in the Mullaitivu district whilst flying a night CASEVAC mission in bad weather. Crew died.
7 January 1998	Mi-17 CH-594	No 6 Squadron	Destroyed by LTTE mortar fire whilst on the ground at the Olamadu Army Helipad, Vavuniya.
12 June 1998	Super Scout	No 11 UAV flight	Lost for unknown reason over the Killinochchi area.
24 June 1998	Mi-24 CH-620	No 9 Squadron	Disappeared south of Vavuniya, explosion in mid-air observed. Suspected LTTE attack. Crew of four died.
29 March 1999	Super Scout	No 11 UAV flight	Lost for unknown reason.
17 December 1999	Mi-24 CH-618	No 9 Squadron	Shot down whilst attacking Sea Tigers' boats in the Kilali lagoon.
17 February 2000	Bell-212 CH-538	No 7 Squadron	Lost whilst flying a CASEVAC mission over Jaffna Peninsula. Probably shot down by a MANPAD.
24 May 2000	Mi-24 CH-624	No 9 Squadron	Hit by gunfire or MANPADS and crashed in the Puliyankulam area. One crew member KIA.
23 July 2000	F-7BS CF-704	No 5 Squadron	Crashed on landing at Katunayake AB. Pilot ejected successfully.
16 September 2000	Mi-17 CH-592	No 6 Squadron	Crashed in central Sri Lanka due to poor visibility, killing all on board.
19 October 2000	Mi-24 CH-615	No 9 Squadron	Hit by gunfire over Jaffna Peninsula. Crew survived.
23 October 2000	Mi-24 CH-613	No 9 Squadron	Shot down by enemy MANPADS whilst strafing LTTE mortar positions in the Trincomalee area. Crew of four KIA, including Wing Cdr. Jagath Rodrigo, the squadron CO.
15 June 2001	Mi-24 CH-626	No 9 Squadron	Crashed due to engine failure.
24 July 2001	Kfir C.7 CF-722	No 10 Squadron	Destroyed by LTTE Black Tigers during Katunayake AB attack.
24 July 2001	Kfir C.7 CF-723	No 10 Squadron	Destroyed by LTTE Black Tigers during Katunayake AB attack.
24 July 2001	MiG-27M CF-732	No 5 Squadron	Destroyed by LTTE Black Tigers during Katunayake AB attack.
24 July 2001	K-8 CTF-741	No 14 Squadron	Destroyed by LTTE Black Tigers during Katunayake AB attack.
24 July 2001	K-8 CTF-743	No 14 Squadron	Destroyed by LTTE Black Tigers during Katunayake AB attack.
24 July 2001	K-8 CTF-745	No 14 Squadron	Destroyed by LTTE Black Tigers during Katunayake AB attack.
24 July 2001	Mi-17 CH-590	No 6 Squadron	Destroyed by LTTE Black Tigers during Katunayake AB attack.
24 July 2001	Mi-17 CH-597	No 6 Squadron	Destroyed by LTTE Black Tigers during Katunayake AB attack.
18 August 2001	MiG-27M CF-737	No 5 Squadron	Crashed after hitting a telephone wire during a low-flying pass to commemorate Ukraine's aviation day. Pilot Capt. L. Veralli died.
22 October 2001	Kfir C.2 CF-719	No 10 Squadron	Crashed due to engine failure, pilot ejected successfully.
?? December 2001	MiG-27M	No 5 Squadron	Crashed in an accident.

The 2000 Great Rush for aircraft

The successive defeats suffered at the hands of the LTTE, culminating in the fall of Elephant Pass in 2000, prompted the government to loosen its financial restrictions in an effort to strengthen the embattled armed forces—a move that greatly benefited the SLAF. This funding boost allowed the SLAF not only to regain lost capabilities and expand existing ones but also to acquire entirely new assets.

Reinforcements and expansions were as follows:

- No. 9 and No. 10 Squadrons were reinforced with the addition of six Mi-35 attack helicopters and four Kfir C.2s and four Kfir C.7s, enhancing their strike capabilities.
- No. 2 Squadron received a major boost, acquiring two C-130E Hercules aircraft (delivered in March and September 2000) and three additional An-32B transport aircraft, significantly enhancing airlift capacity.
- In 2001, the SLAF restored its UAV reconnaissance capability with the acquisition of two Searcher Mk. II UAVs and a single ground control station, improving its real-time intelligence gathering.
- Additionally, the SLAF received two new Bell 412 helicopters, specifically configured for VIP transport, which were assigned to No. 4 Squadron.

These acquisitions significantly strengthened the SLAF's strike, transport, and reconnaissance capabilities, allowing it to better support ground operations and increase its operational flexibility in the ongoing conflict.

The SLAF's training aircraft fleet was rejuvenated with the acquisition of 10 CJ-6 basic trainers from China, which were allocated to No. 1 Flying Training Wing (FTW) to replace the ageing SF-260W fleet. However, the CJ-6 proved to be something of a mixed blessing. While the aircraft were recently manufactured, their outdated design presented several challenges. Maintenance proved particularly difficult, not least due to the aircraft's lack of ergonomic design, which complicated servicing and operations. Despite these shortcomings, the CJ-6 remained in service, fulfilling the SLAF's basic pilot training requirements during this period.[15] Additionally, due to the growing number of jet combat aircraft in the SLAF fleet, the air force placed an order for six Karakorum K-8 advanced jet trainers in 2000. The Bae Hawk and L-39 Albatros had also been considered but were ultimately rejected for cost reasons. The K-8s were delivered from China by sea and were used to establish a new training unit, No. 14 Advanced Flying Training Unit, with assistance from Pakistan Air Force advisors and a team of Chinese technicians. The unit was scheduled to be formally inaugurated at Katunayake Air Base on 24 July 2001. However, on that very day, the LTTE launched a devastating attack on the airbase, destroying three of the brand-new K-8 trainers. Despite this setback, No. 14 Squadron still became operational just a few days later, utilising the three surviving aircraft to begin training SLAF pilots in advanced jet operations.

Botched-up Flogger acquisition

The SLAF had also determined that it required a new combat jet and initially considered acquiring Su-27 or MiG-29 aircraft, both of which were available for sale at relatively affordable prices in Ukraine. However, at the time, the SLAF was already inducting a significant number of new aircraft while also maintaining an intense operational tempo. As a result, the air force could not afford to send experienced jet pilots abroad for lengthy conversion courses, which would have temporarily reduced its already limited pool of operational fighter pilots. At the same time, SLAF airmen were reassessing their actual combat needs, concluding that what they required most was an aircraft capable of high-speed, low-level bombing runs rather than an air superiority fighter. A seemingly ideal solution presented itself almost by chance during a visit to Ukraine by O.D.N.L. Perera, then SLAF Director of Aeronautical Engineering:

> During one of my visits to Ukraine, I started chatting with a cab driver, who happened to be an ex-Soviet MiG-21 pilot. He told me that there were many retired MiG-27 pilots who were prepared to fly as mercenaries immediately.[16]

This led to the swift acquisition of a batch of six MiG-27M ground-attack aircraft and one MiG-23UB trainer, along with a group of Ukrainian pilots willing to fly combat missions. The first four MiG-27Ms were delivered in June 2000 and were immediately deployed in combat operations. Assigned to No. 5 Squadron, three of these aircraft flew their first airstrikes on 8 August 2000, targeting multiple LTTE positions in the Jaffna Peninsula. During the mission, one MiG-27 was damaged by ground fire while emptying its rocket pods, but the pilot successfully returned the aircraft to Katunayake Air Base. The remaining two MiG-27Ms and the single MiG-23UB trainer arrived in October 2000, enabling the beginning of conversion training for SLAF pilots on the new aircraft.

While the MiG-27Ms were undoubtedly potent war machines, capable of delivering up to six FAB-500 bombs—a total of three tons of ordnance in a single strike—they also proved to be maintenance-intensive and prone to technical failures. The primary weapons loadout included S-8 80mm rockets, FAB-250 bombs, and OFAB-250 bombs, but the aircraft's long-term reliability issues soon became apparent. Out of the seven MiGs delivered in 2000, the SLAF suffered multiple losses:

- 24 July 2001: One MiG was destroyed, and another was damaged during the LTTE attack on Katunayake Air Base.
- 18 August 2001: CF-737 crashed when its Ukrainian pilot, Capt. L. Veralli, collided with an aerial power line while conducting an unauthorised low-level pass near Katunayake AB to celebrate Ukrainian Aviation Day.
- December 2001: Another MiG-27M was lost in a training accident.
- 9 June 2004: CF-734 crashed in yet another training accident.
- July 2004: The remaining three MiGs were grounded due to technical issues, effectively ending their operational use.

The high rate of losses and technical failures strongly suggests that, despite being acquired at a low price with favourable payment terms, the SLAF's MiG-27Ms may not have been thoroughly overhauled before delivery. This lack of proper refurbishment likely contributed to their short service life and mechanical unreliability.[17]

Disaster at Katunayake

The most devastating LTTE attack against the SLAF took place at the very end of Eelam War III, targeting Katunayake Air Base—considered the heart of the air force—and the adjacent Bandaranaike International Airport, Sri Lanka's only international airport. Since both facilities shared the same runway, the attack had immense strategic and economic consequences.

Despite previous LTTE assaults on SLAF bases, security at Katunayake remained inadequate, a vulnerability that would be tragically exposed. The LTTE had already demonstrated its capability to strike air force installations on two earlier occasions. During Eelam War II, a small Black Tiger team successfully infiltrated Palali Air Base and destroyed a single Bell 212 helicopter before being neutralised. The second attempt occurred on the night of 5 March 1997, when an assault team of approximately 15 Black Tigers, supported by mortar fire, launched an attack on China Bay Air Base. Initially, the suicide squad succeeded in breaching the perimeter and reached the tarmac, where they destroyed a Y-12 aircraft (CR-856) using RPG fire. However, at this stage, they became pinned down by intense defensive fire from SLAF personnel. At least one Mi-24 from No. 9 Squadron arrived, ready to strafe the insurgents, forcing them to withdraw. In the aftermath, the LTTE left behind the bodies of three of their fighters.

Despite these earlier high-profile attacks, weaknesses in base security remained unaddressed, enabling the LTTE to plan and execute its most destructive assault yet on Katunayake Air Base and Bandaranaike International Airport—a strike that would send shockwaves across Sri Lanka.

During the year 2000, the LTTE began preparing for a far more ambitious operation, with its National Intelligence Wing closely monitoring Katunayake Air Base and Bandaranaike International Airport. Over time, LTTE agents gathered an immense wealth of intelligence, including detailed blueprints of the base, potential infiltration routes, and strategic locations for safe houses. The meticulous reconnaissance ensured that every aspect of the attack was carefully planned and that the infiltrators would have the best possible chance of success. A successful strike on these two targets promised significant rewards. Katunayake Air Base housed the SLAF's most potent strike assets, making it a critical military target. At the same time, an attack on the airport, which served as the main gateway for international travel, would unfold in full view of foreign passengers transiting through the terminal. This guaranteed global media coverage, potentially discouraging tourists from visiting Sri Lanka and dealing a severe blow to the state's revenue. Given the importance of the mission, the planning of the attack was directly overseen by Velupillai Prabhakaran, the LTTE's supreme leader, alongside Pottu Amman, head of the Intelligence Wing, and Shankar, the founder of the Sky Tigers. Their direct involvement underscored the operation's significance and the strategic calculations behind choosing such a high-profile target.

The LTTE leadership ultimately chose 24 July 2001 as the date for the attack, marking the anniversary of the infamous Black July pogrom of 1983. The operation was entrusted to a team of around 20 Black Tigers, primarily drawn from the Chiruthaigal Padai Ani, with additional members from the Radha Padai Ani and the National Intelligence Wing. These elite fighters were infiltrated into Colombo, primarily by sea, before regrouping at a safe house in the Gampaha district on 22 July 2001. Their weapons—G-3 and Type 56 assault rifles, LAW rocket launchers, 40mm grenade launchers, hand grenades, explosive charges, and night vision goggles—had already been stockpiled in the safe house ahead of their arrival. Each commando had undergone intensive training for the mission, studying their target in detail using scaled models built with intelligence gathered by LTTE spies. On the evening of 23 July, the assault team left the safe house in a private bus, preceded by LTTE intelligence agents tasked with scouting the route and monitoring the area around the airport. Still dressed in civilian clothing, the group stopped at a playground, where they had their final meal before changing into SLAF uniforms. Once disguised, they reboarded the bus and resumed their journey toward the airport, exploiting the scheduled blackout that routinely plunged the area into darkness between 9:45 PM and 11:15 PM.

The group infiltrated the air base perimeter using a water drainage canal, allowing them to bypass the minefield that surrounded the base. Once inside, they deactivated the fence alarm system before proceeding with their planned sabotage. Their first move was to plant explosive charges on three power transformers, which detonated between 03:00 and 03:35 AM, plunging the entire base into darkness. With the power disabled, the Black Tigers split into several teams to carry out their objectives. One three-man unit took control of the control tower, establishing a vantage point to provide covering fire for the other teams. The remaining operatives methodically destroyed SLAF aircraft within their reach, advancing towards the civilian section of the airport to sabotage commercial aircraft. Throughout the operation, they carefully avoided harming civilians, recognising that the blowback from killing Western tourists would have been catastrophic for the LTTE's global image. Initially caught completely by surprise, Sri Lankan security forces eventually mobilised reinforcements and launched a coordinated counterattack at dawn. Troops systematically hunted down the insurgents, forcing several of them to commit suicide once cornered or after exhausting their ammunition. By 08:30 AM, the airport was secured, with 14 Black Tigers killed, along with six Sri Lankan military personnel. No civilians were killed, though several were wounded. The damage was extensive. The SLAF lost eight aircraft, including three K-8 trainers, two Kfir C.7s, two Mi-17 helicopters, and one MiG 27M, while several other aircraft were damaged. Meanwhile, SriLankan Airlines suffered the destruction of four Airbus aircraft—two A-330s (4R-ALE and 4R-ALF), one A-320 (4R-ABA), and one A-340 (4R-ADD). As the LTTE had intended, the attack proved a major humiliation for the Sri Lankan government, with widespread international media coverage amplifying its impact. The assault forced multiple passenger aircraft to be rerouted, turning what was already a devastating military and economic blow into a global embarrassment for the state.[18]

3
RIVIRESA

Since the resumption of the war, the Sri Lanka Army (SLA) focused on preparing an all-out offensive to recapture the Jaffna Peninsula, despite the reservations of several senior officers who considered such an undertaking virtually impossible. The planning and logistical buildup were spearheaded by Major General Rohan Daluwatte, the Army Chief of Staff since June 1995, and Colonel Anuruddha Ratwatte, the Deputy Defence Minister (effectively the acting Defence Minister). Ratwatte personally lobbied for and oversaw the procurement of weapons, ammunition, and supplies required for the offensive, placing particular emphasis on securing the logistical means to sustain a prolonged and gruelling campaign. By mid-October 1995, the Sri Lanka Navy and Air Force had transported an astonishing 54,000 tons of equipment and ammunition to the Jaffna Peninsula, ensuring that supply lines would support sustained combat operations. These preparations also included the activation of a dedicated Joint Operations Headquarters to oversee the offensive, along with four newly established divisional commands to manage the rapidly growing force concentration at Palali complex. The new divisions, numbered 51 to 54, each commanded three brigades, all reinforced with engineer, artillery, and armoured units. In total, the SLA amassed approximately 40,000 troops within the Palali complex. However, a portion of this force, particularly those assigned to 54 Division, remained responsible for garrisoning Palali and were therefore not available for offensive operations. Meanwhile, the SLA conducted a series of short-term operations and raids, typically lasting one or two days, designed to expand the Palali perimeter, weaken LTTE forces, and maintain constant pressure on enemy positions. These included Operation Hard Knock (27 July 1995), followed by Jaya Handa (4 August), Shake Hand 1 (8 August), Dragonfire (21 August), Barrel Warmer (26 August), and Shake Hand 2 (12 September). While these operations inflicted steady attrition on the LTTE, their secondary purpose was to hone the combat effectiveness of the troops who would soon be committed to the main offensive.[1]

The LTTE was fully aware of the SLA's build-up in Palali, despite the army's efforts to maintain operational secrecy. Given the limited number of main roads connecting the Kankesanthurai-Palali complex to Jaffna, it was evident that any large-scale advance would have to follow one or more of these routes—just as the Indian Peacekeeping Force (IPKF) had done years earlier. Recognising this, the LTTE reinforced existing defensive positions originally built to resist the IPKF and undertook extensive new fortification efforts. They constructed a series of successive blocking positions along the main roads, ensuring that any SLA advance would be met with layer after layer of resistance. The bunkers were carefully positioned to create interlocking fields of fire, while communication and combat trenches allowed troops to move safely between positions without exposure. Additionally, these fortifications were integrated into vast and densely laid minefields, while obstacles and cover positions, including civilian houses, were extensively booby-trapped to inflict heavy casualties on advancing troops. The LTTE also established an even stronger defensive line at Neerveli, barring the most direct approach to the outskirts of Jaffna. This fortified sector featured underground command bunkers, weapons depots, and multiple concrete firing positions, designed to withstand prolonged bombardment and assaults. Because of the strength of these fortifications and their underestimation of the scale of the SLA build-up, the LTTE leadership remained confident in their ability to block any large-scale offensive towards Jaffna. Their confidence was reflected in a boastful article published in one of their English-language magazines on 24 July 1995, proclaiming their ability to hold the city against any assault[2]:

> The LTTE's military formations are geared up to face any offensive operations by Sri Lanka's armed forces in the Jaffna peninsula. The LTTE leadership is confident that it has a resourceful and highly educated liberation force capable of confronting the aggressive designs of the enemy.[3]

Thunder Strike

The campaign for Jaffna commenced on 1 October 1995 with Operation Thunder Strike, involving 53 Division under the command of Brigadier Janaka Perera. This force, consisting of approximately 5,000 troops, spearheaded the initial assault. Heavily supported by artillery fire and airstrikes, the division's three brigades advanced from the southern side of the Palali perimeter, pushing towards Atchuveli, Avarankai, and Puttur. The LTTE, initially stunned by the intense bombardment, gave ground in the early phase of the offensive. However, as the battle progressed, the insurgents mounted fierce resistance and, on 3 October, launched a large-scale night counterattack against 531 Brigade. The SLA troops held their ground, successfully repulsing the LTTE assault and inflicting heavy casualties on the attacking forces. Over the following days, 53 Division achieved its primary objectives, securing key positions that would serve as launching pads for the larger corps-sized offensive to follow. Controlling this area was strategically vital, as it enabled the use of the Point Pedro-Jaffna road and ensured that any potential LTTE counteroffensive from the Valvettithurai area could be neutralised. By the end of the operation, 53 Division had suffered 54 soldiers killed in action and another 123 wounded. The SLA claimed to have recovered the bodies of 125 LTTE fighters, marking the first significant territorial gain in the battle to reclaim Jaffna.

At this stage, it became clear that the SLA had carefully studied LTTE tactics and had developed effective countermeasures. The army's operations were now meticulously planned, ensuring that advancing units maintained cohesion and avoided leaving vulnerable gaps in their formations. Unlike in previous years, artillery support had improved significantly, providing a level of firepower far superior to anything previously available. Additionally, armour and infantry units had refined their coordination, enabling them to operate with greater tactical efficiency on the battlefield. Operation Thunder Strike demonstrated that the LTTE's confidence in its ability to halt a large-scale offensive against Jaffna was misplaced. The SLA had evolved into a formidable force, as disciplined and tactically astute as the IPKF had been eight years earlier. The rapid and systematic advances of the army exposed the limitations of the LTTE's defensive strategy, marking a turning point in the campaign for Jaffna.[4]

Table 7 Operation Riveresa order of battle, mid-October 1995

Unit	CO	Comment
Joint Operation Headquarter	Maj. Gen. Rohan de S. Daluwatte	
51 Division	Brig. Gen. Neil Das	C Squadron, 5 SLAC, attached with 10 T-85
511 Brigade	Col. Mahendra Wijeratne	
512 Brigade	Col. Ananda Hamangoda	
513 Brigade	Col. Gamini Jayasundera	
52 Division	Brig. P.A. Karunatillake	A and B Squadrons, 4 SLAC, attached with 20 T-55
521 Brigade	Brig. K.B Egodawela	
522 Brigade	Col. Jayambathy Wijeratne	
523 Brigade	Col. Lawrence Fernando	
53 Division	Brig Janaka Perera	B and C Squadrons, 3 SLAC, attached with 10 T-85 and 10 T-86
531 Brigade	Col. Hiran Halangode	Also known as the Airmobile Brigade. 1 & 4 GR, 7 GW.
532 Brigade	Col. Lakshaman Rajasinghe	6SLLI, 6 SLSR, 8 VIR
534 Brigade	Col. Percy Fernando	Also known as the Independant Brigade. 2 Commando, 1 and 2 Special Forces.

Sunrays over the Peninsula

Operation Riviresa (Sunrays) commenced in earnest on 17 October 1995, with the SLA finally revealing its main axes of advance. The offensive was structured around two parallel thrusts, separated by five kilometres, designed to steadily push towards Jaffna. 51 Division advanced along the Palali-Jaffna road, while 52 Division moved along the Point Pedro-Jaffna road, with its southern flank protected by the Uppu Aru lagoon. Meanwhile, 53 Division was held in reserve, ready to exploit breakthroughs or reinforce key sectors. To divert LTTE forces away from the main offensive, SLA troops based on Mandaitivu Island launched harassment attacks across the Jaffna Peninsula, forcing the Tigers to keep some of their units tied down elsewhere. The first day of the offensive turned into a brutal struggle, as leading SLA battalions suffered heavy casualties, losing 54 soldiers killed in action while managing to advance only 200 metres. However, once the LTTE's initial defensive belt was breached, the pace of the advance improved, though progress remained slow at an average of just 400 metres per day. This was due to fierce LTTE resistance, the dense minefields, booby traps, and IEDs laid by the insurgents, and the SLA's methodical approach to combat operations. The army employed a deliberate and systematic assault strategy, ensuring that enemy firing positions were first identified and then neutralised with heavy support weapons before advancing further. Armoured vehicles played a key role, at times demolishing houses with their tracks to create clear fields of fire for their main weapons. Once an LTTE bunker or stronghold was captured, SLA units would pause to reorganise before continuing their advance. While this method was highly effective in preventing LTTE infiltration behind SLA lines, it also allowed the Tigers to withdraw to their next defensive position, where the entire process would begin again. At one stage, the LTTE even deployed improvised armoured vehicles, but these proved completely ineffective and were quickly neutralised. Over time, some infantry battalions, particularly the 6th Gemunu Watch (6th GR), began adopting more flexible tactics, focusing on outflanking enemy positions rather than engaging in direct frontal assaults. Despite this, the overall pace of the advance for both divisions remained slow, as each new LTTE defensive position had to be painstakingly cleared before progress could continue.

A squad of LTTE infantrymen in Jaffna, preparing to move toward the front. (Albert Grandolini Collection)

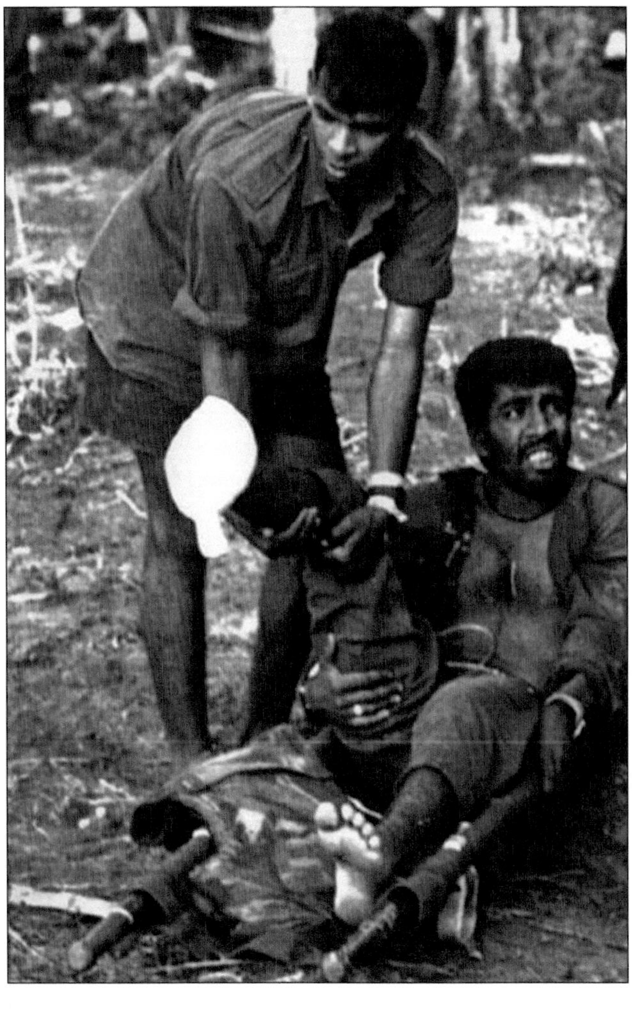

Above: The insurgents proved not only unable to stop the 51 and 52 Divisions during the first weeks of Riviresa, but took heavy casualties too, as shown by this picture of the SLA, showing killed fighters and captured equipment, foremost Type 56 LMGs and Type 69 RPGs. (Albert Grandolini Collection)

A major cause for the SLA losses were the immense amounts of mines, IEDs and booby-traps laid down by the insurgents. (Albert Grandolini Collection)

At last, the two SLA divisions reached the LTTE's strongest defensive belt, with 52 Division facing the most intense battle of the entire campaign at Neerveli. The fighting was brutal and prolonged, but on 30 October, the SLA finally broke through the enemy defensive complex, thanks largely to the overwhelming firepower it had brought to bear. The sheer volume of artillery support was staggering; the Type 83 howitzers alone had fired 50,000 122mm shells since the beginning of the offensive. However, just as the army seemed poised to press forward, heavy and unrelenting rains brought operations to a standstill for the next ten days. Even tracked armoured vehicles struggled to move through the waterlogged terrain, while mortars became almost useless, as their base plates sank into the mud upon firing, making accurate targeting impossible. This unexpected lull gave the LTTE valuable time to construct yet another defensive belt, this time running from Urumpirai to Kopay. Once the weather improved, the SLA resumed its advance, with 51 Division attacking Urumpirai and 52 Division assaulting Kopay. Both localities fell within a matter of days, further weakening the LTTE's ability to hold Jaffna. At this stage, the Joint Operations Headquarters undertook a complete reshuffling of forces to optimise the final push towards the city. 51 Division was withdrawn and redeployed, tasked with securing the vast territory gained since the start of the campaign. Meanwhile, 53 Division, which had been held

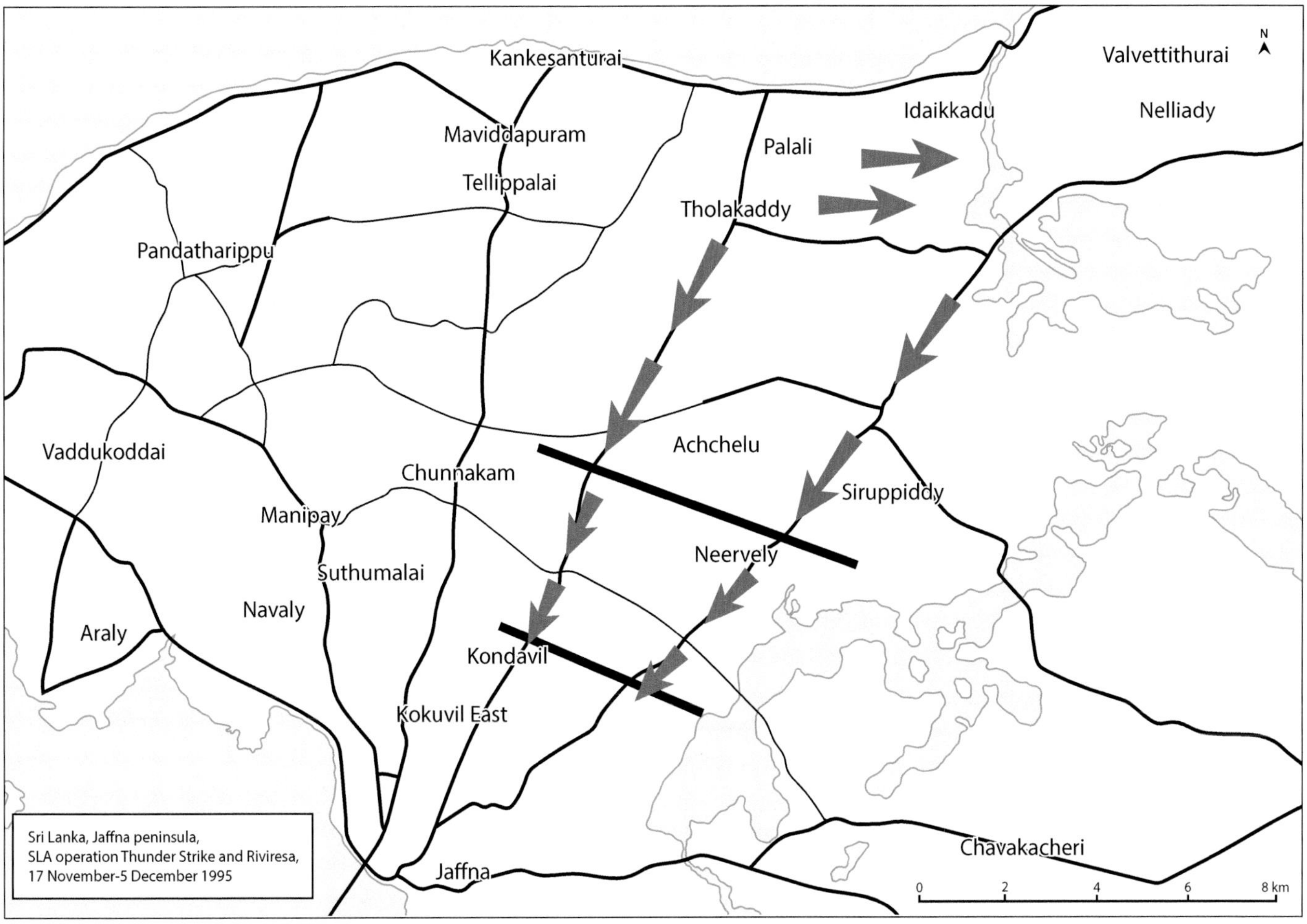

Map showing operation Thunderstrike, and then the first phase of Operation Riviresa, which led to the capture of Jaffna city. (Map by George Anderson)

in reserve, was brought forward and given the decisive mission of investing Jaffna itself. 52 Division, in turn, was assigned to secure 53 Division's flanks and rear, ensuring that the final assault could proceed without the risk of encirclement or counterattack.[5]

Fall of Jaffna

From 18 November 1995, the SLA's advance was significantly bolstered by the arrival of a new and highly potent weapon—the Mi-24V Hind attack helicopters, freshly inducted into the SLAF. The three gunships, still crewed by Russian instructors and SLAF trainees, arrived at Palali Air Base and immediately commenced strike missions against LTTE positions. Armed with guns and S-8 80mm rockets, the Mi-24Vs flew a total of 72 combat missions during Operation Riviresa, delivering devastating firepower to enemy fortifications and troop concentrations. The impact of the Hinds was especially pronounced given the limited effectiveness of previous SLAF air support. Until then, the bulk of close air support had been provided by SF.260 aircraft, which, while nimble, were poorly armed and highly vulnerable to LTTE ground fire. During the campaign, No. 5 Squadron's F-7 jets carried out only a handful of bombing runs, leaving most air support operations to the SF.260s, which managed just 16 combat sorties throughout the offensive. In contrast, the arrival of the Mi-24Vs provided the SLA with a heavily armed, armoured, and far more survivable aerial asset. The ruggedness of the Mi-24V was tested almost immediately. On 19 November, CHF-612 was severely damaged by ground fire just after completing a strike near Jaffna University. The damage was extensive—four of the five rotor blades were struck by bullets, while the main rotor gearbox and hydraulic systems sustained serious hits. Despite these catastrophic failures, the Russian pilot managed to keep the helicopter airborne and nurse it back to Palali Air Base. With its landing gear rendered inoperable, ground crews hurriedly assembled a makeshift landing pad using a mattress of tyres, allowing the pilot to execute a controlled emergency landing, saving both the aircraft and the crew. This incident highlighted the Hind's battlefield resilience and reinforced its reputation as a formidable close air support platform—one that would play an increasingly vital role in the SLA's ongoing campaign to retake Jaffna.[6]

Despite the firepower advantage and steady SLA advances, 53 Division still encountered sporadic but determined LTTE resistance. One of the most challenging obstacles faced by 531 Brigade was what its soldiers referred to as the 'explosive line'—a series of mined houses rigged to detonate as soon as SLA troops reached them, significantly slowing progress. Meanwhile, 534 Brigade, advancing along a parallel route, found itself subjected to a flanking LTTE night counterattack at Thirunelvely. However, the insurgents had the misfortune of running into the 1st Special Forces Regiment, whose battle-hardened operators repulsed the assault with devastating effect, reportedly recovering over 100 enemy bodies in the aftermath. With this threat neutralised, 534 Brigade resumed its advance, systematically overwhelming heavily defended enemy positions at Nallur before securing key portions of the Jaffna-Kandy road in the early hours of 22 November, bringing the SLA to the very heart of the city. 532 Brigade was also advancing along the same axis, tightening the noose around the remaining LTTE positions. As the final push into Jaffna commenced, 53 Division adopted a careful and methodical approach, investing the city street by street. By this stage, LTTE resistance had largely dissipated, with the exception of one sustained firefight at the local hospital, where insurgents made their last stand. By 2 December 1995, Jaffna was declared cleared of LTTE presence, marking the successful completion of the first phase of Operation Riviresa. However, victory came at a heavy cost—the SLA suffered 16 officers and 337 soldiers killed in action, with at least 1,500 wounded. The recapture of Jaffna, a major political and strategic milestone, sent shockwaves through the LTTE, forcing them to abandon conventional warfare in the region and retreat into the jungles of the Vanni, where they would regroup for future conflicts.[7]

Exodus

However, unbeknownst to the Sri Lankan military at the time, there was another crucial factor that explained the comparatively swift recapture of Jaffna town. While the SLA's firepower and tactics had certainly played a major role, the LTTE's own strategic decision-making was just as significant.

Attempting to halt the SLA's relentless advance had come at a tremendous cost for the Tigers, with 438 LTTE fighters killed in action during Operation Riviresa. In the aftermath of the fall of Neerveli, the LTTE leadership realised that continuing to defend Jaffna at all costs would only lead to the senseless depletion of its forces. Rather than sacrificing more fighters in futile urban combat, they made the strategic decision to withdraw the bulk of their forces and preserve their strength for future battles. From that moment onwards, only the absolute minimum number of militants were deployed to engage in delaying actions, buying precious time for the movement to evacuate its fighters, stockpiles of weapons, and ammunition from the Jaffna Peninsula to the Vanni mainland. In doing so, the LTTE effectively abandoned Jaffna as a military stronghold and established its new de facto capital at Kilinochchi. This strategy was not without precedent—the LTTE had used similar tactics when facing the IPKF's offensive years earlier. However, this time, the withdrawal was even more comprehensive, allowing the movement to consolidate its forces in the Vanni and prepare for the next phase of the war. While the Sri Lankan government celebrated the fall of Jaffna as a decisive victory, the LTTE's retreat was, in reality, a calculated move, ensuring that its military capabilities remained intact for future confrontations.

From 30 October onwards, the LTTE ordered all civilians living in Jaffna town and its surrounding areas to flee towards the Thenmarachchi division, triggering a massive exodus within hours. Entire families abandoned their homes, carrying only what they could, as thousands poured onto the roads in a desperate attempt to escape the looming battle for Jaffna. The scale of the displacement was unprecedented, with men, women, and children walking for miles, often under fire, as SLA artillery and airstrikes intensified. Many had nowhere to go, forced to seek shelter in the open, while others relied on temples, schools, and makeshift camps. The humanitarian crisis deepened as food and water became scarce, and illness spread among the displaced. One of the countless refugees later recalled the harrowing experience, describing the panic, uncertainty, and fear that gripped those forced to leave behind their homes, livelihoods, and entire lives in the face of the Sri Lankan military's advance and the LTTE's strategic withdrawal:

> Imagine a 15-foot-wide road. By nightfall, the road was so jammed with people, beast, and the odd car, here and there, believe me, there was virtually no movement. You could take no more than a couple of steps at a time.[8]

Thus, when 53 Division finally entered Jaffna, they found themselves in a ghost town, with only a handful of residents remaining. The scale of the exodus was staggering, with estimates suggesting that roughly 450,000 civilians fled—either voluntarily or under duress—within the Jaffna Peninsula. Of these, approximately 100,000 made their way into the Vanni, a perilous journey that required crossing the Kilali lagoon using the dangerous boat shuttle system operated by the LTTE. From the LTTE's perspective, however, this mass displacement served multiple strategic purposes. First, by forcing civilians to leave Jaffna, the movement ensured that it retained control over as large a population as possible in its new strongholds in the Vanni. Second, the sight of hundreds of thousands of people fleeing ahead of the SLA's advance became a powerful propaganda tool. The LTTE was quick to capitalise on the humanitarian crisis, using it to portray the Sri Lankan military as a force of destruction. In one of its official communiqués, the movement framed the exodus as evidence of the population's rejection of government rule, reinforcing its narrative of resistance against what it depicted as an occupation force:

> The mass exodus of Tamils from Jaffna peninsula has dealt a severe blow and signalled a political defeat to the Chandrika administration. It has made meaningless the political objective behind the Jaffna invasion.[9]

However, this attempt at damage control did little to mitigate the sheer magnitude of the disaster for the LTTE. The loss of Jaffna, the historical heart of Tamil irredentism in Sri Lanka, was a severe symbolic and strategic blow. Along with the territory itself, the LTTE also lost access to vital local resources, further weakening its operational capabilities in the North. Moreover, the mass exodus ultimately proved temporary. While the LTTE had initially forced civilians to flee, it had no means of preventing their return indefinitely. As security in Jaffna gradually stabilised under government control, displaced civilians began making their way back to their homes. By the end of 1996, approximately 150,000 refugees had already returned to the Valikamam division, diminishing the LTTE's ability to claim that the population had permanently rejected Sri Lankan rule.[10]

Riviresa II & III

With the Valikamam administrative division fully secured, including Jaffna town, the SLA turned its attention to the next phase of Operation Riviresa—the capture of the Thenmarachchi division, where a large number of refugees from Jaffna had gathered. The offensive began on 19 April 1996, led by 52 and 53 Divisions, each reinforced with an armoured regiment. Advancing along two distinct axes, the SLA encountered sporadic but at times intense LTTE resistance, which resulted in dozens of fatalities. However, the insurgents harboured no illusions about halting the SLA's advance. Their strategy was simply to inflict as many casualties as possible in areas where the terrain provided a defensive advantage. Despite these efforts, by 2 May, the entire Thenmarachchi division had fallen under army control, and tens of thousands of refugees were returned to Jaffna. The third and final phase of Riviresa followed just two weeks later, on 15 May 1996. This time, 53 Division, reinforced by 533 Brigade, advanced into the Vadamarachchi division, an area historically significant to the LTTE, as it included key strongholds such as Valvettithurai—Velupillai Prabhakaran's birthplace. However, the LTTE did not offer any resistance, having already withdrawn its forces from the region. By 25 May 1996, the entire Vadamarachchi division was under government control, and more importantly, the years-long siege of Elephant Pass was finally broken. With the entire Jaffna Peninsula firmly in government hands, it appeared that Colombo was well on its way to "taming the Tigers". Furthermore, by the end of 1996, most of the civilians who had been displaced by the LTTE had returned to their homes, further solidifying the government's hold over the region. However, the LTTE had used the opportunity to infiltrate operatives back into the Peninsula, reinforcing the network of dormant cells it had left behind before withdrawing. Unsurprisingly, small-scale insurgent activities soon resumed, with the LTTE focusing on IED attacks. These were often deadly, such as the incident on 18 March 1996, when a military truck was blown up, killing 18 soldiers and wounding 23 others. The insurgents also carried out high-profile assassinations, the most notable occurring on 5 July 1996, when a female Black Tiger suicide bomber infiltrated a public gathering in Jaffna town, where Housing Minister Nimal Siripala was present. The Minister survived, but the blast killed 27 people, including Maj. Gen. A.S.S.K. Hamangoda, the commanding officer of 512 Brigade. Though LTTE attacks remained at a relatively low intensity, they were highly effective in tying down large numbers of security personnel, forcing the Sri Lankan military to divert resources to counterinsurgency operations. The Tigers had lost Jaffna, but they were far from defeated.

Above: The aftermath of the Black Tiger attack against the Orugodawatte tank farm on 20 October 1995. (Albert Grandolini Collection)

Right: Shocked civilians just after the massive explosion which gutted the Central Bank Building, only a few blocks away, on 31 January 1996. (Albert Grandolini Collection)

Nonetheless, Operation Riviresa delivered a crushing defeat to the LTTE. The loss of Jaffna Peninsula, the LTTE's historical stronghold, marked one of the most significant military victories for the Sri Lankan government up to that point. At first glance, SLA casualties appeared relatively limited given the scale of the operation, with 408 soldiers killed in action. However, the true cost of the victory was far higher, with a staggering 2,906 troops wounded in action—a figure that underscored the intensity of the fighting and the ferocity of LTTE resistance. [11] Despite these losses, the morale within the SLA soared. The successful execution of a large-scale conventional operation reinforced a sense of confidence and accomplishment within the military ranks. This sentiment was captured in the words of General Gerry de Silva, who, in the aftermath of the operation, expressed the prevailing optimism and self-assurance that had taken root within the army:

> Pre-operational training paid off and the dynamic leadership of junior field commanders at battalion/regimental level and the senior commanders at brigade levels must be lauded. These brilliant field commanders who were also personally in the 'thick of battle', with their intelligent appraisal from experience gained, were instrumental in devolving a plan to move on a broad front which ensured quick achievement of the objective on taking Jaffna.[12]

At a much lower level in the chain of command, 2nd Lt. Sylvester Perera, serving as a platoon commander in the 6th GW, concluded that:

> For the first time in the history of Sri Lanka, the armed forces launched an offensive operation involving three divisions. Our two infantry divisions launched the operation along a narrow front on converging axes using conventional tactics. We were vulnerable to LTTE indirect fire, but the concentration of force, which was applied at the right time and place, helped to outnumber the LTTE and subsequently demoralized them. Unprecedented concentrated fire from artillery, mortars, and tanks, combined with air and continuous ground assaults, broke the will and cohesion of the LTTE forces.[13]

Tiger reprisals

The campaign to recapture the Jaffna Peninsula had devastating repercussions far beyond the battlefield, reaching into the political and economic heart of Sri Lanka. The LTTE leadership, determined to retaliate, sought to strike major economic targets in the capital while also launching terror attacks on an unprecedented scale. These attacks were orchestrated by the highly secretive National Intelligence Wing, one of the LTTE's two intelligence services, which had maintained a well-established network of operatives in Colombo since the late 1980s. This clandestine infrastructure enabled the Tigers to strike with precision and maximize the psychological impact of their attacks. The first major strike occurred on 7 August 1995, when a Black Tiger suicide bomber detonated himself near the Office of the Chief Minister for the Western Province, killing 22 people and injuring dozens more. The next assault came on 20 October, when a small commando unit from the Johnny Miller Padai Ani launched a daring attack on two vital economic targets—the Kolonnawa refinery and the Orugodawatte tank farm on the outskirts of Colombo. The insurgents managed to destroy eight oil tanks with RPG fire before engaging in a fierce firefight with security forces, who had rushed to contain the attack. Less than a month later, on 11 November 1995, another Black Tiger suicide bomber struck outside Sri Lanka Army Headquarters, killing eleven civilians and wounding 52 others. The frequency and scale of these attacks signalled a shift in LTTE strategy, demonstrating that even as the movement suffered territorial losses, it could still project power deep into government-controlled areas, causing chaos and economic disruption.

Far worse was to come when the LTTE's terror campaign reached its deadly climax on 31 January 1996. Late that morning, a truck loaded with several tons of explosives managed to approach the Central Bank building—close to the World Trade Centre—in the heart of Colombo, just a short distance from the Presidential Residence. As the truck reached the security checkpoint, three Black Tigers leapt out and opened fire on the guards, clearing the way for the vehicle to advance. The driver then accelerated towards the building before triggering the massive bomb, unleashing an explosion of unprecedented scale. The blast devastated not only the Central Bank itself but also severely damaged several surrounding buildings, leaving the area in ruins. The attack resulted in at least 80 deaths and over 1,200 wounded, making it one of the deadliest terrorist attacks in Sri Lankan history. As if this atrocity was not enough, the LTTE struck again several months later, on 24 July 1996. This time, a time bomb hidden in a train detonated at Dehiwala Railway Station, killing 57 civilians and injuring 356 others. The scale and frequency of these attacks underscored the LTTE's ability to strike at will, bringing terror to Colombo's streets even as the war raged in the North. [14]

4
DISASTER IN THE VANNI

Once the LTTE's withdrawal into the Vanni was complete, the region became the movement's new heartland, serving as the political, military, and logistical nerve centre of the organisation. The Vanni now housed Kilinochchi, the LTTE's new de facto capital, along with a vast network of headquarters, training camps, hospitals, depots, and workshops. These facilities were scattered across dozens of heavily fortified camps, many of which included underground bunkers and were well concealed within the dense jungle terrain. From early 1996 onwards, the LTTE focused on consolidating its position. It not only reorganised its forces and re-established the infrastructure evacuated from the Jaffna Peninsula but also embarked on a massive recruitment and training drive to compensate for its losses and expand its strength. In 1995 alone, the LTTE had lost 1,505 fighters, necessitating an aggressive effort to replenish and strengthen its ranks. This expansion also extended to the Sea Tigers, who had been forced to relocate the bulk of their naval assets from the Vadamarachchi area to the eastern coast of the Vanni, where they could continue their maritime operations despite the loss of Jaffna.

In this context, the Sri Lanka Army (SLA) camp at Mullaitivu became a significant obstacle for the LTTE leadership, posing a direct threat to the movement's heartland for several reasons. Firstly, the base itself was a major strategic concern. Although completely isolated, its coastal location meant it could be reinforced easily by sea, making it a potential launching pad for a government offensive deep into LTTE-controlled territory. Only a few kilometres separated Mullaitivu from several key LTTE camps and logistical hubs in Puthukkudiyiruppu, which had been operational for years. A well-supplied and fortified Mullaitivu posed a clear danger to the LTTE's operational security in the region. Secondly, the base housed a small Sri Lanka Navy (SLN) detachment, which played a critical role in monitoring and disrupting LTTE naval activities. This unit not only assisted in unloading supplies brought in by Navy ships but also operated a coastal radar system that allowed the SLN to track and counter Sea Tiger movements. By keeping watch over the waters between Kankesanthurai and Trincomalee, this radar significantly hindered the LTTE's ability to operate freely at sea, making it a priority target for the insurgents. Lastly, beyond its strategic importance, Mullaitivu had immense symbolic value. Despite the LTTE's propaganda efforts, the fall of Jaffna had been a crushing defeat, deeply damaging the movement's martial reputation. A high-profile military victory was desperately needed to restore morale and reassert the LTTE's dominance. As a result, from early 1996, the LTTE leadership—under the direct supervision of Velupillai Prabhakaran—began meticulously planning an assault on Mullaitivu. The attack, which would come to be known as Operation Oyatha Alaikal (Unceasing Waves), was seen as a crucial opportunity to reverse the movement's fortunes. As always, the LTTE approached the operation with extensive preparation and intelligence gathering. The entire force of available fighters was mobilised for the attack, with many being sent to Pooneryn for training, though they were kept unaware of their real target. Meanwhile, LTTE intelligence operatives—the Spy Tigers—conducted continuous infiltrations into the base, gathering detailed information on its layout, defensive strength, and troop movements. The LTTE also studied potential government rescue operations, preparing to counter them effectively. To simulate the assault, detailed sand-table models of the base were built, allowing fighters to rehearse every phase of the attack. Meanwhile, night after night, LTTE operatives painstakingly cleared multiple paths through the minefields surrounding the camp, ensuring that the assault force could move in undetected when the time came. The scale of the preparation and the sheer number of fighters committed demonstrated that the LTTE viewed this battle as a turning point in the war.[1]

A giant with feet of clay

At first glance, the Mullaitivu base appeared to be an impregnable fortress. Spanning 2.9 kilometres in length and 1.5 kilometres in width, its location provided natural defensive advantages on three sides. The eastern flank ran along the beaches of the sea, while the western front was shielded by the Nandikadal lagoon. The northern perimeter was further secured by the estuary connecting the lagoon to the sea, leaving only the southern flank as a viable route for a large-scale ground assault. By mid-1996, the garrison had been heavily reinforced in anticipation of an LTTE attack. The recently activated 25 Brigade, under the command of Brigadier Lawrence Fernando, was responsible for the base's defence. The brigade controlled two infantry battalions—the 6th Vijayabahu Infantry Regiment (VIR) and the 9th Sri Lanka Sinha Regiment (SLSR)—with additional engineer, police, and navy detachments stationed within the camp, bringing the total garrison strength to approximately 1,500 men. Firepower was another formidable aspect of the base's defences. The garrison was supported by three artillery troops, manning two 122mm Type 83 howitzers and four 120mm mortars, which complemented the 15 81mm and 41 60mm mortars assigned to the two infantry battalions. Ammunition stocks were sufficient for a period of intense combat, with 610 122mm shells and 377 120mm mortar bombs readily available—more than enough to inflict devastating casualties on any massed infantry assault. Beyond its internal firepower, the Mullaitivu base could call upon rapid air and naval support. The Sri Lanka Air Force (SLAF) maintained close air support assets at Palali, Anuradhapura, and China Bay air bases, ensuring that reinforcements and air strikes could be deployed at short notice. Additionally, Sri Lanka Navy (SLN) combat vessels stationed in Trincomalee were only a few hours' sailing away, ready to provide fire support or emergency reinforcements if necessary. Given these formidable defensive measures, heavy weaponry, and access to air and naval support, the Mullaitivu base was a well-fortified stronghold. On paper, it seemed highly capable of withstanding an LTTE assault.

However, beneath the illusion of security, the Mullaitivu base was riddled with vulnerabilities—many of which the LTTE's meticulous intelligence-gathering practices had identified over time. These flaws, overlooked or ignored by the Sri Lankan military, would ultimately prove fatal when the Tigers launched their attack. One of the greatest weaknesses was the garrison's lack of active patrolling. Since 1990, the LTTE had largely left the base undisturbed, leading to a gradual erosion of defensive discipline. Over the years, the garrison ceased to conduct regular patrols or raids in the surrounding areas, effectively ceding the territory outside the perimeter to the insurgents without resistance. This passivity allowed the LTTE to operate freely in the area, strengthening their positions and observing the base's routines undetected. The observation posts, always positioned in the same locations near the perimeter, were easily avoided by the Tigers, who learned to move unnoticed, even while conducting activities in the immediate vicinity of the camp. Another critical flaw was the degradation of the minefields. The garrison constantly lacked barbed wire, meaning that the boundaries of the minefields could not be properly marked or maintained. As a result, wild animals frequently triggered the mines, and crucially, these were not replaced. The problem reached such an extreme that during one engineer survey, it was discovered that only two functional anti-personnel mines remained in an entire 400-metre stretch of the perimeter. This severe oversight made the task of LTTE sappers far easier, as they could clear access paths through the minefields with minimal risk. The structural layout of the base itself was another major vulnerability. Due to the camp's limited width, the first and main defensive lines were often separated by as little as 50 metres. This narrow gap completely undermined the defensive strategy, as there was no adequate killing field between the lines. Instead of acting as a fallback position, the second defensive line could be overrun almost immediately once the first was breached. The lack of communication trenches between these positions further exacerbated the issue, meaning that retreating soldiers would be constantly exposed to enemy fire with no cover or safe routes to reorganise. Instead of offering depth to the defence, the tight layout played directly into the hands of any well-coordinated assault team. Even the trenches themselves became a burden rather than an asset. The loose, sandy soil caused them to collapse frequently, requiring constant maintenance. Soldiers spent more time digging and repairing trenches than focusing on combat readiness, further draining their morale. The psychological toll on the garrison was immense—many of the same troops had been stationed there for years, with little rotation and no prospect of relief. Their isolation was compounded by prolonged periods of food shortages, with rations that were both scarce and of poor quality. To make matters worse, the base's firepower was concentrated in a single, highly vulnerable location. All 122mm howitzers, 120mm mortars, and 81mm mortars were positioned together on the beach, 150 to 200 metres from the sea, near the Brigade Headquarters at the centre of the camp. This disastrous placement meant that a single, well-coordinated attack could neutralise the camp's entire artillery capability in one strike. In sum, while Mullaitivu appeared on paper to be a fortress, its defensive weaknesses were deeply ingrained. The absence of patrols, the failure to maintain minefields, the poor layout of defensive lines, the exhausting trench maintenance, low morale, and the disastrous artillery positioning all combined to make the base ripe for a devastating assault. The LTTE had taken careful note of these weaknesses—and they would soon exploit them to full effect.[2]

Killing blow

During June and the first half of July 1996, the LTTE undertook a massive build-up in the Mullaitivu area, assembling an estimated 4,000 fighters drawn from its most elite and battle-hardened units. Combatants from the Charles Anthony, Chiruthaigal, Jeyanthan, and 2nd Lt. Malathi Padai Ani regiments were concentrated in preparation for the impending assault, marking one of the most significant military mobilisations of the war. Simultaneously, the Sea Tigers were also preparing for their role in the operation. At least three dozen combat, suicide, and fast transport craft were readied, along with the necessary tractors and launch equipment positioned on the surrounding beaches. These preparations ensured that the naval wing of the LTTE could rapidly deploy reinforcements, evacuate casualties, and disrupt any attempts by the Sri Lankan Navy to intervene. This carefully orchestrated build-up underscored the scale and ambition of the operation. The LTTE's leadership was fully committed to the assault, pooling vast resources and manpower to achieve a decisive victory. With its forces massed and ready, the insurgents awaited the signal to strike, preparing to unleash an attack that would shake the Sri Lankan military to its core.

The meticulously prepared onslaught commenced at 01:30 AM on 18 July 1996, with the LTTE executing a well-coordinated, multi-pronged attack. Fortuitously for the insurgents, both the Brigade and 9 SLSR commanding officers were away at the time, further weakening the already vulnerable chain of command. The initial assault targeted the northern side of the perimeter, where LTTE fighters swiftly breached the two defensive lines. At the same time, infiltrated insurgents who had already entered the base began lobbing grenades into bunkers, spreading chaos and disorder among the defenders. Simultaneously, Sea Tiger boats rushed toward the centre of the base, rapidly disembarking assault squads who immediately attacked the main artillery position, overwhelming it within minutes. With the artillery captured, the same force advanced on the Brigade headquarters, which was swiftly overrun. Within a staggeringly short span of time, the defenders lost both their central command structure and their ability to call in indirect fire support. As the battle raged, another amphibious assault came from the Nandikadal lagoon, targeting the middle of the camp. The insurgents breached the defence lines with alarming ease, driving deep into the base. Pressing their advantage, they advanced toward the sea, making a junction with the Sea Tiger units that had attacked from the beachfront. Within less than an hour, the entire camp was effectively split in two, severing communication and coordination among the defenders. At this stage, the garrison fell into disarray, its cohesion shattered by the relentless and coordinated LTTE offensive. The insurgents pressed their advantage, pouring more and more fighters into the battle, systematically overrunning the remaining defensive positions from multiple angles. By early morning, the entire base had effectively fallen, although isolated pockets of resistance remained. These hastily improvised defensive stands were formed by scattered groups of soldiers and officers who, despite the general chaos, fought on with fierce determination. However, their efforts were ultimately in vain, and the last of these holdouts were systematically eliminated by the afternoon of 19 July. In a single night of intense combat, the LTTE had achieved one of its most decisive battlefield victories, completely annihilating a key Sri Lankan military installation.

The almost instantaneous penetration of the base's defensive perimeter severely compromised the efficiency of SLAF air support. By 02:45 AM, the SLAF scrambled a Pucara, followed shortly after by a Y-12, which was to act as an airborne command post. This marked the beginning of a series of night airstrikes involving the lone Pucara, pairs of Mi-24 gunships and SF-260TPs, and eventually, a duo of Kfirs that conducted a bombing run at 07:25 AM. Despite this swift aerial response, the situation on the ground rendered air support almost ineffective. With LTTE fighters already inside the base, targeting the enemy without also hitting the defenders proved impossible. As a result, all strafing and bombing runs were redirected towards the insurgents' avenues of approach, attempting to disrupt reinforcements and supply lines rather than directly engaging the forces already inside the base. However, this tactical adjustment came far too late to alter the course of the battle. By the time SLAF airstrikes intensified, the LTTE had already established control over most of the camp, rendering aerial intervention largely symbolic rather than strategically decisive.[3]

Still from a LTTE video taken from a Sea Tiger attack craft showing the naval engagement off Mullaithivu on 19 July 1996. (Adrien Fontanellaz Collection)

Still from the same LTTE video showing the last moment of SLNS *Ranaviru,* just after it had been rammed by the first out of three Black Sea Tiger suicide craft. (Adrien Fontanellaz Collection)

LTTE fighters waiting in their trenches before a new assault. (LTTE)

A female infantry squad of the 2nd Lt. Malathi Padai Ani relaxing before a new combat operation (LTTE)

Tigers busy carrying away one of the two Type 83 122mm howitzers captured in the Mullaithivu camp, before the SLAF could target these with airstrikes. (LTTE)

An insurgent machine gunner during the operation Sath Jaya. Of note is his Minimi 5.56mm LMG. (LTTE)

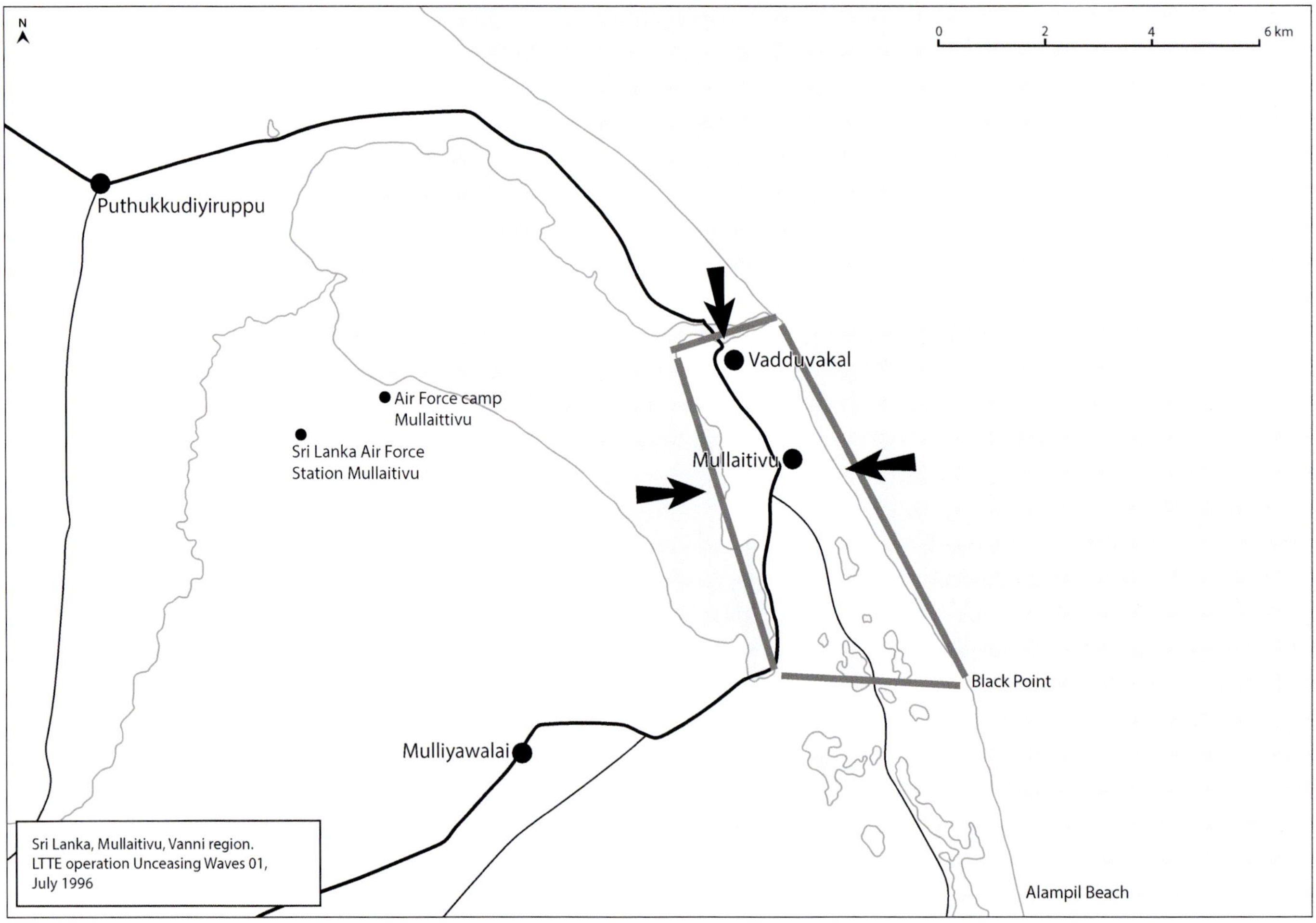

The LTTE assault against the Mullaithivu camp. (Map by George Anderson)

In 1995, the 5 SLAC was equipped with a total of 30 Chinese-made Type 63-II armoured personnel carriers. They rapidly proved a disappointment and were dubbed 'Ice Cream Vans' because of their thin armour – which could be penetrated even by 7.62mm rounds, in use by nearly all of assault rifles of the LTTE. Inserts show tactical insignia of the 5 SLAC as applied on its APCs. (Artwork by David Bocquelet)

The Chinese-designed Type 83 gun calibre 122mm proved far more suitable for deployment from the often water-soaked soil of Sri Lanka than the Soviet-designed D-30 howitzer of the same calibre. Therefore the Sri Lankan Artillery Corps acquired relatively large numbers and allocated all of them to its three regiments, although in the People's Republic of China, this weapon with a range of 15 kilometres, was available in relatively small numbers only. (Artwork by David Bocquelet)

Except for additional tube artillery, in 2001 the Sri Lanka Artillery Corps also acquired a total of 24 RM-70 multiple rocket launchers, with 40 tubes for artillery rockets calibre 122mm from the Czech Republic and Slovakia. Thanks to their ability to fire the entire salvo of 40 rockets in less than two minutes, and then quickly reload, these weapons significantly increased the firepower of the corps. (Artwork by David Bocquelet)

In 1998, Colombo acquired a small batach of BTR-80A wheeled armoured personnel carriers. Thanks to their 30mm autocannon, they proved particularly useful in facing the LTTE's road ambushes. The batch delivered seems to have received a camouflage pattern similar to the woodland pattern of the US Army. (Artwork by David Bocquelet)

Highly satisfied by their Czech-manufactured T-55s, the Sri Lankan Armoured Corps continued the acquisition of this main battle tank, primarily in the form of purchasing additional batches of T-55AM2s. These arrived equipped with an improved fire-control system and additional armour on the turret and the bottom of the hull. The first 18 T-55AM2s reached Sri Lanka in January 1998, while another 36 followed in 2001. (Artwork by David Bocquelet)

During the Eelam War III, the LTTE is known to have operated a single T-55 captured in the Pooneryn area in 1993. The vehicle was primarily deployed to provide fire-support for insurgent assault teams, but became involved in several ambushes against ships of the Sri Lankan Navy, too. (Artwork by David Bocquelet)

Over the years, the LTTE developed several types of suicide boat for its Sea Tigers service. All were very fast and often received improvised armour in form of steel plates protecting the crew space from the fire of enemy machine guns during their final dash towards the target. This example also received a navigation radar and a Browning machine gun calibre 12.7mm. (Artwork by David Bocquelet)

One of most successful warships of the Sea Tigers was the *Miraj* attack boat. Armed with a ZPU-2 heavy machine gun, and up to three other medium machine guns, this class proved a redoubtable weapon – even more so because the ammunition for the ZPU-2 was derived from anti-tank ammunition from the period preceding the Second World War. That said, individual *Miraj* attack boats were no match for far more powerful patrol craft of the Sri Lankan Navy: this is why, as a rule, they never operated alone. (Artwork by David Bocquelet)

As described in Volume 3, the Sri Lankan Navy originally acquired 12 *Dvora* Mk I fast patrol craft. They were highly regarded and intensively deployed to patrol the waters around northern Sri Lanka during the Eelam War II. However, they also proved highly expensive and they were never available in sufficient numbers. (Artwork by David Bocquelet)

The resumption of diplomatic relations with Israel in 1995 was followed not only by the acquisition of IAI Kfir fighter-bombers and Super Scout UAVs, but also led to the delivery of six *Super Dvora* Mk II fast patrol craft. Between 1995 and 1998, these were outfitted by even more powerful engines than the Mk I. Their primary armament of two Oerlikon autocannon calibre 20mm was frequently enhanced by up to six additional machine guns calibre 7.62mm and 12.7mm. (Artwork by David Bocquelet)

Always in need of a larger number of fast patrol craft, but lacking the money necessary to purchase them from abroad, the Sri Lankan Navy eventually ordered the construction of the *Colombo*-class. Essentially, this was a locally-manufactured – and licenced – variant of the Israeli-made *Shaldag*-class. Some had the same weapons configurations as the *Dvora* Mk Is, but others had one ZPU-2 mount aft, replacing the Oerlikon, while several were equipped with a ZU-23-2 fore, and a single ZPU-2 aft. (Artwork by David Bocquelet)

In 1998, the Sri Lankan Navy continued the practice of acquiring larger patrol vessels from the People's Republic of China, through purchasing a pair of *Lushun*-class gunboats. Named the SLNS *Prathapa* (P340) and SLNS *Udara* (P341), they were armed powerfully, including two twin autocannon calibre 37mm, and a single ZPU-2. (Artwork by David Bocquelet)

Representing some of first modern warships indigenously designed and constructed in the People's Republic of China, the *Shanghai II*-class fast gunboats – also known as the *Type-62* – displaced 115 tons and were usually crewed by 35 officers and other ranks. They were fast vessels, capable of reaching speeds up to 30 knots. Armed with two twin autocannon calibre 57mm and one twin autocannon calibre 25mm, they remained the most powerful warships of the Sri Lankan Navy through the 1990s and 2000s. (Artwork by David Bocquelet)

Commissioned on 14 July 1992, the SLNS *Ranarisi* (P 322) was a fast gunboat of the *Shanghai* III-class. It saw action throughout the Eelam War II, Eelam War III, and Eelam War IV and participated in dozens of combat operations against the Sea Tigers. Additionally, the vessel ran regular fire-support operations along the coast. (Artwork by David Bocquelet)

What made vessels of the *Shanghai* II- and III-class so valuable for the Sri Lankan Navy was their mechanical reliability, their high operational speed and powerful armament. This typical *Shanghai*-II vessel has received not only the usual pair of twin 57mm and one twin 25mm autocannon: it also had a significantly smaller superstructure, to offer space for the installation of two multiple rocket launchers calibre 122mm: one fore (between the front 57mm mount and the bridge) and the other aft. (Artwork by David Bocquelet)

As mentioned in Volume 3, Mil Mi-17s were some of the first pieces of heavy equipment acquired by Sri Lanka from former members of the Warsaw Pact in Eastern Europe. In 1993, the SLAF placed an order for two batches of Mil Mi-17 assault helicopters in Moscow. One batch was manufactured in Kazan, and the helicopters in question (like CH-586, shown in Volume 3, or CH-589) were painted in 'sand and spinach' (beige and olive drab). The other batch was manufactured by the factory in Ulan-Ude, and helicopters (like CH-588 and CH-596) painted as illustrated here, in light blue-green and blue-grey. While operated by No. 6 Squadron based at the Vavaunya AB, following an accident, most of Mi-17s had their rear cabin doors entirely removed. (Artwork by Tom Cooper)

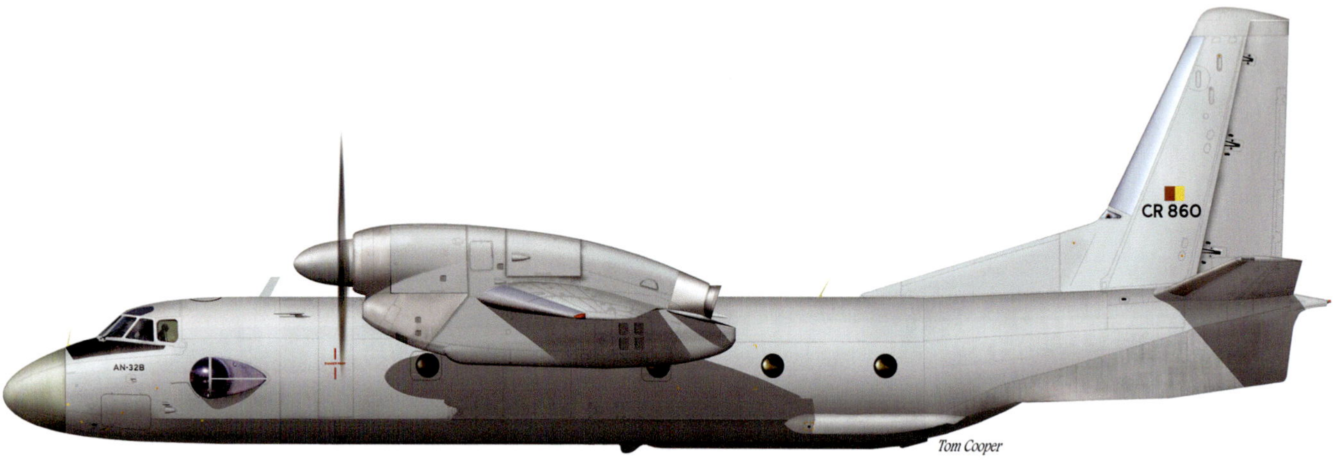

Through 1994-1996, the SLAF transport fleet – home-based at the Ratmalana AB - suffered losses and accidents. Not only Y-8s and HS.842s mentioned in earlier volumes were shot down, but the An-32B with registration CR-865 was lost, while the CR-860 – the first aircraft of this type delivered, shown here – was badly damaged when its nosewheel collapsed. Accidents stopped once the Ukrainian flight crews were sent home. Nevertheless, Ukrainian technicians remained in Sri Lanka and helped repair CR-860. The fleet was not only utilised intensively for hauling supplies around Sri Lanka, but – together with Y-8s – made frequent flights to Pakistan, China and Thailand, to pick up additional armament and spares. Sri Lankan An-32s of this period were painted in mid-grey overall, and wore only small tail flashes and their registrations on the tail. (Artwork by Tom Cooper)

Aiming to improve its firepower, in early 1995 Sri Lanka acquired the first six Mil Mi-24V helicopter gunships from Ukraine. They arrived wearing a very worn-out 'sand and spinach' camouflage pattern, and registrations CH-610 to CH-615. Operated by the newly-established No. 9 Squadron, home-based at the Minneriya AB, they saw strenuous action and heavy fighting both over the land and the sea. Out of the eventual 13 Mi-24Vs purchased from the same source, three were claimed shot down by the LTTE, while three (CH-611, CH-612, and CH-613) have been returned to Ukraine, and replaced by seven completely overhauled and significantly upgraded Mi-35Ps. (Artwork by Tom Cooper)

With its small fleet of IA.58 Pucara COIN aircraft rapidly dwindling, in May 1995 the SLAF initiated the acquisition of IAI Kfir fighter-bombers. For this purpose. No. 10 Squadron was officially established in Katunayake AB, on 1 January 1997. Seven days later, the first two Kfir C.2s and a single TC.2 two-seat conversion trainer (all overhauled and upgraded to C.7-similar standard) were delivered. All were painted in colours similar to BS381C/676 light weatherwork grey on upper surfaces and sides, and BS381C/627 light aircraft grey on undersurfaces. Sri Lankan Kfirs flew their first combat sorties within a week of delivery: nominally a multi-role platform, single-seaters were exclusively deployed for ground attacks, primarily armed with Pakistani-made Mk.82 and Mk.83 bombs (of US design), while the sole two-seater was kept back for conversion- and refresher training. (Artwork by Tom Cooper)

The other three Kfir C.2s from the first batch ordered in 1995, were delivered in April 1996. They were pressed into service in such a rush that they initially carried no other insignia but their registrations on the tail. Principal armament configuration consisted of a single multiple ejector rack under the centreline, usually loaded with four or five Mk.82 bombs, and two drop tanks with a capacity of 1,600 litres. For missions over shorter ranges, Mk.82s were loaded on hardpoints under intakes, too. The insert shows one of the Super Scout reconnaissance UAVs, which the SLAF deployed extensively – both for surveillance and reconnaissance purposes in support of ground forces, and to find targets suitable for air strikes by fighter bombers. (Artworks by Tom Cooper)

In reaction to the LTTE's Operation Oyatha Alaigal, in 2000, the SLAF placed an order for MiG-27Ms in Ukraine. The urgency of this acquisition was such that the first four single-seaters received only a minor overhaul and some adaptations of their communications equipment at the Lviv Aircraft Repair Works. They received an overall livery in a colour similar to the BS381C/682, applied before their shipping to Sri Lanka. Arriving together with a group of Ukrainian pilots and ground crews that operated them until enough native personnel was qualified for the job, they were assigned to No. 5 Squadron and flew their first combat sorties already on 16 August 2000. Another pair of MiG-27Ms and a single MiG-23UB conversion trainer followed in December 2000. Standard armament consisted of FAB-500M-62 bombs or (insert) B-8M pods for unguided rockets calibre 80mm. (Artworks by Tom Cooper)

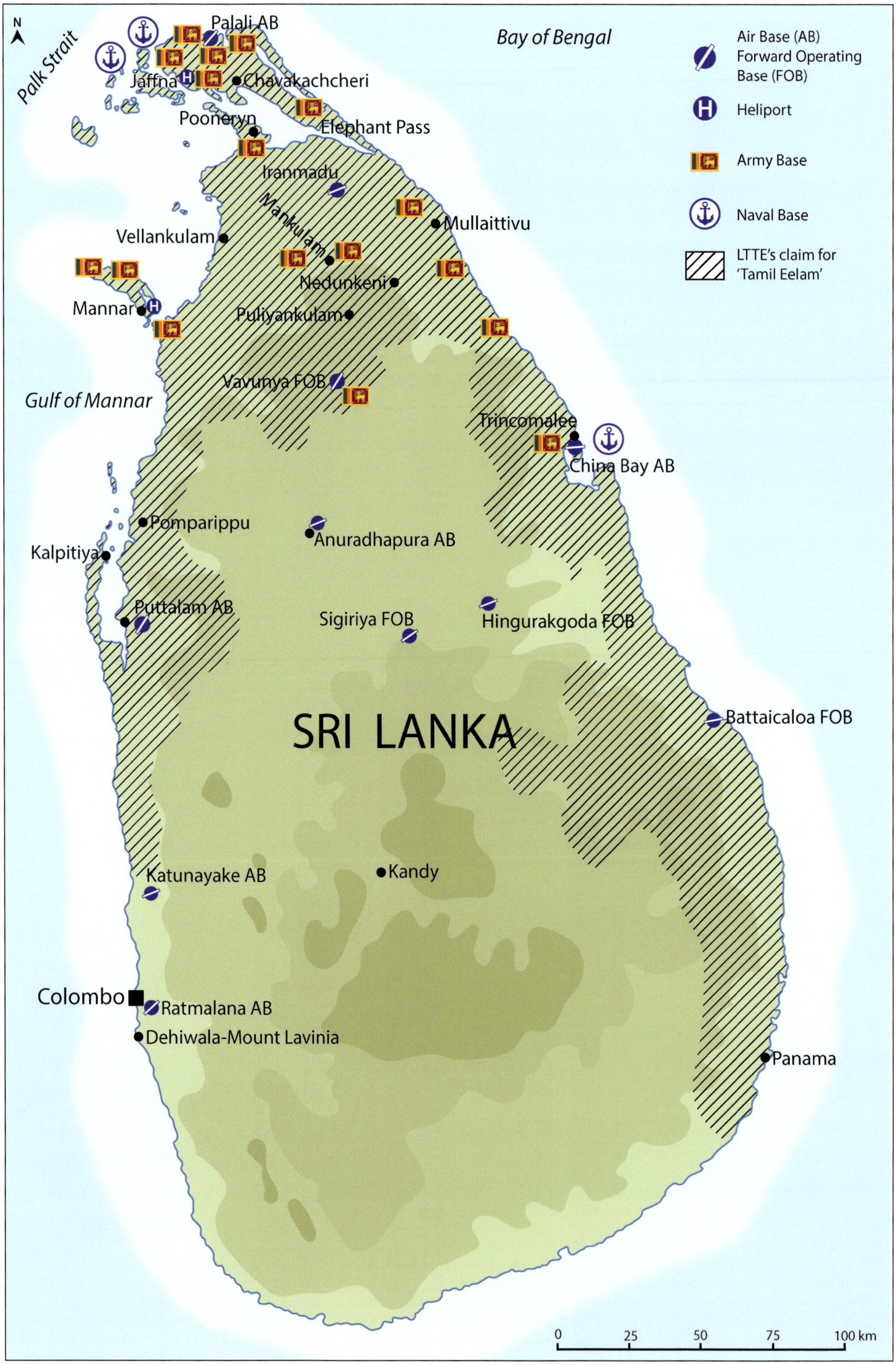

(Map by George Anderson)

Thrivida Pahara

As soon as the attack on Mullaitivu became known, the three branches of the armed forces began planning a combined rescue operation, codenamed Thrivida Pahara (Three Strikes), under the overall command of Maj. Gen. Srilal Weerasuriya. This operation aimed to deploy reinforcements via both sea and air landings to relieve the besieged garrison. The first phase of the operation commenced on 18 July at 15:30 PM, when a formation of five Mi-17 helicopters and two Bell-212s, carrying 180 operators from the 1 SF (under Lt. Col. Fazly Laphir), took off from China Bay Air Base, accompanied by two Mi-24 gunships acting as escorts. Their intended Landing Zone (LZ) was at Alampil, a coastal area approximately five kilometres south of Mullaitivu. However, the LTTE had anticipated this move. Recognising the southern approach as the easiest land access to the base, they had pre-positioned a large number of fighters in the area specifically to counter such an eventuality. In addition, Sea Tiger combat craft were patrolling the coastline to prevent the Sri Lanka Navy (SLN) from deploying reinforcements by sea. Earlier that morning, at around 08:00 AM, a naval engagement had already taken place off the coast of Mullaitivu. A swarm of a dozen Sea Tiger boats had engaged the Sri Lanka Navy vessels, including the Fast Gun Boat (FGB) *Ranaviru* and Fast Attack Craft (FAC) P455 and P473. The intensity of the assault forced the three SLN ships to withdraw from the immediate vicinity, preventing them from providing support for the airborne relief force. The LTTE's well-coordinated defensive preparations ensured that any attempt to reinforce the beleaguered garrison would be met with fierce resistance.

To make matters worse, the two Kfir jets of No 10 Squadron, which were supposed to bomb the Landing Zone (LZ) just before the helicopters arrived, were delayed, and as a result, the airstrike was called off. This left the troop-carrying helicopters vulnerable, forcing them to approach Alampil directly from the sea without any preparatory bombardment. As the Mi-17 helicopters moved in for the landing, the pair of Mi-24 gunships began strafing the tree line just behind the beach, alternating between rocket salvos and gunfire to suppress any enemy presence. However, as the helicopters descended toward the beach, dozens of LTTE fighters suddenly emerged from hidden foxholes, dug directly into the sand and camouflaged with canvas covered in sand. In a well-coordinated ambush, they opened fire with small arms, catching the airborne reinforcements completely off guard. As the helicopters hovered just above the ground, their rotors kicked up a thick sandstorm, adding to the chaos and confusion. Several helicopters managed to disembark their troops, but in the utmost disorder—many soldiers jumped from the helicopters while they were still several meters above the ground, only to immediately come under heavy enemy fire. The landing zone had turned into a kill zone, with LTTE fighters engaging the Special Forces troops in brutal close-quarters combat. Meanwhile, the two Bell 212 helicopters that had been part of the formation began circling the battlefield, attempting to provide suppressive fire from their door gunners. However, as the ground situation deteriorated rapidly, Squadron Leader S.R. Gunaratne, who was commanding the helicopter formation, made the difficult decision to abort the landing. He ordered the helicopters to withdraw toward the sea, leaving the pinned-down troops on the ground to fight for survival against overwhelming odds:

> The five Mi-17s and two Bell-212 flew out about five kilometres over the sea, regrouped, and planned our future action. We discovered that we had dropped a total of about 70-80 troops and if they were not reinforced, we knew they would be massacred. I checked for battle damage, and although three of the aircraft had been hit the damage was not critical. The decision was taken that the rest of troops in Mi-17s Nos. 1, 2, 3 and 5 had to be dropped. The Mi-17 and the two Bell-212s which had already dropped their load were to circle the area. After about three to four minutes, we headed back to the beach. We approached the beach cautiously. Obviously, the Mi-24s which were in the area could not fire onto the beach as army troops were already on ground. As we came to about 300 metres from the landing zone we saw that the troops had done their part and had eliminated all the LTTEers who had been on the beach. [...] We then did a routine troop drop without any problem and took off immediately for China Bay.[4]

The Special Forces operators swiftly rushed to the treeline, seeking cover in the scrub jungle beyond, where they managed to establish a defensive perimeter away from the exposed beach and landing zone (LZ). With their position secured as best as possible under the circumstances, they dug in and waited for the second wave of reinforcements, which was set to arrive aboard the same helicopters that had just completed the first drop. At 1830 PM, the nine helicopters—comprising Mi-17s and Bell 212s—took off once again from China Bay, carrying another 189 Special Forces operators. Overhead, the Y-12 aircraft continued its mission as an airborne command post, coordinating the operation from above. However, once again, things went terribly wrong. As the formation approached the intended LZ, they could not locate the agreed-upon red smoke signal that the ground troops were supposed to deploy to mark their position. The situation became even more precarious when Sea Tiger combat craft suddenly appeared, racing toward the approaching helicopters. Once within range, the insurgent boats opened fire with heavy machine guns (HMGs), forcing the pilots to take evasive manoeuvres to avoid being hit. In response, the two Mi-24 Hind gunships broke away from their escort formation and engaged the Sea Tiger boats directly, unleashing strafing runs with their 30mm cannons and S-8 rockets to suppress the enemy fire. Meanwhile, the transport helicopters continued their desperate search for the red smoke marker, circling anxiously over the area while under threat from both enemy ground forces and the Sea Tigers below. At last, the signal was spotted—but not at the originally planned LZ. Instead, the smoke emanated from a small fishing settlement, a location unexpected by the pilots. One of the Bell 212 pilots later recalled the critical moment when they finally sighted the signal:

> I was flying in the northernmost helicopter giving limited air cover to the Mi-17s with the door-mounted machine guns fitted to my Bell-212. My helicopter was carrying ten troops who were to be dropped, and a total of four crew-pilot, co-pilot and two gunners. The ten soldiers were briefed to disembark rapidly, five from either side. After making two attempts, the formation was finally able to spot the red smoke and the Formation Leader instructed us to follow him and land on a particular site. As we came in for the landing there were LTTE boats in the area.
>
> I instructed my gunners to keep on firing on the boats. When I was just about to land the distance to the boats was around 200 metres. The initial Mi-17 landed and immediately we were subjected to fire. Tracers started flying all over the area. About twenty five metres on the front of me on the shore

The armoured force was composed of:

- 30 T-55 tanks from the 4 SLAC, forming the backbone of the assault.
- Nine Type-63II APCs and nine BMPs from the 5 SLAC, offering both fire support and troop transport.
- Six Type-85 light tanks from the 3 SLAC, adding further strike capability.
- A composite troop from the 1 SLAC, consisting of a mix of older British-designed vehicles: one Saladin armoured car, two Saracen APCs, and one Ferret scout car.

With armour leading the charge, the 53 Division's advance gained momentum, pushing deeper into LTTE-held territory. The concentration of firepower and mobility allowed the SLA to overpower LTTE fortifications that had previously been difficult to breach. The LTTE, though highly adept at countering armoured threats, found itself under immense pressure as the SLA leveraged its mechanised assets in a way rarely seen in the conflict up to that point.

The offensive began with a massive artillery barrage, intended to soften LTTE defensive positions before the SLA's armoured and infantry forces advanced along a broad front down the A9 highway. To divert insurgent forces, 542 Brigade launched a feint towards the east, drawing attention away from the main assault axis. However, the LTTE had heavily fortified the area, preparing three successive defensive lines featuring dense trench networks, fortified bunkers, anti-tank berms, and extensive minefields. Supporting the LTTE's defensive efforts were multiple mortar batteries from the Kutti Sri Padai Ani, providing continuous indirect fire on advancing troops, and specialised anti-tank teams from the Victor Padai Ani, who played a crucial role in repelling armoured thrusts. Notably, this battle marked the first recorded use of anti-tank guided missiles (ATGMs) by the LTTE, which added a new layer of lethality to their defensive capabilities. By the end of 4 August, the SLA's offensive had stalled, turning into a grinding battle of attrition. The armoured spearhead suffered significant losses, with at least three BMPs and nine T-55 tanks destroyed or disabled. Yet, despite the setbacks, 53 Division persisted, launching repeated assaults on LTTE defences in the following days. The LTTE, adept at active defence, harassed SLA build-up areas, supply lines, and rear positions with sniper fire, ambushes, and indirect fire, preventing the Sri Lankan forces from consolidating their gains. The battle quickly escalated into a costly and prolonged engagement.

With LTTE defences holding firm, the SLA's assault stalled, leading to the operation being called off on 8 August. Recognizing the need for reinforcements and better coordination, the newly formed 54 Division under Brigadier Wasantha Perera was brought in, comprising 541, 542, and 543 Brigades. Once troop reinforcements and logistical build-up were completed, Sath Jaya resumed on 22 September 1996. The renewed offensive began with a large-scale diversionary manoeuvre. An entire brigade advanced eastward toward Mullaitivu in what appeared to be a new push against LTTE strongholds in the region. However, after drawing LTTE attention and forces to the Eastern front, the brigade withdrew back to its starting positions, having successfully misled the insurgents. Meanwhile, another infantry brigade, reinforced by 4 and 5 SLAC armoured units, moved westward before executing a wide flanking manoeuvre, turning eastward toward Kilinochchi. Anticipating the impending threat, the LTTE launched a massive counterattack on 26 September, throwing in significant numbers of fighters in a bid to halt the advance. The battle was brutal and costly for both sides, with the insurgents suffering 90 KIA and the SLA taking similar losses, but despite their efforts, the LTTE failed to halt the government forces. Recognizing that prolonged urban combat would favour the SLA due to its superior firepower and logistical support, the LTTE made the strategic decision to withdraw from Kilinochchi rather than engage in a protracted and costly battle on unfavourable terms. On 30 September 1996, Kilinochchi fell to the SLA, marking a symbolic victory that Colombo had desperately sought to offset the devastating loss at Mullaitivu. The SLA suffered significant casualties during the three-phased operation, with 11 officers and 293 other ranks killed in action. However, the capture of Kilinochchi was a major psychological and strategic blow to the LTTE, demonstrating the government's ability to seize key strongholds. As always, the SLAF played a crucial role in the offensive, conducting 63 strike missions in total. This included 22 missions by Pucara aircraft, 17 by Kfir jets, 16 by SF.260TP trainers used for ground attack, and eight by Mi-24 gunships. The LTTE acknowledged losing 241 fighters between 4 August and 30 September 1996, underlining the high cost of defending the town.[10]

5
CONTESTED SEAS

As operations Unceasing Waves 01 and Thrivida Pahara demonstrated, the Eelam War had a critical maritime dimension, as control of the sea was vital for both sides. For the Sri Lankan military, naval dominance was essential to prevent LTTE reinforcements and resupply, while for the Tigers, maritime access was a matter of survival. Despite controlling large portions of Northern Sri Lanka and being able to levy taxes on Tamil communities in the East, this alone was insufficient to sustain their war effort. The LTTE's survival and expansion depended on its global network of front organizations, which funded the insurgency through the Sri Lankan Tamil diaspora. This diaspora network, particularly strong in Canada, India, the UK, Germany, France, Switzerland, and Australia, provided the lifeblood of LTTE financing. By 2001, an estimated 600,000 to 800,000 Tamils lived abroad, with around 450,000 residing in Western countries and Australia. The LTTE's fundraising operations generated substantial sums annually. To cite a few examples, the movement collected approximately $12 million from Canada, nearly $8 million from Switzerland, and around $4.5 million from the UK every year. While these numbers appear significant, they were far from abundant given the enormous costs of sustaining a large-scale insurgency.[1] This funding, while crucial, was never enough to fully support a growing war machine, particularly as the conflict shifted from guerrilla warfare to a semi-conventional war requiring greater supplies of weapons and ammunition. Despite developing a cottage industry for manufacturing arms and capturing significant quantities of enemy equipment, these efforts were never sufficient to meet the movement's expanding needs. Consequently, the LTTE remained heavily dependent on external supply lines to procure arms, ammunition, and other essential supplies. This reliance on maritime supply routes became even more pronounced after 1991, following the assassination of Rajiv Gandhi. Before this, the LTTE had used Tamil Nadu as a key rear base, facilitating the movement of supplies, fighters, and finances. However, after India turned against the LTTE, access to Tamil Nadu was largely lost, forcing the Tigers to rely entirely on long-range maritime smuggling networks. Given Sri Lanka's island geography, maintaining these sea-based logistical channels was a constant challenge—one that would define much of the LTTE's strategic thinking in the years to come.

K.P. Department

Given the critical importance of maritime logistics to the LTTE's survival and expansion, it is hardly surprising that from 1984 onward, the movement developed its own maritime wing, commonly known as the Sea Pigeons or the K.P. Department. This department operated under the leadership of Kumaran Pathmanathan (alias of Shanmugam Kumaran Tharmalingam), an exceptionally talented businessman and organizer who took charge in 1986. At the heart of the K.P. Department's operations was its fleet of ocean-going merchant vessels, which by 2001 numbered around a dozen ships. These vessels were crewed by members of the Sea Tigers, even though the department itself functioned almost entirely independently. However, the procurement and operation of these ships were merely the visible tip of a far more complex and clandestine operation. To maintain this fleet and disguise its true purpose, the K.P. Department had to manage an ever-evolving network of front companies and shipping firms, constantly changing the registration of its vessels to conceal their real ownership. These tactics allowed the LTTE to circumvent international scrutiny and continue its maritime operations without direct attribution to the insurgent group. Beyond its primary function of weapons procurement, the K.P. Department also engaged in a range of legal and illegal enterprises, including human trafficking, contraband smuggling, and drug running. These illicit activities were not only highly profitable but also enabled the department to partially self-finance its operations, reducing its reliance on direct financial contributions from the Tamil diaspora. The department maintained several offices across South Asia, which served as logistical hubs for its sophisticated web of financial and shipping transactions. Weapons procurement remained the core mission of the K.P. Department. Initially, arms were sourced from the black market, but as the department's expertise grew, its operatives learned to bypass middlemen and deal directly with manufacturers. By the early 1990s, Cambodia was a key supplier of arms to the LTTE, but as the decade progressed, Ukraine and North Korea became primary sources. North Korean arms deals, however, required an added layer of deception—since the country's ports were closely monitored by international intelligence agencies, LTTE merchant ships would load their cargoes in Chinese ports instead, avoiding detection. The department's ability to conduct shadow operations reached astonishing levels, as exemplified by the May 1997 diversion of a Sri Lankan government arms shipment. The shipment, consisting of 32,000 81mm mortar shells, was originally

MV *Horizon* afire in the morning of 14 February 1996, after having been stricken by SLN ships and a SLAF Pucara. (Adrien Fontanellaz Collection)

Still from the film taken by a Super Scout UAV showing the MV *Stillus Limmasul* bombed by either a SLAF Kfir or a Pucara, on 2 November 1997. (Adrien Fontanellaz Collection)

Velupillai Prabhakaran, followed by Soosai (in blue uniform, alias of Thillaiyampalam Sivanesan), the head of the Sea Tigers, inspecting a guard of honour from one of the Naval Wing female units. (LTTE)

ordered by Colombo from Zimbabwe Defence Industries. However, through a well-planned deception, the LTTE managed to intercept the shipment in the port of Beira, Mozambique, where it was loaded onto the MV *Stillus Limassol*, an LTTE-controlled vessel. This episode was one of the most audacious acts of maritime deception in the war, demonstrating just how sophisticated and resourceful the K.P. Department had become.

For years, the LTTE's gun-running operations into Sri Lanka followed a straightforward yet highly effective method. At regular intervals, one of the merchantmen from their clandestine 'Ghost Fleet' would approach LTTE-controlled coastal areas and rendezvous with Sea Tiger boats, typically 30 to 40 nautical miles off the coast. These transshipment points were carefully chosen to minimize the risk of detection by the Sri Lanka Navy (SLN) while allowing for a swift transfer of arms and supplies. To facilitate these operations, the K.P. Department preferred to use small tankers, rather than conventional cargo ships. This was because tankers could be filled with water ballast, allowing them to adjust their draft and stabilize themselves during the delicate mid-sea transshipment to the high-speed motorized barges used by the Sea Tigers. These barges, while built for speed, had limited cargo capacity, meaning multiple trips were often required to complete a single transfer. Security during these operations was paramount. The transshipment barges were always escorted by an array of Sea Tiger attack and suicide crafts, ready to engage any SLN patrol vessels that approached. These tactics allowed the LTTE to maintain a near-continuous flow of arms and supplies between its merchant fleet and the Tamil Eelam-controlled coastline. Between 1995 and 2002, the K.P. Department's activities remained largely uninterrupted, despite escalating efforts by the Sri Lankan military and intelligence agencies to disrupt them. However, the LTTE's reliance on this supply chain nonetheless came with significant risks, and the movement suffered major losses during targeted SLN interdiction operations and intelligence-led strikes on its logistics network.[2]

Operation Dragnet

On February 8, 1996, the Sri Lanka Navy (SLN) received a rare piece of actionable intelligence from Interpol, alerting them that a suspected LTTE vessel had departed from Phuket, Thailand, carrying a shipment of 2,000 tons of weapons procured in Cambodia. In response, the Fast Gun Boat (FGB) SLNS *Ranawickrema* and Fast Attack Craft (FAC) P465 were dispatched from Trincomalee to patrol theEastern coast, initiating Operation Dragnet. On February 13, after days of surveillance, the SLN vessels spotted the merchant ship MV *Horizon* approximately 80 miles off the coast, still outside Sri Lankan territorial waters. The two navy vessels trailed the merchantman, maintaining a discreet watch while SLN intelligence worked to confirm its connection to the LTTE. Meanwhile, the SLN reinforced its operation by deploying the FGB SLNS *Weeraya* along with FAC P454 and P473 to support the pursuit. Once intelligence confirmed that MV *Horizon* was LTTE-owned, the SLN ordered the vessel to divert to Trincomalee for a thorough inspection. However, at 1:00 AM on February 14, instead of complying, the ship's crew suddenly removed plywood coverings to reveal two concealed 14.5mm heavy machine guns (HMGs). They opened fire on the nearest SLN ships, forcing them to temporarily withdraw under heavy gunfire. Seizing the opportunity, MV *Horizon* accelerated toward Mullaithivu, making a desperate attempt to escape. By dawn, the SLN closed in once more, this time just 13 nautical miles off Mullaithivu, well within Sri Lankan territorial waters. The SLN vessels unleashed a relentless barrage from their rapid-fire guns, striking the ship's hull. Soon, explosions erupted as fuel and ammunition ignited, engulfing MV *Horizon* in flames. The LTTE crew, realizing that capture was inevitable, abandoned ship, some fleeing on rafts while others jumped overboard.

As several Sea Tiger craft were spotted launching from the coast, the Sri Lanka Navy (SLN) immediately called for air support to counter the threat. In response, the Sri Lanka Air Force (SLAF) scrambled a Y-12 aircraft to serve as an airborne command post, followed shortly by a Pucara CA-604 and two SF.260TP light attack aircraft. At 6:30 AM, the Pucara arrived on the scene and conducted two attack passes on MV *Horizon*, emptying its rocket pods into the vessel's hull. Afterward, the pilot turned his attention to the incoming Sea Tiger boats, which were advancing at full speed to rescue the merchantman. Making two strafing runs, the Pucara inflicted damage on the enemy craft, but in return, was hit by their concentrated fire. Despite suffering damage to three electrical trimmers, the pilot managed to retain control of the aircraft and successfully return to base. By the time the Pucara disengaged, the pair of SF.260TP aircraft had arrived and immediately launched attacks on the Sea Tiger boats. Their repeated strafing runs eventually forced the LTTE vessels to abandon their rescue attempt and turn back. The pilots later reported sinking at least one enemy boat, though this could not be independently verified. What was undeniable, however, was that by 9:00 AM, MV *Horizon*—ripped apart by relentless fire and internal explosions—sank to the bottom of the sea. The destruction of the vessel marked a significant victory for the SLN and SLAF, effectively eliminating a major LTTE weapons shipment and delivering a severe blow to the insurgents' maritime supply network.

A far more unusual and dramatic incident unfolded on 2 November 1997, resulting in the destruction of another LTTE merchant vessel under curious circumstances. That day, Fast Attack Craft (FAC) P461, along with P441, was escorting the passenger ship SLNS *Hansaya* on its routine shuttle between Trincomalee and Kankesanthurai, when they sighted a merchantman moored just 500 metres off the coast near Mullaitivu. The vessel was surrounded by small boats clearly engaged in offloading its cargo onto the shore. As it turned out, the vessel in question was none other than the MV *Stillus Limmasul*, infamous for having hijacked a shipment of Zimbabwean mortar bombs just a few months prior. For reasons that remain entirely unclear, the ship had taken the reckless and near-suicidal risk of mooring so close to the coastline—a move that proved fatal. Realizing the opportunity at hand, the Sri Lanka Navy (SLN) swiftly launched a response. Orders went out to all available ships from the Eastern and Northern Naval Commands, including SLNS *Ranawickrema* and the FACs P460, P480, and P492, to converge on the scene. Simultaneously, the Sri Lanka Air Force (SLAF) was called in for support. A Super Scout UAV was dispatched to loiter at 10,000 feet, providing real-time surveillance of the developing situation. Not long after, two Kfir jets from No. 10 Jet Squadron arrived overhead, each armed with eight Mk.82 250 kg bombs, which they dropped directly onto the merchant vessel. The resulting explosions inflicted critical damage. A short while later, a Pucara and two Mi-24 gunships arrived and conducted multiple attack runs, targeting not only the stricken vessel but also the surrounding small craft and several trucks positioned on the nearby beach, likely involved in the unloading operation. By 5:17 PM, the MV *Stillus Limmasul*, devastated by repeated air and sea strikes, finally sank beneath the waves, bringing an end to one of the LTTE's most audacious—and baffling—logistical operations.[3]

The K.P. Department and the Sea Tigers swiftly adapted to the loss of the MV *Horizon* and MV *Stillus Limmasul* by refining their logistics and smuggling tactics. Over time, they began to increasingly rely on civilian fishing trawlers for the final leg of transshipment operations toward the Sri Lankan coast. These vessels, ubiquitous in local waters, were far less conspicuous and more difficult to detect than cargo ships. Moreover, the LTTE cunningly exploited trawlers nominally owned by Sinhalese individuals, and once a smuggling run was completed, the boats would be loaded with fish and sail to government-held ports such as Negombo, thereby avoiding suspicion. Fishing trawlers also had an important operational advantage: they could function effectively in rough seas, particularly during the northeast monsoon, whereas the Sri Lanka Navy's FACs, with their planning hulls optimized for speed, were unable to operate in sea conditions above Sea State 3. This seasonal vulnerability provided the LTTE with an opportune window to run supplies more freely. Simultaneously, the K.P. Department evolved a two-tiered shipping system. Larger mother ships remained in international waters, transferring their cargoes to smaller merchant vessels, each carrying roughly 50 tons of supplies. These smaller ships would then undertake the riskier journey into Sri Lankan waters. This approach reduced the overall loss in the event of an interception by either the Sri Lankan or Indian navies. Despite these innovations and the department's relative success, its capabilities should not be overstated. Nor should the LTTE's financial resources be exaggerated. Within Sri Lanka itself, the movement operated under severe constraints, constantly forced to conserve resources and reuse whatever was available. For instance, undetonated bombs dropped by SLAF aircraft were routinely salvaged and repurposed as explosive charges for Sea Tiger suicide boats.[4]

From the top: Sea Tiger *Miraj* Class attack craft parading, showing their main armament - a ZPU-2 mounting. The latter's 14.5mm calibre rounds are renowned for their penetration capabilities. (Adrien Fontanellaz Collection)

A closer view of a ZPU-2 naval mounting, seized from a SLN FAC, and 'manned' by a female fighter of the Naresh Padai Ani. (Adrien Fontanellaz Collection)

A view of the *Thrikka* Class high-speed carrier *Arrivu* during the second half of the 1990s. All Sea Tiger craft had a distinctive name. (Adrien Fontanellaz Collection)

Another view of a *Miraj* Class attack craft, showing its secondary armament with no less than three GPMGs. These were instrumental in allowing the craft to keep its target under fire whilst turning away from it. (Adrien Fontanellaz Collection)

Above: One of the Sea Tigers' *Idayan* Class suicide craft, which can be recognized thanks to its protuberant rostrum, containing detonators linked to the explosive charge. Some suicide craft could be comparatively large, because they needed to operate in rough weather and in the high seas. (Adrien Fontanellaz Collection)

Right: This still shows a single 23mm gun mount. Some of the Sea Tigers' attack craft even carried a single 37mm gun as their main armament. (Adrien Fontanellaz Collection)

This still from one of the LTTE TV channels shows a 'Stealth' Class suicide craft. In the background is a *Suddai* class attack craft. (Adrien Fontanellaz Collection)

ensuring a constant stream of suppressive fire. In addition to their firepower, the *Miraj* boats were fitted with basic communications gear, most notably radio sets, GPS units, and at least one civilian radar system. Interestingly, the Sea Tigers were known to use this radar in unconventional and highly effective ways, exploiting its capabilities well beyond its commercial design—as noted by a former senior officer of the Sri Lanka Navy:

> The Sea Tiger attack craft even used radar to control their forward guns with increasing firing efficiency. They used a small radar with a six-inch display and used the Variable Range Marker (VRM) to set the effective firing range. It is a very simple but effective mechanism which enables the forward gunner to wait until the SLN target comes inside the effective firing range of the weapon.[5]

The Sea Tigers also used another family of attack crafts, the *Suddai* class, which were equally fast, but smaller, with a crew of six and a single heavy machine gun and at least another 7.62mm GPMG. As described by a former officer of the Navy SBS, the Sea Tigers' craft were surprisingly robust considering their construction and size, which reached a maximum length of 21 metres and a maximum with of 5.5 metres because of the necessity to load them on trailers.

> ... The LTTE build their boats very robustly to carry multiple weapons and fibre glass construction caused the hits to penetrate through the material without causing serious damage unless high explosive projectile had exploded on the boat. Secondly, inflammable fuel was carried in aluminium tanks placed below the water level thus reducing the risk of fire and explosion on hitting the fuel tank. More importantly, the hull profile of the attack craft served for a steady ride even in considerably rough sea conditions.[6]

Following the attack craft, the Sea Tigers deployed a range of suicide boats, typically crewed by one or two Black Sea Tigers. Over time, a wide variety of these vessels were developed, but the most commonly used were the two-man *Idayan* class and the later *Kafir* class, which emerged in the late 1990s. Built purely for speed and lethality, these boats carried explosive payloads ranging from 150 to 200 kilograms—typically C-4—connected to redundant triggering mechanisms. These included impact detonators, often mounted on protruding horns at the bow, as well as manual triggers that could be activated by the crew. Most suicide boats featured armour plating around the cockpit and the explosive compartment to protect both the crew and the payload until impact. Their compact design helped reduce radar cross-section and visual detectability. The *Kafir* class, in particular, was said to incorporate some stealth features, although the level of sophistication remains unknown. These boats were also built with endurance in mind, allowing them to operate in tandem with the larger attack craft over extended periods. The last major category of Sea Tiger vessels was the *Thrikka* class. These high-speed troop carriers were manned by four crew members and typically armed with one or two 12.7mm heavy machine guns or 7.62mm GPMGs. Powered by four 250hp outboard motors, they featured an internal compartment capable of transporting up to a dozen fighters or approximately six tons of cargo. Nearly all Sea Tiger craft were powered by petrol-fuelled outboard motors (OBMs) ranging from 50 to 250 horsepower. This configuration enabled rapid acceleration and manoeuvrability at sea. Crucially, the Sea Tiger boats were inexpensive to build and could be produced in large numbers by LTTE boatyards, which continually tweaked and enhanced their designs to meet evolving operational needs.

The Sea Tigers' naval engineers also experimented with the design and limited production of more specialized craft, including semi-submersible suicide vessels and a small number of rudimentary midget submarines. One such midget submarine was even captured by the Sri Lankan military during Operation Riviresa in early 1996, offering a rare glimpse into the LTTE's ambitions beneath the surface. Despite the ingenuity behind these innovations, however, none of these experimental platforms had any significant impact on the course of Eelam War III.[7]

The Packs

What made the Sea Tigers so deadly was not just their diverse fleet, but the way they employed it. The first layer of their classical operational pattern was built around a network of shore-based radar stations, some of which were capable of detecting targets as far as 75 nautical miles away. This radar coverage was paired with a systematic, ongoing effort to monitor and decode Sri Lankan Navy radio traffic, giving Sea Tiger commanders near real-time awareness of enemy movements. When a suitable target was identified, orders were swiftly issued, and craft stationed at appropriately located Sea Tiger bases were towed to nearby beaches and launched into the sea. These boats would then rendezvous just offshore, assembling into battle formations while still close to the coast—making them difficult to detect by the SLN's offshore radar systems. Attacks were typically launched at night, taking advantage of darkness to conceal their low-profile vessels. The larger SLN Fast Attack Craft (FAC), by contrast, were more visible targets under these conditions. Although the SLN equipped its FACs with 1,000 candlepower Xenon searchlights to improve target acquisition, these lights came with a serious drawback: while they enabled accurate fire on a specific boat, they also instantly revealed the Navy vessel's position to all surrounding enemy craft—an invitation to coordinated counterattack. This fusion of early-warning systems, radio interception, rapid deployment, and nighttime swarming tactics made the Sea Tigers a uniquely formidable maritime insurgent force.

The Sea Tiger craft operated in structured subunits, typically organized into groups of three attack boats. These subunits then combined to form larger formations of nine to twelve attack craft, sailing in arrowhead formations and often reinforced with one or two Black Sea Tiger suicide boats. In most engagements, two to three of these groups were deployed simultaneously, resulting in swarms of 25 to 30 boats, including at least five suicide crafts. These formations would close in on their targets at full speed, aiming to overwhelm enemy ships in a fast-paced melee. The goal was to create confusion and exploit openings, with each three-boat subunit focusing its efforts on a single target. The attack craft prioritized disabling the engines of their targets to render them immobile and vulnerable. This multi-craft targeting strategy also significantly enhanced the survivability of individual Sea Tiger boats. Since the enemy ship was forced to divide its defensive fire among several rapidly approaching threats, it was rarely able to concentrate on any one attacker for long—allowing the Sea Tigers to press home their assault with a higher chance of success.

Meanwhile, the Sea Black Tigers' suicide craft would lie in wait, poised to strike at the most opportune moment. Their mission was clear: to dash forward and ram any enemy vessel that had been rendered vulnerable—either due to damage inflicted by the attack craft or because it had paused to reload its heavy weapons. This layered tactic allowed the Sea Tigers to overwhelm naval opponents who, under normal circumstances, would have been able to neutralize individual threats quickly thanks to their superior firepower and the inherent advantage of operating from more stable firing platforms. By exploiting moments of weakness and combining saturation attacks with precision suicide strikes, the Sea Tigers effectively neutralized the SLN's technological and firepower superiority—a fact acknowledged by the former commander of the SLN Fast Attack Flotilla himself:

> It was in the mid-nineties, that is 1995-1996 onward, that the swarming came up nicely because earlier it was a maximum of two boats or two-boat groups. But after 1995, they came up with this formation of swarming attacks, there were always three boats together, operating as one unit and there would be a number of such units. These tactics succeeded. I would say from the 1990s and 2000 even up to the ceasefire it was a success and we found it very difficult to deal with these swarming attacks. Our analysis in every encounter where 1 FAC dealt with 3 enemy groups, 1:3 ratio we lost the FACs. But in all 1:1 encounters we destroyed the enemy.[8]

Indeed, given the limited number of Fast Attack Craft (FAC) available at any given time, the SLN typically conducted patrols in pairs—either two FACs or two Fast Gun Boats (FGBs). This approach, while economical in terms of coverage, left the Navy ships highly vulnerable to being overwhelmed by the much larger swarms fielded by the Sea Tigers. The FACs did, however, retain one key advantage: their superior speed, which allowed them to disengage at will if necessary. Aware of this, the Sea Tigers occasionally attempted to lure SLN vessels into ambush zones closer to the coastline—areas where they had deliberately emplaced and concealed their heaviest long-range weapons, such as the captured T-55 tank from Pooneryn in late 1993, or one of the Type 83 122mm howitzers seized during the battle for Mullaithivu. These traps were designed to exploit the vulnerability of SLN ships operating too close to shore. Even so, the Sea Tigers grew increasingly bold. From 1996 onward, they began using their fast-moving swarms to directly target Navy transport ships operating on the critical Trincomalee–Kankesanthurai supply route. In these encounters, the FAC escorts had no option but to stand and fight, knowing that any withdrawal would leave the slower transport vessels exposed and defenseless—a risk the Navy simply could not afford to take.[9]

Underseas infiltrators

The Sea Tigers continued to rely heavily on their two Underwater Demolition Team (UDT) units to strike enemy ships while they were anchored in harbours or moored in secure areas. These operations were typically preceded by an extended phase of reconnaissance, during which the target's location, defences, and routines were carefully studied. Once preparations were complete, the attacks were launched with precision, often under the cover of darkness. At times, the UDT missions were also coordinated with other Sea Tiger assets, such as suicide boats, to maximize the chance of success and sow confusion among the defenders. This combination of stealth, detailed planning, and multi-pronged assaults made the UDT units a crucial component of the Sea Tigers' naval warfare strategy.

On 16 July 1995, combat divers from the Angaiyarkanni Padai Ani successfully placed an explosive charge on the hull of the surveillance and command ship SLNS *Edithara*, while it was moored off Kankesanthurai. The initial detonation caused damage to the vessel, prompting an immediate follow-up attack by four Black Sea Tiger suicide boats. Three of these boats were destroyed before they could reach their target, while the fourth withdrew under heavy fire. Amid the confusion, another LTTE combat diver managed to attach a second explosive charge beneath the ship's waterline. This second blast proved decisive, and *Edithara* sank as a result. The attack claimed the lives of three Sri Lankan Navy sailors and wounded five others. One of the female combat divers involved in the operation was captured.

On 17 October 1995, another Underwater Demolition Team (UDT) from the Sea Tigers successfully infiltrated Trincomalee Harbour and placed a powerful explosive charge beneath the hull of the Sri Lanka Navy auxiliary ship *A512*. The resulting detonation was devastating, slicing the large trawler in two and sinking it. The attack once again demonstrated the effectiveness and reach of the Sea Tigers' underwater operations, even in one of the Navy's most heavily guarded ports.

A combined Sea Tiger attack against Colombo Harbour on the night of 12 April 1996 met with entirely different results. Two suicide boats managed to enter the harbour but were quickly detected and destroyed by the Fast Gun Boat *SLNS Rangala* and another FAC. Amidst the confusion, two Underwater Demolition Team (UDT) divers attempted to infiltrate the harbour by swimming in under cover of darkness, but were spotted by sentries and killed before they could place any charges. A more complex operation followed against the small naval base at Karainagar on 11 and 13 June 1996. In this instance, Sea Tiger combat divers were more successful, managing to sink P232 and P244 and damage P234 and P243 while the vessels were moored at the base's old pier. However, this proved to be the swansong of the Sea Tigers' UDTs. Although numerous infiltration attempts continued throughout the remainder of the war—particularly against Trincomalee Harbour—most failed. The Navy, having identified several nearby inlets as staging areas for Sea Tiger operations, responded by keeping them under close surveillance and laying mines at their entrances. These countermeasures proved highly effective, and most subsequent missions were foiled before reaching their targets. Unlike their successes, these failed attempts were never publicized by the LTTE, and the names of the fallen Sea Black Tigers remained unannounced.[10]

More of the same

During those years, the Sri Lanka Navy (SLN) was constantly forced to adapt to the Sea Tigers' evolving tactics, yet it often found itself one step behind. As one former high-ranking Sri Lankan officer bluntly put it, "if the enemy had this, we had to buy that to protect us." The Navy was widely seen at the time as a supporting force, primarily tasked with ensuring maritime mobility for the Army and keeping open the critical supply artery to the Jaffna Peninsula. It wasn't until much later in the conflict that the SLN began acquiring the capabilities necessary to operate in deeper waters and actively hunt the LTTE's elusive Ghost Fleet. In the interim, the Navy concentrated its efforts on expanding its Fast Attack Craft (FAC) fleet, which bore the brunt of the confrontations with the Sea Tigers. This point was driven home by a former commander of the 4th Fast Attack Flotilla, who emphasized just how central the FACs were to the Navy's warfighting strategy during that period:

> We failed to see anything beyond that. As a result the FAC Flotilla was the workhorse for the Navy. I used to say if the

FAC turns back the fleet turns back. When the fleet turns back, the Navy turns back. When the Navy turns back, the whole country turns back. So much reliance and dependability was on the FAC. I would say we could have thought of another kind of fleet or flotilla, for example the Offshore Patrol Vessels (OPV). At one point of time OPVs were looked upon as a kind of a burden, high value assets you have to protect but merely doing surveillance and nothing else. But it proved its mettle in the destruction of the warehouse."[1]

The *Dvora*'s Mystery

The mainstay of the Sri Lanka Navy (SLN) continued to be its Fast Attack Craft (FAC), operated by the 4th Fast Attack Flotilla, which expanded dramatically in both size and importance. At its peak, the flotilla operated more than 30 FACs simultaneously. These vessels were widely known—both within the SLN and among the LTTE—as *Dvoras*, after the fast Israeli design that had become synonymous with naval speed and firepower in the region. The original fleet included twelve Super *Dvora* Mk I boats (hull numbers P453 to P458 and P463 to P468), purchased during the 1980s. The resumption of diplomatic ties with Israel in the mid-1990s opened the door to new acquisitions, and by the end of 1996, four *Super Dvora* Mk II craft had been delivered. These were followed by two more in 1998, bringing the total number of Israeli-built fast craft to 18. However, the high operational tempo and persistent threat from the Sea Tigers meant several of these were lost in action, and their replacement came at a significant financial cost. To compound the challenge, the SLN still relied on older and far less capable vessels—specifically, ten 40-ton FACs built domestically in the early 1980s (hull numbers P231–P235 and P241–P245). These lacked the firepower, speed, and resilience of the Israeli *Dvoras*. Additionally, there were only three South Korean-designed *Killer*-class FACs (P473–P475), which offered some improvement but were not sufficient to meet the evolving maritime threat posed by the LTTE's increasingly aggressive and sophisticated Sea Tiger fleet.

The turning point for the SLN's FAC program came in 1995, when an agreement was reached with Israel for the delivery of two *Shaldag*-class fast attack craft, along with comprehensive technical support to enable licensed local production by Colombo Dockyard Limited. This marked the beginning of an ambitious and vital shipbuilding initiative that would eventually see the SLN's fast attack fleet dramatically modernised and expanded through several iterations of domestically produced vessels. Production began with two Colombo Mk.1 craft, followed by seven Mk.2s and then 14 Mk.3s. The Mk.2 had a full-load displacement of 57 tons, a top speed exceeding 40 knots, and an endurance of 600 nautical miles. The Mk.3 version improved on these capabilities even further, achieving speeds in excess of 50 knots, making it among the fastest craft in the SLN's inventory. The precise configurations of these vessels' armament varied. Some carried two 20mm cannon—one mounted forward, the other aft—while others were equipped with a single forward-mounted 20mm gun and an aft ZPU-2 14.5mm heavy machine gun. A third configuration combined a forward-mounted 23mm ZU-23-2 with an aft ZPU-2. All versions featured multiple general-purpose machine guns (GPMGs) on single mounts to provide additional suppressive firepower during close-quarters combat.[12] The *Shaldag/Colombo*-class FAC programme proved to be a linchpin of the SLN's strategy. It allowed the 4th Fast Attack Flotilla not only to sustain operations during six consecutive years of intense maritime conflict but also to expand its operational strength—despite suffering heavy losses. The ability to locally produce and adapt these vessels to the demands of the war was critical in maintaining pressure on the Sea Tigers and ensuring the Navy could continue to safeguard vital sea lanes and support land operations.

A post-war picture of SLNS *Udara*, one of the two *Lushun* class Fast Gun Boats commissioned by the Sri Lanka Navy during Eelam War III. (Adrien Fontanellaz Collection)

The *Dvora* Mk.1 Fast Attack Craft P402, after modernization of its main armament. (Adrien Fontanellaz Collection)

The Coastal Patrol Craft P235, seen in 2019. Less known as their FAC counterparts, they played a crucial role during Eelam War III by ceaselessly patrolling the water surrounding government held areas. (Rehman Abubakr)

The Fast Attack Craft P465, seen during a naval parade in 2019 but still fitted with a typical Eelam War III armament complement, with one ZSU-23/2 mounting fore and one ZPU-2 mounting aft, together with several GPMGs. At least three, if not more, Sea Tiger attack craft were needed to overwhelm such a ship. (Rehman Abubakr)

The *Sa'ar* 4 SLNS *Suranimila*, also seen in 2019. Whilst the two *Sa'ar* 4 were commissioned late into Eelam War III, they drastically increased the service available firepower, as can be seen with the 76mm gun mounted aft and the 40mm gun station fore. (Rehman Abubakr)

OPV at last

By the end of 1994, the SLN's 3rd Fast Gun Boat Squadron fielded a total of ten *Shanghai*-class fast gunboats, comprising SLNS *Sooraya* (P310), *Weeraya* (P311), *Ranakamee* (P312), *Dakshaya* (P313), *Balawatha* (P314), *Jagatha* (P315), *Rakshaka* (P316), *Ranasuru* (P320), *Ranawiru* (P321), and *Ranarisi* (P322). In 1995, the squadron received three additional vessels: *Ranajaya* (P330), *Ranadeera* (P331), and *Ranawickrema* (P332). These were followed in 1998 by the delivery of three further gunboats—*Abeetha II* (P316), *Edithara II* (P317), and *Wickrama II* (P318)—though these were not commissioned into service until 2000. Altogether, these reinforcements more than offset the losses of *Sooraya*, *Ranasuru*, and *Ranawiru*, which were sunk in 1995 and 1996. The continued expansion and replenishment of the 3rd Fast Gun Boat Squadron ensured the SLN retained a capable and numerically strong surface force in the face of persistent and evolving threats from the Sea Tigers.

The Sri Lanka Navy increasingly shifted its focus toward acquiring larger, more capable vessels in the latter half of the 1990s. In early 1996, it inducted its first *Hainan*-class submarine chaser, *SLNS Parakramabahu* (P351), a relatively powerful platform equipped with multiple rocket launchers and two twin mounts each for 37mm and 14.5mm guns. This was followed in 1998 by the addition of two lighter but similarly armed *Lushun*-class gunboats, *SLNS Prathapa* (P340) and *SLNS Udara* (P341). While *Parakramabahu* was assigned to the 7th Surveillance and Command Squadron and frequently served as a flagship, the other two vessels joined the 3rd Fast Gun Boat Squadron. A significant shift in naval doctrine came in late 1999, when Colombo signed a landmark contract with Tel Aviv for the acquisition of two former Israeli Navy *Sa'ar 4* fast attack craft: *INS Moledet* and *INS Komemiyut*. These 415-ton, 58-metre-long vessels represented a step-change in capability for the SLN. Each was armed with an OTO Melara 76mm gun and a Bofors 40mm cannon, vastly increasing the Navy's surface firepower. Additionally, Israel provided four Gabriel Mk.II surface-to-surface missiles as part of the deal. The cost per vessel reached USD 26 million, and a complement of 116 Sri Lankan sailors and officers was dispatched to Israel for training. The ships were delivered in August 2000 and recommissioned as *SLNS Suranimila* (P702) and *SLNS Nandimiththra* (P701). The same year, the SLN expanded its long-range patrol capabilities with the induction of the former *INS Sukhanya*, a 101-metre-long offshore patrol vessel. Renamed *SLNS Sayura* (P620), the ship was armed with three 40mm Bofors guns and marked a notable enhancement in the Navy's blue-water operational reach.

By early 1995, the Sri Lanka Navy operated a diverse fleet of landing, transport, and supply vessels. Among its assets were the *SLNS Kandula* (A537), *SLNS Pabbatha* (A538), *SLNS Gajasingha* (L839), and *L820*. For fast personnel transport, the Navy employed *SLNS Hansaya* (A540) and *SLNS Lihiniya* (A541). The auxiliary fleet included *A512*, as well as six merchant vessels converted into motherships: *SLNS Abeetha* (P714), *SLNS Edithara* (P715), *SLNS Wickrema* (P716), *SLNS Mahaweli* (A24), *SLNS Lanka* (A25), and *SLNS Kanthi* (A26). Expansion of the fleet continued through the mid-1990s. In 1995, the SLN received a second *Yunan*-class landing ship, *L821*, along with two similar vessels built by the Colombo Dockyard: *SLNS Ranavijaya* (L836) and *SLNS Ranagaja* (L839). Additionally, a third fast personnel carrier, the *SLNS Jetliner* (A542), was acquired.[13] This was followed by the commissioning of another Chinese-built landing ship, *SLNS Shakthi* (L880), in May 1996, further enhancing the Navy's capacity for amphibious and logistical operations.

Table 9: Known active Sri Lankan Navy combat ships 1995-2001

Fast Attack Crafts	P422, P430, P440-443, P452-458, P460-463, P465-468, P472-475, P480, P483-484, P490-492, P494-498.
Fast Gun Boats	Shanghai II Class: *Sooraya* (P310), *Weeraya* (P311), *Ranakamee* (P312), *Dakshaya* (P313), *Balawatha* (P314), *Jagatha* (P315), Rakshaka (P316), *Abeetha II* (P316), *Edithara II* (P317) and *Wickrama II* (P318) Shanghai III Class: *Ranasuru* (P320), *Ranawiru* (P321), *Ranarisi* (P322) Haizhu Class: *Ranajaya* (P330), *Ranadeera* (P331) and *Ranawickrema* (P332) Lushun Class: *Prathapa* (P340) and *Udara* (P341).
Offshore Patrol Vessels and other large ships	Jayasagara Class: *Jayasagara* (P601) Hainan Class: *Parakramabahu* (P351) Sa'ar 4 Class: *Suranimila* (P702), *Nandimiththra* (P701) Sukanya Class: *Sayura* (P620).

Convoy battles

Eelam War III witnessed dozens of large-scale naval battles, although only a handful have been documented in any detail. One such engagement occurred on 29 August 1995, when the merchant vessel MV *Irish Mona*, carrying 136 civilian passengers, was intercepted by Sea Tiger operatives off the coast of Mullaithivu while on its routine voyage between Trincomalee and Kankesanthurai. Following the boarding, the ship altered course, prompting the Sri Lanka Navy to dispatch the Fast Gun Boat SLNS *Jayasagera* along with the Fast Attack Craft P456 and P463 to investigate and intervene. As the naval vessels approached, disaster struck: a massive explosion tore through P463, likely caused by a direct hit from a heavy-calibre artillery piece positioned onshore by the LTTE. In the immediate aftermath, a swarm of Sea Tiger attack and suicide craft descended upon the remaining Navy ships, initiating a prolonged and chaotic battle close to the coastline. Despite air support being summoned and SLAF pilots conducting multiple strike missions—during which they reportedly evaded surface-to-air missiles—P456 was also sunk in the melee. SLNS *Jayasagera* managed to break away and retreat from the engagement zone. In the aftermath, the Sri Lanka Navy and Air Force claimed to have sunk at least 10 Sea Tiger craft. However, the battle came at a heavy cost: 21 sailors were killed, marking yet another painful reminder of the evolving threat posed by the Sea Tigers during the conflict.[14]

On 2 October 1995, another major confrontation unfolded off the coast of Mullaithivu when a swarm of Sea Tiger boats launched a coordinated attack against the landing craft SLNS *Ranagaja* and its escort. The *Ranagaja*, which was transporting 170 personnel, came under intense enemy fire. The assault left the vessel dead in the water, severely damaged and unable to manoeuvre. The cost was grim: 20 sailors and soldiers were killed, and a further 76 wounded. Eventually, a Fast Attack Craft managed to tow the stricken ship to safety, narrowly avoiding a total loss. Just a few months later, on 30 March 1996, another large-scale naval battle erupted—this time off Vettilaikkerni. A flotilla of Sea Tiger craft targeted the transport vessel MV *Nagoroma* and its escort while the ship was ferrying troops from Kankesanthurai to Trincomalee. The escort responded aggressively, managing to destroy several suicide boats. However, in the heat of the engagement, FAC P458 came under concentrated fire from four Sea Tiger attack craft and was severely damaged. As it lay vulnerable and being towed away by another vessel, a Black Sea Tiger exploited the opportunity and slammed his suicide boat into the hull of the crippled FAC. P458 sank instantly. Of its ten crew members, only one survived.[15]

By October 1996, the Sri Lankan Navy resolved to strike directly at the Sea Tiger concentrations in the Mullaithivu region. On 20 October, it launched Operation Dirithara, targeting a key enemy naval base at Poonathuduwai, which also hosted a radar station. The operation began with Mi-17 helicopters, escorted by Mi-24 gunships, inserting approximately 180 soldiers from the 1st Commando Regiment at multiple landing points around the base. Simultaneously, the Fast Gun Boats SLNS *Ranawickrema* and SLNS *Jagatha*, along with the FACs P457, P466, P467, and P468, appeared off the coast and began shelling the Sea Tiger base. Their bombardment provided covering fire for a group of Inshore Patrol Crafts that closed in on the shore to land 25 Navy Special Boat Squadron (SBS) operatives and 67 Special Forces troops from the 2nd Special Forces Regiment. Despite the IPC P164 being destroyed by an RPG round and P161 sustaining damage, the special forces successfully overran and destroyed the camp. They then withdrew on foot toward Elephant Pass. In parallel, five additional FACs patrolled off the coast near other Sea Tiger bases, which were simultaneously targeted by seven Kfir airstrikes. The LTTE, caught completely off guard by the well-coordinated operation, mounted minimal resistance. As a result, the Army and Navy suffered limited casualties: five killed in action, two missing, and 26 wounded—an acceptable cost for what was widely considered a highly successful joint operation.

In response to Operation Dirithara, the Sea Tigers launched a swift retaliatory strike. During the night of 25 October 1996, they dispatched one of their flotillas—comprising at least ten attack and suicide craft—toward Trincomalee Harbour. However, Sri Lankan Navy sentries spotted the formation well before it could enter the harbour. Reacting immediately, all available Fast Attack Craft cast off and raced to intercept the approaching enemy. Realising they had lost the element of surprise, the Sea Tiger vessels turned away, attempting to evade the naval response. During the ensuing high-speed pursuit, however, a suicide craft managed to strike FAC P457, sinking it in a devastating explosion. All twelve crew members aboard were reported missing, presumed killed.[16]

On 13 March 1997, the Sri Lankan military launched another combined operation against the Sea Tigers, codenamed Thrividaseraya. The objective was to target and disrupt four known Sea Tiger bases in the Mullaithivu area. At dawn, the SLAF initiated the assault with four sorties each by Kfir and Pucara aircraft, delivering precision strikes on enemy installations. Simultaneously, SLA artillery positioned within range opened fire on the same targets, adding to the intensity of the barrage. This aerial and ground assault was swiftly followed by a naval bombardment. A task force comprising the gunboats SLNS *Ranawickrema*, *Ranarisi*, and *Ranajaya*, escorted by Fast Attack Craft P461, P462, P422, and P430, joined the operation by shelling enemy positions from offshore. Notably, the landing craft SLNS *Pabbatha* played a unique role in this operation—it carried a T-55 main battle tank, which fired 85 rounds of 100mm shells at inland targets, adding a powerful punch to the joint assault. The offensive did not end there. In the following months, Operation Thrividaseraya 2, 3, and 4 were launched on 6 April, 10 May, and 2 July 1997, respectively. These follow-up strikes were more limited in scope, consisting solely of air raids conducted by No. 10 Squadron Kfirs, focused again on degrading Sea Tiger infrastructure in the region.

Another major naval operation was quietly taking shape in the wake of Operation Thrividaseraya, intended as a decisive strike against LTTE sea bases. It would ultimately result in a resounding victory for the Sri Lankan Navy—though not in the way originally anticipated. On 23 March 1997, a powerful SLN task force gathered off Trincomalee under the overall command of Commander Navan Tennakoon. The force included the flagship SLNS *Parakramabahu*, the fast gunboats SLNS *Jagatha* and *Ranadheera*, as well as the FACs P460, P452, P441, and P422. Once assembled, the fleet began its northward sail, setting course for the Mullaithivu coast. Unbeknownst to the SLN, the movement of this fleet was picked up by the LTTE's coastal radars and lookout posts stationed near Trincomalee. However, Sea Tiger commanders misread the situation, assuming the ships were part of a routine supply convoy en route to Jaffna. This error would prove critical. At 1:30 AM on 24 March, while the naval force was roughly 25 nautical miles off Mullaithivu, the ships' radars picked up multiple enemy formations heading toward them from the shore. In response, two more FACs—P440 and P443—were dispatched from Northern waters to reinforce the fleet. A total of 33 Sea Tiger attack and suicide boats, arranged in six groups, soon launched a determined assault on the SLN formation. What followed was a brutal four-hour engagement in the darkness. Crucially, the LTTE's failure to amass a sufficient number of craft to overwhelm the powerful SLN formation allowed the Navy to fight off the assault effectively. By the end of the engagement, the Sea Tigers had suffered significant losses—eleven of their craft were destroyed, including three suicide boats that attempted, and failed, to strike SLNS *Parakramabahu*. The SLN, for its part, saw one *Dvora*-class FAC disabled, with one sailor killed and several others wounded. Though unintended in its initial purpose, the engagement ended as a clear tactical victory for the Navy, demonstrating the increasing resilience and coordination of its naval forces.[17]

The Sea Tigers exacted a brutal revenge only months after their defeat at sea. On the night of 19 October 1997, off the coast of Kokkilai, the Sri Lankan Navy lost the FAC P452 when it was rammed by one of two Black Sea Tiger suicide boats, which were operating under the cover of several attack craft. The FAC was sunk in the assault; four sailors were killed, another was wounded, and three went missing in action. Worse was yet to come. On 22 February 1998, the Sea Tigers mounted one of their most devastating attacks during Eelam War III. That evening, a large flotilla of attack and suicide crafts intercepted a SLN supply convoy en route from Trincomalee to Kankesanthurai, just off Point Pedro. The convoy comprised the landing craft SLNS *Pabbata*, the transport vessel SLNS *Shakthi (L880)*, and the civilian ferry *Valampuri I*, escorted by two fast gunboats and two FACs. The ensuing battle erupted around 7:00 PM and raged until 2:00 AM the following morning. In the chaos of the night engagement, multiple suicide boats broke through the naval screen. SLNS *Pabbata* and *Valampuri I* were both struck and sunk by ramming attacks. Only SLNS *Shakthi* managed to escape the onslaught. The losses were grievous: at least 50 sailors and soldiers were killed and another 15 wounded. The LTTE, for its part, acknowledged the death of 11 Black Sea Tigers in the attack. Just days later, on 26 February, the Sea Tigers launched another aggressive operation, this time targeting the naval base at Kilali with around 20 craft. However, on this occasion, the SLN defenders were prepared, and the raid was successfully repulsed.[18]

Then, during the night of 18 to 19 April 1998, the Sea Tigers suffered a significant setback when a formation of approximately 15 craft, apparently en route to Trincomalee, was intercepted off Thiriyaya by several SLN Fast Attack Craft. Supported by SLAF

Mi-24 gunships, the Navy claimed to have sunk five enemy vessels without suffering any losses in return. Later that year, on 30 October 1998, around 20 Sea Tiger attack and suicide craft launched an assault on another SLN supply convoy off Mullaithivu. The convoy's escort—comprising two fast gunboats and several FACs, again supported by Mi-24 helicopters—managed to prevent the Sea Tigers from reaching the two main supply ships. However, the engagement was not without cost: two FACs were damaged, and a third, P498, was left dead in the water. Insurgents quickly seized the opportunity, boarded the immobilized vessel, and stripped it of its armament before it capsized. The Navy lost one sailor killed in action, two more were wounded, and 16 others were declared missing, their bodies never recovered. The LTTE, for its part, acknowledged the deaths of only two fighters. But convoy battles did not always favour the Sea Tigers. On 8 February 1999, two FACs, supported by a single Mi-24, intercepted a Sea Tiger fast supply convoy off Delft Island. Despite the intervention of several insurgent attack craft, the Navy sank one boat and captured another, which was found to be carrying a cargo of medical supplies. The LTTE lost 18 fighters in the engagement. Retaliation came swiftly. On 18 February 1999, just before midnight, 10 Sea Tiger attack and suicide craft were launched from Pooneryn. They succeeded in capturing a Sri Lankan Navy Inshore Patrol Craft sailing in the Kilaly lagoon, marking yet another blow in the ongoing war at sea.[19]

Bloody year 2000

On 7 April 2000, during the height of the Elephant Pass battle, several SLN combat vessels moved in close to shore to bombard LTTE positions in the Vadamarachchi East area, near Nakarkovil. It wasn't long before they came under coordinated attack from both Sea Tiger craft and insurgents positioned along the coast, who used either a recoilless rifle or an anti-tank guided missile (ATGM) to devastating effect. The Fast Attack Craft P463 and P493 were struck in succession and both were sunk. The LTTE later claimed that one of the Mi-24 helicopters dispatched to assist the stricken ships was also damaged. The Navy suffered significant losses: three sailors were confirmed killed, 14 went missing, and another five were wounded. The following day, Sea Tiger divers were dispatched to the wreck sites and succeeded in salvaging weaponry from the sunken ships. Among the items recovered were a 23mm cannon, two 20mm guns, five 12.7mm heavy machine guns, and eight additional light or medium machine guns—another clear blow to the SLN. Just a few days later, on 12 April, the Sea Tigers struck again. The Inshore Patrol Craft P170 had been dispatched from its base at Kuthiraimalai to investigate a suspicious dinghy when it was suddenly rammed by a suicide craft. The attack killed one sailor and wounded two others.[20]

The second major disaster for the Sri Lankan Navy in 2000 occurred on 5 June, when the Sea Tigers launched a concerted attack against a supply convoy off the Vadamarachchi coastline. What followed was a fierce and prolonged engagement that lasted several hours, as the Navy escort clashed with insurgent flotillas composed entirely of attack craft. During the battle, both Fast Attack Craft P482 and P496 were sunk. 21 sailors were reported missing in action, with another wounded. The Sea Tigers also suffered losses, with 11 militants killed and several of their craft destroyed. The Sri Lanka Air Force intervened in force, flying multiple combat sorties in an effort to support the embattled Navy units. However, the damage had already been done. Later that same month, on 26 June, the Sea Tigers struck again, this time successfully sinking the merchant vessel MV *Huan* using Black Sea Tiger suicide craft.[21]

Then, on 23 October 2000, the Sri Lankan Navy suffered its third major blow of the year when the LTTE launched a carefully orchestrated assault on Trincomalee Harbour. The attack began at 5:30 AM when a platoon-sized LTTE team, including mortar and anti-aircraft elements, infiltrated Marble Beach—situated at the mouth of the harbour and nearly opposite the main naval base. Once in position, they began shelling the naval yard, providing covering fire for the next phase of the operation. Soon after, four Black Sea Tiger suicide boats, escorted by several attack craft, charged directly into the harbour. A chaotic and brutal close-range battle ensued. At least one suicide craft rammed the Fast Personnel Carrier SLNS *Jetliner*, causing serious damage, while another Navy gunboat sustained lighter damage in the fray. Meanwhile, Sri Lankan Army troops advanced toward Marble Beach to neutralize the infiltrators, supported by a pair of Mi-24 gunships. During the exchange, one of the helicopters—CH-613—was hit by a Strela-3 shoulder-fired surface-to-air missile and shot down, killing all four crew members on board. The LTTE later acknowledged the deaths of six Black Sea Tigers in the course of the operation, which once again demonstrated their capacity to strike high-value targets even in one of the Navy's most fortified locations.[22]

Despite the LTTE's unilateral ceasefire declaration in late December 2000, naval hostilities resumed only a few months later. On 21 March 2001, a fierce engagement broke out off the coast of Mullaithivu between Sri Lankan Navy combat vessels and a Sea Tiger flotilla. During the clash, Fast Attack Craft (FAC) P495 was sunk, and the LTTE claimed to have captured another FAC, stripping it of its weapons before destroying the vessel. Five sailors were reported missing, while another 13 sustained injuries. A far larger naval confrontation occurred later that year on 16 September 2001. That morning, the Sea Tigers attempted to intercept MV *Pride of South*, a transport ship sailing from Trincomalee to Kankesanthurai. The vessel was carrying 89 policemen, 1,209 soldiers, and a cargo of 2,500 tons of rice. It was initially escorted by the gunboats SLNS *Udara* and *Edithara II*. Around 6:00 AM, approximately 30 nautical miles off Point Pedro, a swarm of about 20 Sea Tiger suicide and attack crafts launched an ambush on the convoy. In response, the Navy scrambled all available combat ships to reinforce the escort, including the SLNS *Jagatha*, 13 FACs, and two smaller patrol craft. Simultaneously, the Air Force deployed Kfir jets and Mi-24 helicopter gunships to the scene. A brutal and extended battle unfolded. At one stage, the Sea Tigers came dangerously close to overtaking the MV *Pride of South*, prompting soldiers aboard to fire back using GPMGs from the deck. Ultimately, the transport vessel managed to break contact and escape toward the open sea, though 58 soldiers were wounded during the clash. The Navy suffered further losses when patrol craft P251 was sunk in the engagement, with all 10 crew members reported missing. On the other side, four Sea Tiger boats were destroyed through the combined efforts of the SLN and SLAF. One Mi-24 narrowly evaded a Strela-3 surface-to-air missile. The LTTE later acknowledged the loss of 10 fighters, including four from its elite Black Sea Tiger units.[23]

Table 10: main Sri Lanka Navy losses 1995-2001

Date	Ships	Comment
19 April 1995	SLNS Sooraya (FGB) SLNS Ranasuru (FGB)	Sunk by combat divers whilst moored at Trincomalee naval base.
16 July 1995	SLNS Edithara (Surveillance & Command ship)	Sunk by combat divers whilst moored off Kankesanthurai naval base in the aftermath of Sea Tigers seaborn attacks repulsed by Navy ships.
29 August 1995	P456 (FAC) P463 (FAC)	Sunk during a naval battle off Mullaithivu.
17 October 1995	A512 (auxiliary ship: trawler)	Sunk by combat divers whilst moored at Trincomalee naval base.
30 March 1996	P458 (FAC)	Sunk during a naval battle off Vettilaikkenii.
11-13 June 1996	P232(Coastal Patrol Craft) P244(Coastal Patrol Craft)	Sunk by combat divers whilst moored at Karainagar naval base.
31 July 1996	SLNS Ranaviru (FGB)	Sunk during a naval battle off Mullaithivu.
20 October 1996	P164 (Inshore Patrol Craft)	Destroyed by a RPG round during an assault on a Sea Tiger base.
25 October 1996	P457 (FAC)	Sunk during a naval battle off Trincomalee.
19 October 1997	P452 (FAC)	Sunk during a naval battle off Kokkilai.
22 February 1998	SLNS Pabbatha (LCM) Valampuri I (Ferry)	Sunk during a naval battle off Point Pedro.
30 October 1998	P498 (FAC)	Sunk during a naval battle off Mullaithivu.
7 April 2000	P463 (FAC) P493 (FAC)	Sunk during a naval battle off Nakarkovil.
12 April 2000	P170 (Inshore Patrol Craft)	Ambushed and rammed by a Black Sea Tiger boat.
5 June 2000	P482 (FAC) P496 (FAC)	Sunk during a naval battle off Vettilaikkeni.
30 September 2000	P183 (Inshore Patrol Craft)	Sunk by Sea Tigers off Kalpity.
21 March 2001	P495 (FAC)	Sunk during a naval battle off Mullaithivu.
16 September 2001	P251 (Coastal Patrol Craft)	Sunk during a naval battle off Point Pedro.

6
JAYASIKIRUI

The year 1997 opened with a devastating blow delivered by the LTTE. On 9 January, the insurgents launched a meticulously planned large-scale assault against Sri Lankan Army (SLA) positions stretched between Elephant Pass and Paranthan. Spearheaded by Special Commander Balraj, the operation involved approximately 2,000 fighters, primarily drawn from the elite Charles Anthony Padai Ani. The main thrust of the attack came from the east of the A9 road and included several Black Tiger infiltrations. Initially, the LTTE achieved significant success, throwing SLA units into disarray and capturing several key artillery support bases. In the process, they destroyed 10 artillery pieces—six Type 83s and four Type 59-I guns. An ammunition depot containing 8,000 shells was blown up, and the insurgents managed to seize two 120mm mortars. The SLA, however, responded swiftly, dispatching reinforcements from the 531 Brigade. These troops eventually managed to halt and repel the LTTE advance, forcing the Charles Anthony Padai Ani fighters to withdraw. Nonetheless, the losses suffered by the army were severe: 165 soldiers killed in action, 65 listed as missing, and 392 wounded. In addition, seven civilian employees were killed, and 17 others injured. The LTTE admitted to losing 170 fighters in the battle, underlining the high cost of the engagement for both sides.[1]

On 9 February 1997, the Sri Lankan Army (SLA) launched Operation Edibala with the objective of reopening the A14 road linking Mannar and Vavuniya, a vital route that had remained cut off since 1990. As part of the plan, 53 Division began advancing along the road, clearing the surrounding areas and establishing a Forward Defence Line (FDL) along its path to secure the route for future use. The operation progressed smoothly, as the LTTE chose not to oppose the advance. By early March 1997, the road had been fully reopened and secured. The insurgents' lack of response appeared to confirm the Army's assessment that the LTTE had been significantly weakened by the events of 1996 and that its available strength in the Vanni heartland was unlikely to exceed 6,000 fighters. This perceived reduction in LTTE capability would play a crucial role in shaping the planning and ambition of the government's next major offensive.[2]

Following the completion of Operation Riviresa, the logistical burden of supplying the Jaffna Peninsula increased dramatically. In addition to supporting the sizeable military garrison stationed there, Colombo was also responsible for providing food and essential commodities to nearly half a million civilians. All supplies had to be transported either by sea or by air, placing considerable strain on the state's logistical apparatus. However, the persistent threat posed by the Sea Tigers forced the Navy to escort civilian shipping convoys, significantly raising transportation costs. Meanwhile, the air bridge maintained by the Sri Lanka Air Force (SLAF) was unable to handle the bulk of goods, not least due to limited airlift capacity and unsuitable infrastructure. Faced with these mounting logistical and financial challenges, the government concluded that the only sustainable solution was to reopen a land route through the Vanni, reconnecting the government-held areas in the South with the Jaffna Peninsula. This strategic imperative gave birth to Operation Jayasikurui—literally translated as 'Victory Assured'—a massive military campaign designed to establish a secure overland supply corridor through hostile territory.

Sri Lanka Army commanders considered two potential main axes for their advance. One option was to push from Mannar along the western coast of the Vanni toward Pooneryn. The second, more direct approach, was a thrust straight along the A9 highway from Vavuniya to Kilinochchi. While this latter route offered the significant strategic advantage of cutting LTTE-held territory in two, it also presented a major tactical drawback: the need to secure both flanks of the advancing force throughout its 80-kilometre push. Ultimately, the Army chose the A9 route due to its directness and potential strategic payoff. However, available manpower posed an immediate challenge. With the 51 and 52 Divisions tied down in securing the Jaffna Peninsula and the 54 Division responsible for holding the key positions at Elephant Pass, Paranthan, and Kilinochchi, only the 53 Division—comprising the 531, 532, and 534 Brigades—was available for offensive operations. To address this shortfall, the Army raised a new formation in March 1997: the 55 Division, consisting of the 551, 552, and 553 Brigades. This was followed by the creation of the 56 Division in October 1997, with its 561, 562, and 563 Brigades. Additionally, in September of the same year, the former 2 Division, previously a territorial unit, was redesignated as the 21 Division. This formation, comprising the 211, 212, 214, and 215 Brigades, remained focused primarily on rear-area security duties.

From the outset, Operation Jayasikurui was conceived as a multi-phase, protracted campaign expected to last anywhere from several weeks to three or four months. Extensive preparations preceded its launch. In addition to amassing vast stockpiles of ammunition and supplies, the Army acquired several dozen bulldozers to carve out new dirt roads through the dense and often impenetrable jungles of the Vanni, ensuring logistical access and mobility for advancing troops. The scale of the operation was unprecedented. The bulk of the Army's armoured corps was committed, alongside a significant proportion of the artillery corps. In total, the 53 and 55 Divisions, together with supporting formations, fielded around 20,000 troops—roughly one-fifth of the Army's total manpower and virtually its entire offensive capability at the time. Major General Asoka Jayawardhane was appointed as the Overall Operations Commander (OOC). The operation's first phase was structured as a two-pronged pincer movement converging on Puliyankulam Junction, located about eight kilometres north of Omanthai. The 55 Division was tasked with advancing directly up the A9 highway toward the junction. Simultaneously, the 53 Division was to advance from the Weli Oya/Manal Aru area, cutting through thick jungle terrain. This more arduous path was considered better suited to the 53 Division due to its inclusion of three elite Commando and Special Forces battalions operating under the 534 Brigade, whose training and experience made them well-prepared for jungle warfare.[3]

Do or Die

The offensive began in earnest on 13 May 1997. The 53 Division launched its advance from Weli Oya, pushing through dense jungle terrain, while the 55 Division moved forward in parallel columns flanking the A9 highway, carefully avoiding the road itself due to the risk of improvised explosive devices (IEDs) and landmines buried beneath it. Contrary to expectations that the LTTE might resort to its usual strategy of dispersal and evasion, Velupillai Prabhakaran chose instead to meet the offensive head-on. He ordered his forces to defend from well-prepared, entrenched positions, withdrawing only when there was a genuine risk of encirclement. As described in earlier chapters, this defensive approach proved highly effective in slowing the Sri Lankan Army's advance to a crawl while minimizing LTTE casualties. The SLA, for its part, unwittingly played into the Tigers' hands by pushing forward along narrow fronts, which allowed the LTTE to concentrate its fighters in specific areas without spreading its forces too thinly. One of the most effective tactics employed by the Tigers was the systematic use of indirect fire. Mortars and artillery were positioned with precision and often pre-registered on likely approach routes. Soldiers reported finding yellow stakes driven into the ground—planted by LTTE forces to assist with pre-targeted artillery strikes. As a result, the majority of SLA casualties were inflicted by well-coordinated barrages of indirect fire. Prabhakaran did not underestimate the potential impact of Jayasikurui. He recognised that, if successful, the operation could split the LTTE's heartland in two. In anticipation, he even made contingency plans for such a scenario. He also ordered a series of large-scale counterattacks, collectively known as the 'Do or Die' operations, which primarily targeted the advancing Army's rear areas. While these counterattacks varied in effectiveness, they succeeded in further delaying the SLA advance, albeit at a high cost in LTTE casualties. To reinforce his forces, Prabhakaran redeployed the Anbarasi and Jeyanthan Padai Ani units—two semi-regular formations drawn from Eastern Sri Lanka—back into the Vanni theatre. Simultaneously, he raised a new unit, the Sothyia Padai Ani, composed primarily of local women recruited from the Vanni, reflecting both the seriousness of the threat and the total mobilisation of available human resources for what was seen as a decisive campaign.

The first of the LTTE's Do or Die counteroffensives came less than a month after the launch of Jayasikurui. In the early hours of 10 June 1997, at approximately 02:30 AM, a force of at least 1,000 LTTE fighters launched a surprise assault on the rear-area headquarters and support elements of the 55 Division, located at Tandikkulam—roughly 10 kilometres behind the frontlines at Omanthai. The attack, launched from multiple directions including from the south, completely caught the Sri Lankan military off guard. The base, sprawling and lightly defended, was quickly overrun in several sections, and for a time the insurgents appeared poised to capture it entirely. What saved the situation from turning into a full-scale rout was the timely and tenacious intervention of three T-85 light tanks from 3 SLAC. These vehicles manoeuvred through the base under intense fire, engaging LTTE fighters at extremely close range—sometimes just 30 to 40 metres—with their coaxial machine guns and 73mm cannons. On several occasions, they intercepted and disrupted LTTE assault formations as they attempted to regroup for renewed multi-company-sized attacks. Supporting artillery also played a key role. Five Type 59-2 130mm guns positioned in a nearby firebase opened fire with direct trajectories, lobbing shells into LTTE concentrations. By dawn, two of the T-85s had suffered barrel jams from overheating after firing continuously through the night. As daylight broke, reinforcements arrived. The 10th Gajaba Regiment and the 10th Vijayabahu Infantry Regiment, supported by a company of commandos deployed by helicopter, launched a coordinated counterattack. Faced with increasing resistance and the risk of being encircled, the LTTE fighters began to disengage and retreat, leaving behind a scene of destruction. In the aftermath, it was clear how close the Army had come to disaster. One Type 86

APC had been destroyed, several artillery pieces were damaged, and numerous ammunition dumps had exploded during the night. A nearby bridge was also demolished. Sri Lankan losses were heavy: 145 personnel, including five officers, were confirmed killed, 12 soldiers were listed as missing in action, and another 200 were wounded. LTTE casualties were never officially disclosed, as was typical, but were believed to be substantial.

The second Do or Die operation followed swiftly. Late on the evening of 24 June 1997, an estimated 1,000 LTTE fighters launched a coordinated assault on both flanks of the 55 Division at Periyamadu, near Omanthai. As in the previous attack, one of the main objectives was the capture of an Army artillery battery—a tactic that had yielded success in earlier engagements. This time, however, the Tigers met stiff resistance. The artillery positions remained firmly in Army hands, and the front-line defences held despite the scale and ferocity of the attack. The only temporary success for the LTTE came in the form of briefly severing the A9 highway, a key supply route, which they managed to cut for a few hours. But even this was short-lived. At 04:00 AM on 25 June, a counterattack launched from Vavuniya pushed the attackers back and reopened the route. Despite holding their ground, the Army paid a steep price for the victory, suffering 74 killed in action and around 200 wounded. However, the LTTE fared worse. In a rare admission, the group later acknowledged losing 95 fighters during the engagement—a significant toll even by their standards. Additional LTTE counterattacks followed on 7 July and again on 31 July. The latter targeted the 551 Brigade headquarters at Omanthai and briefly succeeded in breaching the Army's Forward Defence Lines to reach the HQ perimeter. Yet, these attempts proved far less devastating than the earlier ones and failed to deliver any strategic results. Meanwhile, the main Jayasikurui offensive ground forward, albeit at great cost. The slow, attritional advance of the 53 and 55 Divisions through entrenched LTTE defences continued steadily. By 6 August 1997, after weeks of bitter fighting, the two divisions finally linked up—just two kilometres south of Puliyankulam, the key objective of Jayasikurui's first phase. With the link-up complete, both formations stood poised to launch a full-scale assault on the town.[4]

Highway of Death

However, the LTTE leadership had firmly resolved to make a stand at Puliyankulam. The small town and its surrounding areas were transformed into a heavily fortified stronghold, defended by several companies drawn from the Malathy, Charles Anthony, Jeyanthan, and Imran-Pandian Padai Ani. As always, these units were backed by a formidable network of mortar batteries, pre-sited for maximum effect. The 53 Division launched a series of frontal assaults from the west against the LTTE's forward defence lines, but, predictably, these efforts failed to make any meaningful progress. On 19 August, in an effort to break the deadlock, the SLA attempted a bold manoeuvre. A large armoured column—comprising virtually the entire 4 SLAC, with more than 30 T-55 main battle tanks and approximately 20 other armoured vehicles—set off from Nedunkeni. The objective was to follow a narrow jungle track and strike toward the A9 highway, reaching it behind the LTTE's primary defensive line in a flanking move, then rolling up their positions from the rear. To coincide with the manoeuvre, 55 Division launched another frontal assault from the north. However, the plan faltered early. At the head of the armoured column, one T-55 struck a landmine and threw its track, effectively blocking the narrow route and preventing the rest of the formation from moving forward. As a result, only three T-55s and three BMP-1 infantry fighting vehicles managed to reach the A9, falling far short of the intended massed armoured breakthrough. Nonetheless, the sudden appearance of these six armoured vehicles in the LTTE's rear caused temporary chaos. The surprise was so complete that in the ensuing confusion, some female fighters from the Malathy Padai Ani hesitated to open fire, fearing they might be targeting friendly armour. A disjointed skirmish broke out, during which one BMP was destroyed and its crew killed, while another BMP was captured by the insurgents. The remaining T-55s and a surviving BMP turned and raced along the A9 toward 55 Division's forward positions, eventually managing to reach safety under the cover of confusion and artillery fire. Despite the setback, the raid clearly rattled the LTTE. The following day, a renewed attack by 55 Division—this time well supported by artillery and armoured elements—succeeded in capturing the Puliyankulam railway station on the town's outskirts. However, further progress proved elusive. The LTTE's defences held firm, and subsequent assaults again stalled, bogged down in the familiar and punishing pattern of attrition.

Sri Lankan soldiers on the advance, carrying Type 56 LMGs, the Chinese version of the RPK. Any forward movement had to be extremely deliberate, with the troops risking entering into an enemy field of fire at any moment. In the latter case, obvious elements of cover were booby-trapped. (Albert Grandolini Collection)

A squad of LTTE fighters moving toward their defensive positions, and carrying several boxes of ammunitions, across a channel in the Vanni. (LTTE via Telibrary.com)

Queen of the battlefield - a Sri Lankan Type 66 152mm howitzer fires against LTTE positions somewhere in the Vanni. Such heavy guns were often dispersed in at most battery strength in fire bases. These were, in turn, often targeted by enemy infiltration parties. (Albert Grandolini Collection)

LTTE fighters inspecting a captured section of the FDL protecting Kilinochchi in the aftermath of their victory in early October 1998. Such berms, covered by bunkers at regular intervals could be formidable obstacles and were used throughout Eelam War II, III and IV. (LTTE via Telibrary.com)

A squad of Tigers inspecting a demolished SLA bunker. This picture shows how heavily armed the LTTE infantry could be, with several AK or Type 56 rifles, one Type 56 LMG and two Type 69 rocket launchers. (LTTE via Telibrary.com)

A trio of SLA soldiers pause for the camera in the mid-90s. Such men formed the 'Poor Bloody Infantry' which was the very core of the SLA. (Albert Grandolini Collection)

Burial of a soldier killed in action. These scenes became more and more frequent during Jayasikurui as losses mounted. (Albert Grandolini Collection)

The LTTE single T-55, captured in Ponnaryn in 1993, and operated by the Victor Padai Ani. The tank was engaged from time to time to support the movement offensives. (LTTE via Telibrary.com)

A frequent sight in the skies of the Vanni. A SLAF Mi-24 flying at low altitude toward its target and photographed by an insurgent. (LTTE via Telibrary.com)

Tigers entering the centre of Kilinochchi, in the aftermath of Unceasing Waves 02. (LTTE via Telibrary.com)

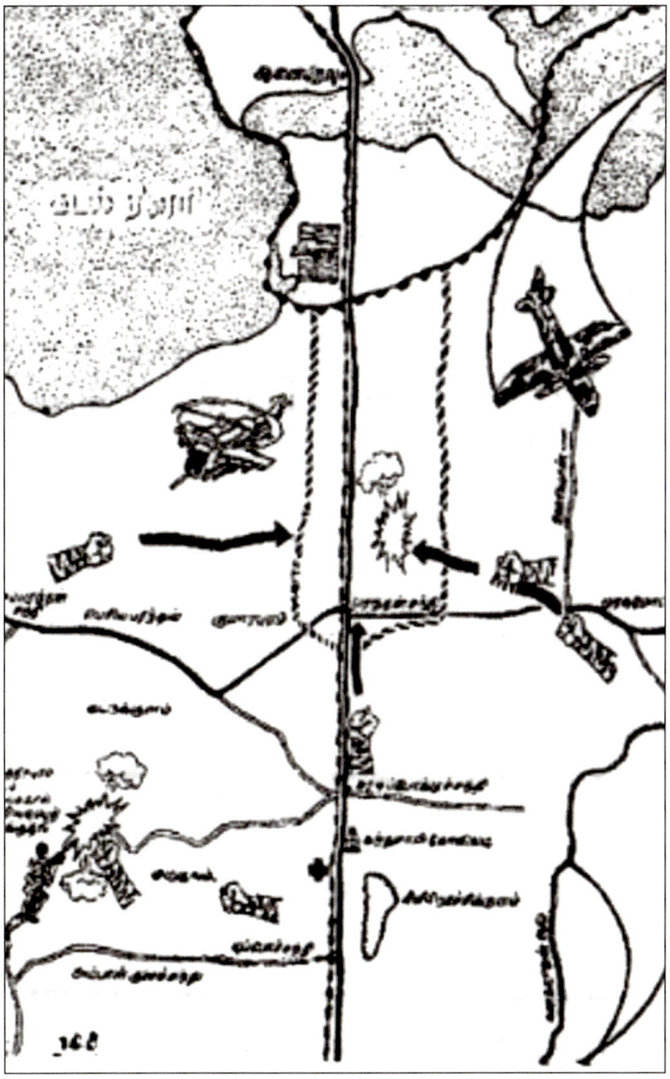

A map published in one of the LTTE newspapers in October 1998, showing Unceasing Waves 02 main thrusts. (LTTE via Telibrary.com)

In late September and early October 1997, the 53 Division initiated a wide envelopment manoeuvre, bypassing the entrenched LTTE defences at Puliyankulam and pushing southward toward Kanagarayankulam—the next significant locality along the A9 highway. Recognising the threat this posed to their defensive posture, the LTTE responded with a new 'Do or Die' counteroffensive on 5 October. In a well-coordinated assault, LTTE fighters launched a large-scale attack on the 53 Division's headquarters and forward logistical depots in the Karappukkuththi area, at a moment when the division was completing its final push toward Kanagarayankulam. To compound confusion and stretch enemy resources, the Tigers simultaneously mounted multiple diversionary attacks elsewhere in the sector. The result was a chaotic five-day battle waged in dense jungle terrain under heavy monsoon rains. At the onset of the attack, the insurgents succeeded in overrunning the divisional headquarters, with the commanding officer narrowly escaping capture. The LTTE held the headquarters for three days before withdrawing. While the Sri Lankan Army did not release official casualty figures, LTTE losses were substantial: the movement acknowledged 163 fighters killed in action. However, they claimed to have seized significant quantities of military equipment and supplies, including large ammunition caches, two 12.7mm heavy machine guns, fourteen 81mm and twenty-two 60mm mortars, and even eight bulldozers. Despite this fierce counterattack, the Army's flanking manoeuvre proved strategically effective. It forced the LTTE to extend their defensive perimeter to an unsustainable length if they wished to continue holding Puliyankulam. Recognising this, LTTE leader Velupillai Prabhakaran ordered a tactical withdrawal from Puliyankulam and directed his forces to prepare a new fortified defensive complex at Mankulam. In the interim, smaller LTTE units were tasked with delaying the advancing Army as much as possible. A few days later, Puliyankulam fell into Army hands without resistance. However, it was only in early November that Colombo officially announced the town's recapture. Around the same time, Maj. Gen. Sri Lal Weerasooriya was appointed as the new Overall Operation Commander of Jayasikurui, replacing Maj. Gen. Asoka Jayawardhane. The new commander was given the ambitious—and ultimately unrealistic—goal of completing the operation by 31 December 1997.[5]

The Mankulam deadlock

From Puliyankulam, the 55 and 53 Divisions advanced along the A9 highway in two parallel columns, maintaining a front of approximately 1,000 metres. Although they did not encounter any major set-piece battles, their progress was nonetheless hampered by a series of determined LTTE delaying actions. Insurgent detachments fell back from one fortified position to the next, engaging the advancing troops before retreating further, in a well-practised effort to buy time. Compounding the challenge, the onset of the monsoon had turned the unpaved roads into rivers of mud, severely hindering mobility and logistics. At Kanagarayankulam Junction, however, the LTTE launched a strong counterattack. Fighters from the Malathy Padai Ani, already holding the line, were reinforced by elements of the Jeyanthan Padai Ani. In the ensuing battle, the LTTE suffered 37 fighters killed, but succeeded in halting the advance of the 53 Division, at least temporarily. This bought them additional time to strengthen their defensive positions around Mankulam. Realising the mounting difficulties of pushing directly along the A9, the Sri Lankan Army command opted for a change in approach. Instead of continuing the frontal assault, the two divisions pivoted southwest and began following the so-called 'Old Kandy Road', a narrow and lesser-used route leading directly to the village of Karuppaddamurippu. This location was strategically important, as the road intersected with the A34, which connected Mankulam to Mullaitivu. This unexpected manoeuvre took the LTTE by surprise. Expecting continued pressure along the A9, they had concentrated their forces and defences accordingly. By shifting direction, the Army forced the LTTE to rapidly redeploy and rethink their defensive posture. By the end of January 1998,

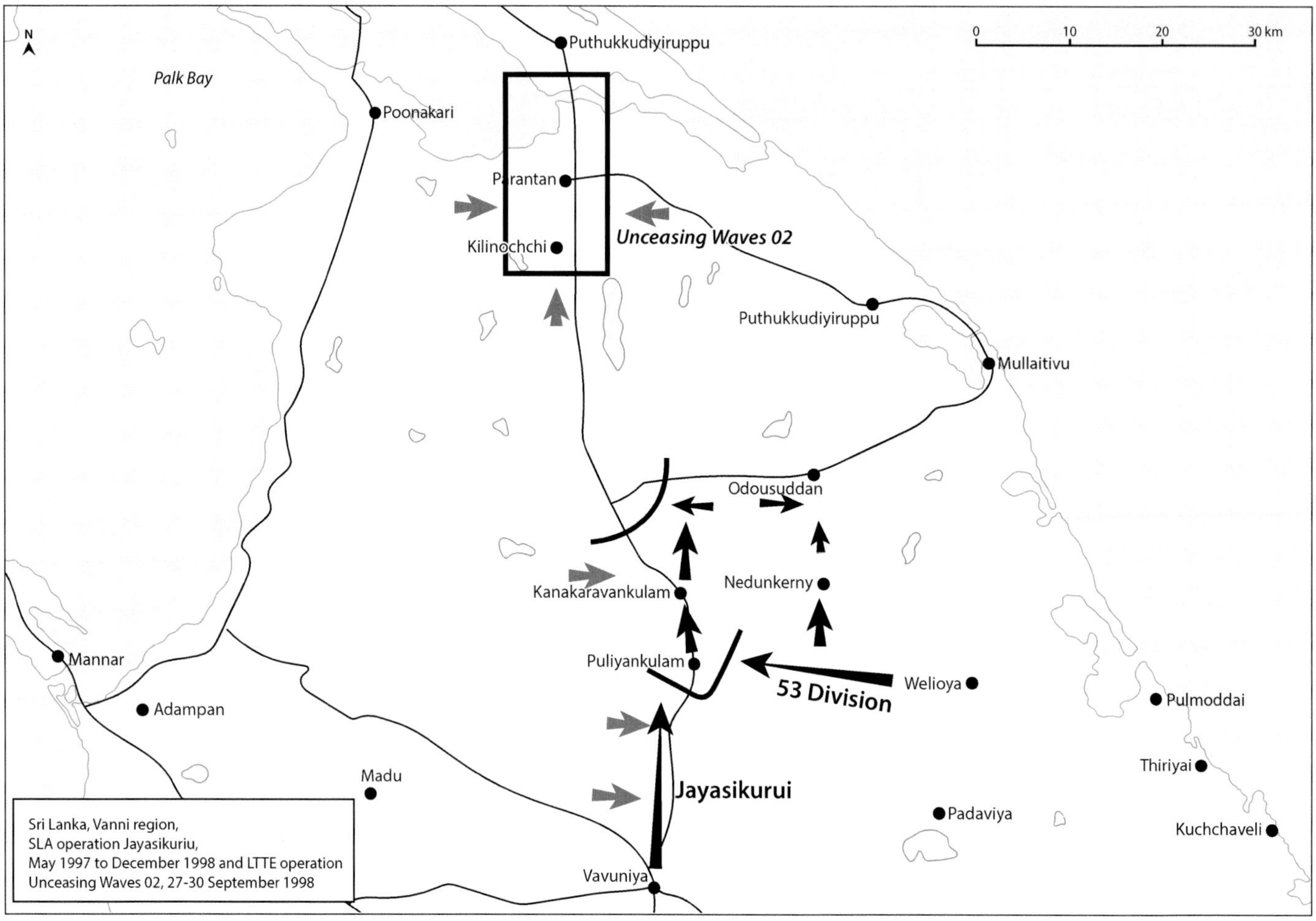

Map showing the SLA advances during operation Jayasikurui, and the LTTE Unceasing Waves 02 offensive.

the Sri Lankan forces had reached positions from which they could launch a direct assault on Mankulam—and the extensive network of trenches, bunkers, and fortified positions the LTTE had spent weeks preparing.

On 24 February 1998, the Sri Lankan Army launched its first assault on Olumadu, a strategically important village situated approximately five kilometres east of the Mankulam Junction. Acting as a critical bulwark on Mankulam's eastern flank, Olumadu was essential to the LTTE's efforts to prevent any advance by government forces along the A34 corridor. However, the initial attack was swiftly and decisively repulsed by a well-coordinated LTTE counteroffensive. Over the following weeks, the Army made several renewed attempts to break through the defences at Olumadu, continuing until mid-April. Yet each effort met the same fate: firm resistance and eventual failure. It soon became apparent that Olumadu was heavily fortified and defended by seasoned companies from the Sothiya, Charles Anthony, and Chiruthaigal Padai Ani formations. A major element of the LTTE's defensive network was positioned along the southern edge of a wide, open expanse just beyond the village. For the Army infantry, this terrain proved a nightmare—an exposed field of fire that left advancing troops vulnerable to relentless machine gun and mortar bombardment. However, what was a death trap for infantry was seen by the Army commanders as an opportunity for their armoured units. They assessed that this open area, while treacherous for foot soldiers, was ideally suited for armoured manoeuvre, where tanks and infantry fighting vehicles could exploit both their firepower and mobility with minimal obstruction. Plans began to take shape for a concentrated armoured thrust that could turn the tide in the Army's favour.

Thus, a large-scale mechanized assault was meticulously prepared under a veil of secrecy. A total of 48 armoured vehicles were assembled for the operation, including 20 T-55 tanks from 4 SLAC (A and C squadrons), 10 T-85s and 12 T-86s from 3 SLAC (A and C squadrons), and six BMPs from 5 SLAC. To avoid arousing suspicion, the vehicles were dispersed across several rear-area camps, well away from the front lines. Additionally, small detachments of T-55s were regularly deployed to conduct fire missions against known LTTE positions, serving as a ruse to mislead the Tigers regarding their true intent. The deception culminated on the evening of 19 April, when a full squadron of T-55s carried out one of these routine fire missions, deliberately generating as much noise and activity as possible. This masked the movement of the remaining squadrons, which were quietly assembling just two kilometres from the open field where the assault was to begin. By nightfall, the Army had successfully concentrated at least 21 armoured vehicles, organized into two assault echelons. The first wave comprised six T-55s and three T-85s, whose role was to punch through the LTTE defensive lines. The second echelon consisted of 12 T-85s acting as armoured personnel carriers, each carrying eight soldiers from the 3rd Battalion of the Sri Lanka Light Infantry (3rd SLLI). These infantrymen were tasked with dismounting and securing enemy positions once the initial breach had been achieved. To enhance the operation's effectiveness and fragment the LTTE's response, two additional infantry battalions simultaneously launched diversionary attacks on other Tiger strongpoints, aiming to fix and divide the insurgents' forces at the critical moment of the mechanized thrust.

The attack commenced on 20 April at 08:00 AM, with artillery delivering a heavy barrage on the insurgent positions at Olumadu.

Initially, the plan unfolded smoothly, with the LTTE unable to counter the overwhelming force of tanks and armoured personnel carriers (APCs) as they charged toward their positions. The sheer momentum of the armour proved too much for the insurgents to halt from a distance. However, once the tanks and APCs breached the first line of the LTTE defensive system, consisting of an earth berm, the situation changed. As the infantry dismounted and moved to secure the ground, the engagement shifted into intense close-quarter combat. The insurgents responded quickly, with mortar fire from the Kutti Sri Padai Ani and anti-tank squads from the Victor Padai Ani rushed to the frontlines. The terrain became chaotic as both sides fought fiercely for control.

The battle raged for several hours, with withering exchanges of fire. By 16:30, the armoured squadrons received the order to withdraw, having accomplished their objective but suffering significant casualties. Two T-55 tanks were destroyed, set ablaze by multiple RPG hits, while a T-85 lost its tracks after another RPG strike. The disabled T-85 had to be destroyed by a 100mm shell from a T-55 to prevent it from falling into enemy hands. The battle left 43 soldiers, including four officers, dead, with numerous others wounded. Despite the heavy losses, the operation demonstrated the power of the mechanized assault but also highlighted the resilience of the LTTE's defensive tactics.

53 and 55 Divisions did not relent, and continued to mount a series of determined assaults against the heavily fortified Mankulam stronghold. One notable attempt occurred on 20 June 1998, when three armoured units supported a two-pronged assault led by the 1st SLSR and 6th GR regiments. Despite suffering significant casualties, the two divisions steadily pressured the LTTE defences, forcing them to eventually withdraw. By 30 September 1998, the government had successfully captured Mankulam, located just 27 kilometres from Kilinochchi. While the official conclusion of operation Jayasikurui was announced on 5 December 1998, the campaign had already reached its zenith after the fall of Mankulam. In the end, the operation's final outcome proved to be far less decisive than anticipated, as the LTTE launched a strategic counter-move that would redefine the balance of power in the region.[6]

Unceasing Waves 02

From early 1998 onward, the LTTE adopted a dual strategy that capitalized on its ability to manoeuvre on interior lines. This strategy involved continuing to resist the Jayasikurui offensive in the South while also consolidating its forces for a significant counteroffensive in the North, specifically targeting the strategically vital Elephant Pass – Paranthan – Kilinochchi complex, which was under the control of 54 Division. The challenge for the LTTE lay in the formidable defences surrounding Kilinochchi. These were extremely dense, with the usual FDL consisting of an earth berm, protected with bunkers reinforced with concrete, railway sleepers or teak logs placed at close intervals, sometimes as close as 30 metres from each other, thus providing excellent interlocking fields of fire. Furthermore, a second, equally strong, defence line was arranged roughly one kilometre behind the first. This area, which formed the head of the Kilinochchi-Paranthan-Elephant Pass complex, was held by 543 Brigade. This was linked by the A9 road to Paranthan and Elephant Pass, which were held by the division's two other brigades. The road itself was protected by two defensive lines, with the usual several metre-high berms, erected on its eastern and western sides, forming a 10 kilometre long and two kilometre wide corridor. The flanks of the A9 road were covered by roughly 2,000 troops and thus much more vulnerable that the Kilinochchi defences. This was unavoidable as 54 Division had to hold a 162 square kilometers perimeter, shaped like an dumbbell, with two strong ends thinly connected.

On 1 February 1998, the LTTE launched a large-scale offensive targeting the defensive perimeter surrounding their former capital, Kilinochchi. The attack was well-coordinated, with the insurgents assaulting five different points simultaneously. This time, the LTTE relied heavily on firepower to overwhelm the defences, firing thousands of artillery and mortar rounds in support of their attack teams. Additionally, the insurgents deployed their unique T-55 tank, along with two other captured armoured vehicles, to provide further strength to the assault. Meanwhile, a diversionary attack was carried out against Paranthan. Two Black Tiger teams were also involved in the operation. One of the teams infiltrated the area and successfully attacked a communications tower, disrupting enemy radio traffic. Another Black Tiger team attempted to destroy a long-range artillery position in the Iyakachchi area, located on the southern tip of the Jaffna Peninsula. However, this attack failed, and five Black Tigers lost their lives in the attempt. Despite initial success, as the battle raged on, the Tigers were able to push 54 Division troops back, forcing them to withdraw from their forward defence line (FDL) along a two-kilometre stretch toward their second defensive line. But after the initial breakthrough, the momentum of the LTTE attack stalled, and repeated attempts to breach the main defence line were unsuccessful. After several days of fighting, the LTTE called off the offensive. The insurgents acknowledged the loss of 150 fighters during the battle, including 14 Black Tigers. On the Sri Lankan Army side, 89 soldiers were killed, 26 went missing, and 405 were wounded. Despite this defensive victory, the triumph was short-lived. Several months later, the Sri Lankan Army high command ordered 54 Division to retake the two kilometres of lost ground. This led to a series of futile frontal assaults, with the last attack on 17 June 1998 ending in a staggering loss: 137 soldiers were killed, 37 went missing, and 636 were wounded due to the heavy machine gun and mortar fire unleashed by the well-entrenched LTTE forces.[7]

The early February 1998 defeat and the subsequent counterattacks by 54 Division did not dissuade the LTTE from attempting to retake Kilinochchi. This time, however, the insurgents reverted to their usual strategy. They deployed dozens of Spy Tigers, their specialized reconnaissance troops, to infiltrate enemy lines. These spies meticulously observed the enemy's positions over weeks, noting their exact dispositions, unit strengths, routines, and potential vulnerabilities. As explained a few years later by Jerry, a senior commander in the LTTE military intelligence apparatus, the movement placed significant emphasis on tactical reconnaissance. According to Jerry, the success of their operations often relied on gathering precise intelligence about enemy defences, weaknesses, and timing. By carefully studying these factors, the LTTE could exploit opportunities for breakthroughs, minimize casualties, and outmanoeuvre the enemy. This approach helped the LTTE remain adaptive and responsive to the changing dynamics on the battlefield, allowing them to continue their struggle despite setbacks:

> Before the spy operation for Unceasing Waves 02 began, we had some surveillance around the military guards in the Kilinochchi area. We accelerated this reconnaissance operation within a month of Operation Unceasing Waves 02. Initially, only special spies saw this. We completed this by involving each unit in this reconnaissance operation to spy on unloading teams into battle. [...] In the last stages they worked

> day and night completely without rest. The full responsibility of the fight rests with the spy. In fact, if a spy is going into dangerous areas without respecting his life, its real purpose is to reduce the casualties of other fighters along the way if he returns alive. If there are problems with the spy, there may be losses, so the spy fighters will realize this and engage in it. If a battle is won, its initial success will depend on the spy. [...] Spy fighters will also be involved in providing combat training to the teams, as their guidance will be essential to the teams.[8]

In the meantime, the LTTE meticulously constructed replicas of the Forward Defence Lines (FDL) sections they planned to attack, ensuring that every detail matched the real defensive positions. At least 1,400 fighters from the Jeyanthan Padai Ani and other infantry units underwent intensive training for three months in preparation for the forthcoming operation. Dubbed Oyaatha-Alaikal 2 (Unceasing Waves 02), the offensive was led by seasoned operational commanders such as Balraj, Theepan, Vithusha, and Karuna Amman. As always, the operation was closely overseen by the LTTE leader, Velupillai Prabhakaran, who monitored the campaign from behind the scenes.

Ironically, while the reconnaissance activities of the Spy Tigers had been noticed by the Sri Lankan Army, as several of the spies were killed by sentries or patrols within the complex, the SLA unknowingly played into the insurgents' hands. In a strategic misstep, the Army sent one infantry and one Special Forces battalion, along with armour and artillery, from 54 Division to reinforce the 53 and 55 Divisions that were engaged in the battle for Mankulam. This move left the 54 Division's own defences weaker, allowing the LTTE to exploit the opportunity for a counteroffensive.

Unceasing Waves 02 began in earnest on 27 September 1998 around midnight. The LTTE launched several diversionary attacks from the south directly on 534 Brigade positions defending Kilinochchi, creating confusion and spreading the Sri Lankan Army's resources thin. Meanwhile, two groups, each consisting of several companies of infantry, launched simultaneous attacks from the east and the west. These forces targeted the weakest part of the entire defensive complex: the two defensive lines protecting the A9 road between Paranthan and Kilinochchi. The insurgents went so far as to sacrifice one or two of their few remaining armoured vehicles, using them as Suicide Vehicle Borne Improvised Explosive Devices (SVBIEDs) to breach the berms. These armoured vehicles, laden with explosives, were driven straight into the heart of the defences, detonating upon impact. Guided by Spy Tigers who had carefully reconnoitred the advance paths, the assault teams breached the defence lines in less than an hour. Once through, they began to entrench themselves, effectively cutting off the 543 Brigade from the rest of the division and leaving the Sri Lankan forces vulnerable to further attacks. Col. Sylvester Perera, who was a mid-ranking officer at the time, later described the LTTE onslaught as a devastating and swift attack that left the defending forces struggling to reorganize. Their ability to coordinate such an assault, using a combination of deception, carefully planned reconnaissance, and overwhelming force, caught the Army off guard and gave the LTTE a significant advantage in the initial stages of the battle:

> I was the commander of Bravo Company, 6th Battalion, Gemunu Watch. [...] Our battalion was holding a defensive line facing southward toward the LTTE stronghold. At around 0100 hours, our defences began to receive small arms fire, along with a heavy barrage of artillery fire. During this attack, the LTTE also started shelling the tactical headquarters of the brigade and battalions. The guerrillas penetrated our defences from the flanks and started firing from our front and rear with massive fire support. [...] The LTTE managed to cut our forces off from the rear and surround our defences. They fired rocket-propelled grenades at the tanks, armoured personnel carriers, ambulances, and other vehicles that were involved in reinforcement and the evacuation of casualties.[9]

As soon as it understood where the Tigers were, the 54 Division HQ reacted by unleashing all the firepower it could on the area, whether with mortar, artillery, or by calling airstrikes, which were followed by fierce counterattacks, fuelled by the arrival of the 531 "Air Mobile" Brigade, which had been dispatched as reinforcements from Mankulam to Elephant Pass and transported by SLAF helicopters. According to Thamizhini, a female Political Wing cadre, the fierceness of the SLA reaction unsettled the LTTE commanders:

> This battle went for three days straight. The places captured by the Tigers on the first day were recaptured by the army on the second day. Apparently, at that time, the Leader [Author note: Velupillai Pirabhakaran] had given Thamiselvan, who was at the main command centre, an important mission. [...] He was asked to report back on the morale of the commanders involved in the attack. Following the Leader's request, Thamilselvan talked to the attack commanders Balraj, Theepan and Vithusha and found they held no great hopes of victory in the attack. When Political Wing leader Thamiselvan informed the Leader of this, it seems he lost his temper and slammed his fist on the table, saying "I'll win this fight and show them!" After this, the Tigers gained Kilinochchi by hammering the army with the new heavy mortar shells the Movement had acquired. Thamilselvan himself told us this story in a gathering, face to face.[10]

However, on 28 September at 03:00, the Army Command decided to withdraw 543 Brigade from Kilinochchi, and the unit left its positions under massive concentrations of enemy direct and indirect fire, whilst another attack was made from Paranthan. The withdrawal turned into a rout, and command and control were lost, with the units splitting into small groups of men fending for themselves. The bulk of brigade elements, supported by a few armoured vehicles, still made it to Paranthan through multiple ambushes, but at a devastating cost. One of its infantry battalions, the 4th SLSR, lost 132 soldiers killed and 286 wounded, whilst another, the 10th SLSR, had 121 KIA and WIA. Altogether, 857 soldiers were killed, 171 went missing and another 936 were wounded during the three-day battle of Unceasing Waves 02. The Tigers acknowledged the loss of 240 fighters in the aftermath of the operation and captured several dozen vehicles and tractors as well as vast amounts of diverse equipment. Thus, Unceasing Waves 02 ended in a triumph for the LTTE, which had both recaptured its lost, and ephemeral capital, thrown the SLA back to Paranthan and decimated an entire brigade in the process. Ironically enough, each side lost a major stronghold and captured an enemy one exactly at the same time. Indeed, the fall of Mankulam was directly linked to the success of operation Unceasing Waves 02 because the LTTE had gambled on withdrawing some of the best troops defending the town to dispatch them to Kilinochchi.[11]

Flawed Battle Cry

As soon as Jayasikirui was officially closed, the SLA launched a follow-up operation, named Rivibala, with 53 and 55 Divisions advancing east from Mankulam and Olumadu. They cleared the Nedunkerni-Oddusuddhan area, capturing both localities, without meeting heavy enemy resistance. However, something much more ambitious was in the making. Namely, the government needed a clear-cut victory against the LTTE, especially as presidential elections were to take place by the end of 1999. This pushed the army to retake the Madhu area, and foremost, the Shrine of Our Lady of Madhu, one of the most revered places among the Sri Lankan tiny, but influential, Catholic community.

On 4 March 1999, the 53rd and 55th Divisions launched Operation Ranaghosa ('Battle Cry') and executed a pincer movement that enabled them to encircle the targeted area. By May, they had captured the shrine along with a 962-square-kilometre area. In parallel, the Army advanced along the western Vanni coast via the A32 road, which connects Mannar to Pooneryn. From June onwards, the two divisions continued expanding the territory under their control, encountering only minimal resistance from the LTTE, aside from occasional artillery raids against army camps. This situation changed in mid-September 1999, when the 53rd and 55th Divisions encountered a series of well-fortified defensive positions supported by intense indirect fire as they began operations in the Pallamadu–Periyamadhu area. Their advance slowed to a halt, and casualties rose sharply, with 114 soldiers killed over the course of two days. The entire operation was called off a few days later. Overall, the Army succeeded in re-establishing control over a substantial portion of the Vanni at relatively limited cost—primarily because the LTTE had chosen not to engage in a prolonged battle prior to September, for reasons that would become apparent in the months that followed.[12]

7
UNCEASING WAVES 3

The year-and-a-half-long Jayasikurui operation shaped the context in which the final years of Eelam War III would be fought. Most notably, both sides had concentrated the bulk of their forces in the Northern theatre, to the detriment of Eastern Sri Lanka. By the end of September 1999, government forces controlled a larger portion of LTTE heartland territory than at any point in the previous decade. However, these gains had severely depleted the Army's strength.

Vanni slaughterhouse

At the outset, the Sri Lankan Army (SLA) suffered grievous casualties during the offensive. By mid-August 1997, it had already lost 600 soldiers killed in action (KIA) and 3,000 wounded in action (WIA), and by the end of the year, these figures had risen to at least 1,000 and over 5,000 respectively. Before long, the A9 highway had earned the grim moniker 'Highway of Death' within the army. This, in turn, further exacerbated already endemic desertions—particularly when considering the nightmarish living conditions on the frontlines during the monsoon season.

By the end of 1999, the situation had deteriorated to the point where several infantry battalions had only around 200 men available, far below their nominal strength of 850. Low morale was widespread.

At the operational level, the Vanni campaign consumed ever-increasing numbers of troops, as newly seized areas required protection through the establishment of forward defence lines (FDLs). For example, to secure the rear communications of the advancing 53rd and 55th Divisions, the SLA was forced to construct two berms with bunkers placed at regular intervals along the entire length of the A9 from Vavuniya to Mankulam. Over time, these FDLs were pushed further away from either side of the road, greatly expanding the area the Army was required to control. A similar situation developed in the Western Vanni after the Madhu area was retaken. As a result, an increasing number of troops were tied down to static defensive duties, particularly within the 22nd and 56th Divisions. These were often reinforced with second-rate or non-frontline units, such as the 20th Sri Lanka National Guard (SLNG)—fit only for rear-area security—or ad hoc Police, Navy, and Air Force march units, many of whom were poorly prepared for ground combat. Manpower shortages were so acute that even the Special Task Force (STF)—a highly specialised counter-insurgency unit crucial to operations in Eastern Sri Lanka—was redeployed to the North. Despite all these efforts, the defensive lines remained thinly held. Bunkers were widely spaced, often manned by just two soldiers each. Moreover, the Army's continuous offensives left almost no strategic reserve. In essence, the SLA had overextended itself. Worse still, it consistently overestimated the losses inflicted on the insurgents and, as a result, underestimated their remaining combat strength. As Major General Kamal Gunaratne would later explain:

> We expanded our area of control beyond our capacity and encircled it with thinly held, long winding FDLs, which consumed troops. When FDLs are only thinly defended, it is mandatory to have a strong reserve force for contingencies. However, even the dedicated reserves for each area, were deployed for ground defence.[...] Our weak defence lines and large expanses of empty jungles were easy for the LTTE to penetrate and carry out reconnaissance. Whilst the LTTE comprehensively planned their attacks with the intelligence so gathered, we were busy formulating plans looking at a map.[1]

The LTTE was acutely aware of the Army's overextension, which is why it allowed the SLA to seize the Madhu area unopposed in 1999—knowing that this very success would tie down an ever-greater number of troops and render the Army even more vulnerable. Another significant shift in operational paradigm during these years was the LTTE's drastic increase in the use of indirect firepower, particularly mortars. This enabled the group to attrit government forces—up to 70% of SLA casualties were reportedly caused by indirect fire—while simultaneously limiting its own losses. The Army typically lacked detailed intelligence on enemy positions and therefore employed its artillery in broad area bombardments. By contrast, the LTTE excelled in intelligence-gathering, allowing it to launch pinpointed, limited, but highly accurate mortar and artillery strikes against specific SLA targets. To minimise risk, the insurgents deliberately avoided massing large numbers of fighters in any single location where possible. Standard LTTE defensive tactics also helped reduce their own casualties. However, their counterattacks—although occasionally successful—were invariably costly in terms of manpower. The LTTE as a whole committed heavily to resisting Jayasikurui, and this came at a steep price: 2,106 fighters, including 507 women, were killed in 1997 alone—representing an increase of approximately 30% compared to losses sustained in 1996. As Thamizhini recalled:

> On the frontlines, where the ground shook from time to time, the fighters were injured or killed in large numbers. At the same time, injured fighters were sent back to the frontlines even before their injuries were healed. There were times when a fighter who was injured 10 times was sent back into battle for the eleventh time. The medics were also worried that those who were suffering from massive blood loss were taking longer to heal because of malnourishment. As far as I knew, at least two fighters died of anaemia.[2]

Furthermore, the insurgents struggled to expand their order of battle and therefore intensified their recruitment efforts, virtually forbidding young Tamils from leaving LTTE-controlled areas. This was particularly evident among the female population. In addition to replacing casualties in existing units, the movement established the Major Sothiya Padai Ani, another dedicated women's formation. To relieve its regular fighters from rear-security duties as much as possible, the LTTE expanded efforts to raise rural, part-time militias, primarily tasked with patrol and home guard duties in uncontested areas. Nevertheless, because the Tigers benefited from operating along relatively small frontlines—and, unlike the Army, did not need to commit large numbers of troops to holding captured territory—they retained the capacity to maintain sufficient reserves. These could then be deployed for large-scale offensive operations, launched at a time and place of their own choosing.[3]

NATIONAL INTELLIGENCE WING'S BLOODY TRAIL

The LTTE continued to utilise its National Intelligence Wing and its network of clandestine cells to launch terrorist attacks in Colombo, as well as in central and southern Sri Lanka. On 15 October 1997, a vehicle-borne improvised explosive device (VBIED) was detonated near the Galadari Hotel and the World Trade Centre, in the heart of Colombo, killing 11 bystanders and wounding another 105. On 25 January 1998, a suicide bomber killed two people and injured 15 others at the highly symbolic Temple of the Sacred Tooth Relic in Kandy—one of the holiest Buddhist shrines in Sri Lanka. On 5 March, another VBIED exploded near a police station in the capital, killing 36 and wounding 270. On 29 September 1998, LTTE operatives shot down Lion Air Flight No. 602 over Jaffna, killing all 54 passengers and crew. On 18 December 1999, a female suicide bomber infiltrated a political rally at Colombo Town Hall, killing 16 and injuring 106. The main target, President Chandrika Kumaratunga, survived but lost an eye in the attack. On the same day, another suicide bomber killed Major General C. L. Algama at a separate election rally, along with 11 others; a further 45 people were wounded. Assassinations remained common throughout the war, with the majority of victims being military officers or politicians from Tamil political parties. Despite ongoing counter-intelligence efforts, the security services failed to dismantle the National Intelligence Wing's clandestine networks, allowing its leader, Pottu Amman, to continue launching attacks at will. These were often timed in retaliation for battlefield setbacks, incidents involving high Tamil civilian casualties, or as a means of increasing political pressure on the government.[4]

The Great Collapse

By the end of October 1999, the LTTE had completed its extensive preparations for a new large-scale operation, named—rather unsurprisingly—Unceasing Waves 03. However, unlike its two predecessors, which had focused on overwhelming a specific area, Unceasing Waves 03 was, in essence, a multi-phased campaign designed to reverse the Army's gains by recapturing territory lost in the Vanni over the previous two years, ultimately seizing Elephant Pass and advancing into the Jaffna Peninsula.

The offensive began during the night of 1–2 November 1999, targeting the Army's forward defence lines (FDLs) running west to east from Mankulam to Oddusudan, and north to south from Oddusudan to Nedunkerni. These two lines roughly formed two sides of a square that protected the north-eastern approaches to the A9, as well as the two divisional headquarters positioned along it—the 55 Division HQ at Mankulam and the 56 Division HQ at Kanagarayankulam. The west-east section was held by naval infantry, while responsibility for the Oddusudan–Nedunkerni line fell to 563 Brigade. Within this sector, the 2nd (Volunteer) Gajaba Regiment (2nd (V) GR) defended Oddusudan, the 3rd Sinha Regiment (3rd SR) held Nedunkerni, and the 8th Vijayabahu Infantry Regiment (8th VIR) manned the FDL connecting the two locations. This entire area was strategically significant due to its proximity to the LTTE's major base complexes in the Mullaitivu region, allowing the insurgents to operate close to their main rear logistical hubs. Consequently, the LTTE had little difficulty concentrating multiple companies from the Charles Anthony, Jeyanthan, Chiruthaigal, and Sothiya Padai Ani, all well supported by mortars and anti-tank teams.

At first, the Tigers infiltrated large-sized units through the FDL, launching attacks from the rear directly against the 2nd (V) GR and 8th VIR headquarters, while other assault teams struck the FDL itself. The resistance of the 2nd (V) GR collapsed after its commanding officer, Major Suranga Amarasinghe, was killed—along with several other officers—by a mortar barrage. By midday on 2 November, Oddusudan was in LTTE hands. The Tigers pressed on with their multipronged assault, and before long, the 8th VIR was also overwhelmed, followed by the 3rd SR, while 563 Brigade Headquarters was hastily withdrawn southwards. Limited reinforcements dispatched from the A9 were swiftly repulsed in a series of ambushes and under mortar fire, as LTTE artillery shelled Army positions at Mankulam and Kanagarayankulam. The Tigers captured Nedunkerni on 3 November, and several of their units advanced towards the A9, threatening to encircle Mankulam and Kanagarayankulam. Consequently, the units defending the two towns and their respective divisional headquarters began to retreat. Crucially, a Buffel MRAP carrying several sets of communications equipment became stuck in the mud during the withdrawal and was abandoned. It was later seized intact by the insurgents, forcing the

Army to suspend its radio communications until countermeasures could be implemented. At this stage, command and control broke down, leading to a collapse in morale across the 55 and 56 Divisions. This, in turn, triggered a chain reaction that engulfed nearly all troops engaged in the central Vanni, as recalled by Major General Kamal Gunaratne:

> When Oddusudan, Mankulam and Nedunkerni were falling, troops in other areas of Operation Jayasikuru also started falling back, abandoning everything. Some troops quickly abandoned their positions, even before their area was attacked, without firing a single shot or sustaining a single casualty. When troops saw their colleagues from the forward areas withdrawing, they simply followed, without knowing why. When the troops of the Navy, Air Force and Police saw the Army retreating, they too followed, for no real reason. It was an avalanche which could not be contained. [...] Command and Control totally disintegrated and armouries full of weapons, ammunition dumps including tank and artillery ammunition, food stores, fleet of vehicles including tractors and bulldozers, were all left behind.[5]

Mankulam fell into LTTE hands on 5 November, followed the next day by Kanagarayankulam and Puliyankulam, as the military continued to retreat towards Vavuniya. The debacle, which threatened to spiral out of control, was halted by Colonel Roshan Silva, commander of the 531 (Air Mobile) Brigade. He ordered his troops to establish a defensive line in front of Omanthai and hold it firmly against advancing LTTE vanguard units, with the support of several artillery batteries. This action allowed the retreating forces and their commanders to regroup and reorganise in Vavuniya. Meanwhile, the Tigers advanced through the eastern Vanni, capturing several camps until they reached the Weli Oya/Manal Aru area.

By that time, the Tigers had launched another series of similar attacks in the Western Vanni, which led to the collapse of the local Army defence line and triggered the same wave of panic that had swept through the Central Vanni. By 18 November, the Madhu Church area was once again under LTTE control, and the Mannar–Vavuniya road was under renewed threat. Thus, the territorial gains made by government forces since early 1997 were reversed within days—and at a remarkably low cost to the Tigers. By 9 November, the LTTE claimed to have lost only 120 fighters killed in action, including 44 women, while the Army suffered at least 1,000 killed. The entire defence establishment was stunned by the blow. President Chandrika Kumaratunga responded by pressuring the Army's top command to dismiss the Vanni Security Force Commander, the commanding officers of the 55 and 56 Divisions, the CO of 561 Brigade, and three battalion commanders.[6]

Above: Bell 212 helicopters were also used for casualty evacuation (CASEVAC). During large-scale battles, the number of wounded was so high that the blood of injured soldiers pooled and congealed on the cabin decking of the helicopters. (Adrien Fontanellaz Collection)

Below: A LTTE company leader and his assistants. One can never emphasise enough how the insurgents' excellent communication network was instrumental into their combat effectiveness, if only because it routinely allowed them to launch extremely precise mortar barrages. (LTTE)

Typical briefing before the launch of another large-scale attack. These were parts of the insurgents' meticulous preparations before any offensive operation. (LTTE)

Fighters of one of the LTTE female units advancing in front of the former 55 Division HQ, in Mankulam, during the first phase of Operation Unceasing Waves 03. (LTTE)

A Saracen of 1 SLAC captured during the beginning of Unceasing Waves 03. Some of these outdated APCs were still serving in the SLA as late as early 2000. (LTTE)

Impregnable fortress

In the aftermath of its triumph in the Vanni, the LTTE concentrated all available forces on its next objective: the Elephant Pass complex. Although fighters from some units were granted a few days' leave to recover from exhaustion, the focus quickly shifted to preparations for the coming offensive.

Capturing Elephant Pass was a formidable challenge, and the insurgents knew it—having failed in their previous attempt in 1991. During that operation, Aakaya Kadal Veli ('Air, Sea, Land'), the LTTE had tried to seize the base, then held by a single infantry battalion. The assault ended in abysmal failure, with the Tigers breaking against the SLA's defensive lines while also contending with a powerful counterattack from a division-sized force that landed at Vettilaikerni, approximately 12 kilometres from the Pass. From 1996 onwards, following the completion of Operation Riviresa, Elephant Pass functioned as the gateway controlling all land access to the Jaffna Peninsula. The peninsula itself remained the symbolic and strategic heart of Tamil irredentism—the ultimate prize for the LTTE—making Elephant Pass an obvious target. The Army was fully aware of this, and by 1999, the Elephant Pass complex had developed into a massive defensive system, stretching 23 kilometres in length and between 8 to 10 kilometres in width. It was under the responsibility of the 54 Division, which by the end of 1999 commanded six brigades (541 to 546), supported by the equivalent of a regiment each of armour and artillery, as well as signals and engineering detachments—amounting to roughly 10,000 men in total. Additionally, it could rely on fire support from long-range artillery batteries based in Palali. Meanwhile, the 51 and 52 Divisions were stationed in the Jaffna Peninsula, but they remained preoccupied with counter-insurgency operations against underground LTTE networks left behind after the group's withdrawal in early 1996. These cells continued to launch regular attacks, including IED placements, terrorist strikes, and small-scale ambushes.

The southern side of the complex was anchored at Paranthan, where well-constructed defensive lines protected the land approaches to the Pass itself. This was considered the most threatened sector and was defended by three brigades, including the 545 and 546 Brigades. In addition, due to the growing strength of the Sea Tigers and the LTTE's increasing capacity to conduct seaborne operations, the 54 Division also had to secure the coastline and the areas north of the Pass. This included protecting its two critical supply lines: the A9 road linking the Pass to Jaffna, and the beaches between Kadaikkadu and Vettilaikerni on the north-eastern coast, where supplies were offloaded by the Sri Lanka Navy—rather than being transported all

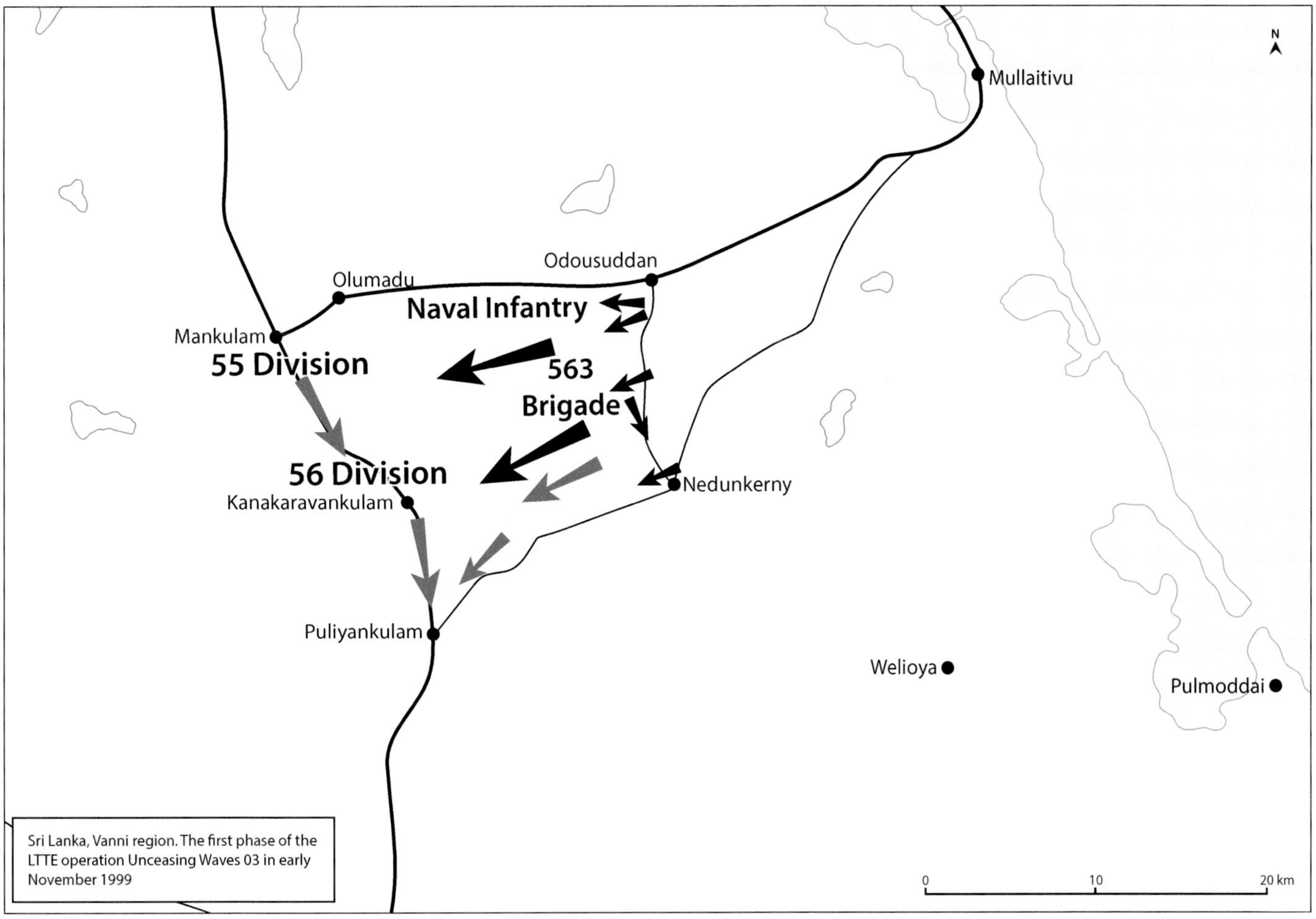

Map showing the opening stage of Operation Unceasing Waves 03, which led to the SLA collapse in the Central Vanni. (Map drawn by George Anderson)

the way from Kankesanthurai by road to Elephant Pass. As a result, at least two brigades were tasked with guarding the northern side of the complex, with fortified positions established in locations such as Kadaikkadu and Vettilaikerni on the north-eastern coast, and Iyakachchi further inland. The latter held crucial strategic value, as it was the only location within the complex with access to drinkable water wells. Although the SLA had installed water purifiers as a backup, these had broken down and had not been repaired. This would ultimately prove to be the garrison's proverbial Achilles' heel.

As with the rest of the SLA, morale among the troops of the 54 Division had been undermined by the series of defeats suffered in previous months, resulting in endemic rates of desertion, further exacerbated by insufficient replacements. On the other hand, the division had been subjected to an intensive regimen of field exercises aimed at improving its combat effectiveness. Meanwhile, the Tigers maintained constant pressure on the southern sector of the complex following the fall of Kilinochchi. They constructed their own entrenchments as close as possible to SLA positions and conducted regular mortar and artillery harassment fire.[7]

First blow

The most obvious axis of attack against Elephant Pass was a frontal assault on Paranthan from the south, and accordingly, this was where the 54 Division's defences were strongest. However, the LTTE leadership chose to pursue an entirely different strategy. While the Paranthan defences would indeed be engaged, the main thrust of the offensive would come via a flanking manoeuvre on the eastern side of the complex, with the ultimate objective of severing its connection to the rest of the Jaffna Peninsula by capturing the A9 road. This plan was feasible only through comparatively large-scale amphibious landings—an operation that would have been unthinkable without the Sea Tigers' ability to contest control of the sea against the Sri Lanka Navy, at least for limited periods. The LTTE had conducted amphibious operations before, notably during Operations Frog in 1993 and Unceasing Waves 01 in 1996, but these had been limited in both scale and the distance involved compared to what would be required to outflank the Elephant Pass complex. This worked to the LTTE's advantage, as the SLA's eastern defences were designed to repel small-scale incursions, not a full-scale assault. As always, the insurgent offensive was preceded by months of meticulous intelligence gathering, followed by weeks of planning and rehearsals.

The first blow of Unceasing Waves 03's second phase came in the early hours of 11 December 1999, when dozens of Sea Tiger transport boats—heavily escorted by attack and suicide craft—landed multiple companies from the Malathi Padai Ani and the Jaffna regional command on the beaches between Kaddaikadu and Vettilakerni. This entire area formed a narrow strip of land between the sea and a saltwater lagoon. The fighters surged from the beach and began infiltrating the defensive positions of the 2nd (V) Gemunu Watch (2nd (V) GW), which was tasked with defending the sector, sparking a fierce battle. Simultaneously, other LTTE units advanced from the south through the Chandikulam bird sanctuary and assaulted Pullaveli, thereby catching the SLA's eastern flank in a pincer movement. Meanwhile, the Kittu Padai Ani's heavy guns shelled the complex from Pooneryn, targeting brigade and divisional headquarters.

Furthermore, another infantry force, transported by Sea Tiger craft across the Kilali Lagoon, attacked the eastern flank of the complex and engaged positions held by the 11th (V) Gajaba Regiment (11th (V) GR), thereby revealing the LTTE's overall objective: to sever the Jaffna Peninsula at its narrowest point and isolate Elephant Pass. This was followed by another assault launched from the Kilali Lagoon on the morning of 12 December. Covered by heavy mortar fire from Pooneryn, elements of the Jeyanthan and Imran Pandian Padai Ani, under the overall command of Sornam, landed near Thanankilappu, posing a direct threat to Chavakachcheri. This move successfully forced the Sri Lankan military to divert significant artillery and air assets to the area, as well as dispatch reinforcements. Indeed, as soon as the offensive began, the 51 Division was ordered to send its only reserve battalion southward, while the brigade defending Palali redeployed two of its three battalions. Despite this swift and determined reaction, the LTTE detachment managed to retain a foothold in the area for the following months, effectively tying down SLA forces.

Further east, events did not unfold as intended for the LTTE either, as the 11th (V) GR managed to repel the insurgents' landing parties within a few hours. The Sri Lanka Air Force (SLAF) played a significant role in the fighting, and a few days later, Mi-24 helicopter CH-618 was shot down while engaging Sea Tiger boats. All four crew members were killed.

The female fighters of the Malathi Padai Ani proved far more successful at Vettilakerni, gradually wearing down the 2nd (V) GW's defences and infiltrating further inland. By the afternoon of 12 December, the battalion was ordered to withdraw to more defensible positions. The retreat was conducted in good order, and, with the arrival of reinforcements, the 54 Division managed to establish a new defensive line further west, anchored on the seawater lagoon and blocking access to the A9. The sudden offensive thus ended with mixed results. The insurgents succeeded in capturing a three-kilometre-long beachhead along the Eastern coast between Vettilakerni and Kaddaikadu, effectively severing the Elephant Pass complex from its maritime supply line. However, they failed to cut its other major logistical artery, the A9, thereby turning the operation into a protracted engagement. Up to that point, the battle had proven less deadly than previous operations, with the LTTE admitting the loss of 64 fighters killed in action in the preceding days. This allowed them to retain the capacity to renew their offensive at will. Meanwhile, the 53 Division was rushed from the Vanni to the Jaffna Peninsula by air and sea.[8]

Loss of Paranthan

It was not long before the LTTE resumed its offensive against the complex. This time, the blow fell on the 546 Brigade's lines at Paranthan. Aware they were targeting the strongest section of the entire complex, the insurgents concentrated all available firepower to support their assault. In addition to multiple mortar teams from the Kutti Sri Padai Ani and the heavy guns of the Kittu Padai Ani, this included their sole T-55 tank. From 16 December 1999 onwards, these assets relentlessly pounded the Paranthan defences. The artillery preparation proved devastating; the 8th Gajaba Regiment (8th GR) alone suffered 150 soldiers killed in action on the first day of the bombardment. The scale of casualties was such that SLA civilian employees had to be requisitioned to man sections of the defensive line, while the intensity and precision of the shelling made it impossible to send reinforcements. During the night of 19 December 1999, multiple assault teams from the Charles Anthony and Malathi Padai Ani infiltrated the forward defence lines, triggering a particularly fierce battle. The battered Sri Lankan units were eventually forced to withdraw from Paranthan. Together with 545 Brigade, they attempted to establish a new defensive line at Umayalpuram, but the Tigers pressed on with their assault, still supported by their mortar array. By 21 December, both brigades had been driven from the area, and the 545 Brigade headquarters at the Paranthan Chemical Factory had to be evacuated. The LTTE ended up in full control of the southern approaches to Elephant Pass.

The insurgents did not immediately press their offensive further, leading the 54 Division command to believe that the situation had stabilised. However, the LTTE continued to launch small-scale probing attacks on both the eastern and southern flanks of the complex, carried out frequent mortar and artillery barrages, and repeatedly infiltrated Spy Tigers—some disguised in SLA uniforms and fluent in Sinhalese—into enemy lines to gather intelligence. Other infiltration teams were deployed for additional purposes. On 17 February 2000, a Bell 212 helicopter (CH-538) was shot down while conducting a CASEVAC mission over the peninsula. The SLA did not remain passive either. On 1 January 2000, the 54 Division launched an attack from Iyakachchi, but quickly suffered 28 soldiers killed and over 100 wounded. Similar offensives were launched in the same area over the following weeks, but these failed to pose a serious threat to the LTTE beachhead. In March, the 55 Division was redeployed from the Vanni to the Jaffna Peninsula.[9]

The Box

On the evening of 26 March 2000, around 600 fighters led by Theepan launched a northward attack from Vettilakerni and began investing the SLA defence line at Thayaladi. Simultaneously, three teams of four Black Tigers each infiltrated the Palali complex and targeted two artillery batteries within its perimeter. They succeeded in destroying two 130mm and three 152mm guns—nearly a quarter of the artillery pieces stationed at the base at the time—as well as an ammunition depot, before withdrawing, with four operatives killed in the process. However, these actions were in support of a third move—one that was completely unexpected.

Namely, at least 12 infantry companies from the Charles Anthony, Sothiya, and Malathi Padai Ani, along with several anti-tank teams and mortar batteries from the Victor and Kutti Sri Padai Ani—totalling around 1,200 fighters under the command of Balraj—had been secretly concentrated south of Vettilakerni, along with all the fast transport boats the Sea Tigers could assemble. This comparatively large amphibious force, escorted by flotillas of attack and suicide craft, set sail in the evening, covering the 11-kilometre distance to Kudarappu, near Nakarkovil—the intended landing site, which had been cleared by infiltrated Spy Tigers positioned behind SLA lines defending Thayaladi.The first wave of fighters landed unopposed, quickly securing the beach and its surroundings, allowing subsequent waves shuttled by the Sea Tigers to disembark safely. Meanwhile, Balraj sent forward elements across the narrow lagoon separating the landing zone from the rest of the peninsula, using small fishing boats to transport heavy equipment. Before long, these units reached their ultimate objective: the A9 road. Within hours, the 1,200 fighters had established a box-shaped defensive perimeter, six kilometres long and 1.5 kilometres wide, centred on Kudarappu to the east and the village of Ittavil, situated directly on the A9.

This sudden severing of the A9 was nothing short of a disaster for the SLA. Once the scale of the threat was realised, the 53 Division was ordered to counter-attack and regain control of the road, triggering an extremely fierce battle that would last for 24 days. However, the urgency of the crisis led to the 53 Division being committed piecemeal, with its brigades hurling themselves at the entrenched insurgents one after another, rather than overwhelming them before they could consolidate their positions. Fortunately for Balraj's fighters, by 29 March, Theepan's companies had broken through the now-isolated SLA defenders at Thayaladi and linked up with the Kudarappu force, establishing a land corridor between Balraj's command and LTTE-held areas. This allowed the LTTE to sustain the beachhead, rotate troops, and bring in reinforcements. On the afternoon of 2 April, the 53 Division launched a large-scale assault, spearheaded by at least a dozen tanks and armoured vehicles. The insurgents responded immediately with a counter-attack involving approximately 600 fighters, successfully isolating the Sri Lanka Armoured Corps from its accompanying infantry. This initiated a several-hours-long engagement that lasted into the evening. The LTTE destroyed two T-55 tanks, four T-63 II armoured personnel carriers, and claimed to have captured two Buffels. Still, the protracted battle was becoming a gruesome ordeal for the insurgent detachment as well—at least according to Balraj:

> It was the real battle. For 24 days we faced all types of attack from artillery shells, mortar attacks, air-raids, air strafing, tank formations, armoured vehicle attacks, commando operations, etc. One day our enemy would capture a few hundred metres from us but next day we would chase them out and capture more territory. This process continued for 24 days. Furthermore, it was a completely open area so we had nowhere to go but to remain inside the bunkers. Everything from cooking, sleeping and treating wounded soldiers was done inside the bunkers.[10]

Indeed, and largely due to their powerful and precise mortar and artillery support, the Tigers not only succeeded in repelling the 53 Division's initial counterattacks but also managed to construct their own defensive positions approximately a kilometre beyond the original box-shaped perimeter. With the A9 still under LTTE control, the Sri Lankan forces had no choice but to resort to an alternative route running along the coast beside the Kilali Lagoon to continue supplying Elephant Pass. A new north–south defensive line was also established to protect this route from any potential advance by Balraj's forces. However, this improvised road lay just three kilometres at most from LTTE positions, was built on sandy soil, and was barely usable for heavy vehicles. As a result, supply trucks were frequently bogged down, especially when heavily loaded. Unsurprisingly, the insurgents regularly targeted the four-kilometre-long and fragile logistical artery with interdiction artillery and mortar fire. Thus, the 53 Division was forced not only to hold its defensive line under constant pressure but also to launch repeated counterattacks—all of which were repelled, despite the support of armour and artillery. Yet, the supply situation for Balraj's detachment was also precarious, as illustrated by this account of Women's Wing political cadre Thamizhini's journey to Ittavil:

> As the Tigers' stations were set up in a condensed space, the army swept the area endlessly with shells. A heavy artillery team was travelling in a boat ahead of us. Tragically, the boat was struck right before our eye, and the boat and the fighters in it were submerged in flames as I watched in shock. When we reached Vithusha's station, having somehow survived, we only found temporary bunkers with sticks over them, and sandbags piled on top. At the same moment I heard her voice on the high frequency walkie talkie, the whole place shook, and the sandbags and sticks flew into the air.[…] The battles that had taken place on that saltwater lagoon had claimed many lives.[11]

A SLA machingunner in position in the Elephant Pass area, holding his Type 56 LMG. (Albert Grandolini Collection)

The Elephant Pass complex was defended by extensive field fortifications, as shown by this well-protected Type 56 85mm divisional gun, the Chinse variant of the Soviet D-44. (Albert Grandolini Collection)

Balraj giving his instructions to his commander before the launch of their amphibious operation, with the ultimate goal of cutting the A9. (LTTE)

A female fighter posing in front of Paranthan, in the aftermath of the particularly vicious battle that allowed the insurgents to seize the town in December 1999. (LTTE)

Female crew of the Kutti Sri Padai Ani towing their 120mm mortars through a saltwater lagoon. A few of these were assigned to Balraj's command. (LTTE)

One of the 4 SLAC T-55's destroyed in battle whilst supported the 53 Division counterattacks along the A9 road. (LTTE)

A view of a typical SLA First Defence Line, part of the Elephant Pass complex. (LTTE)

Fighters inspecting a captured section of a SLA defensive line in the aftermath of the Elephant Pass battle. (LTTE)

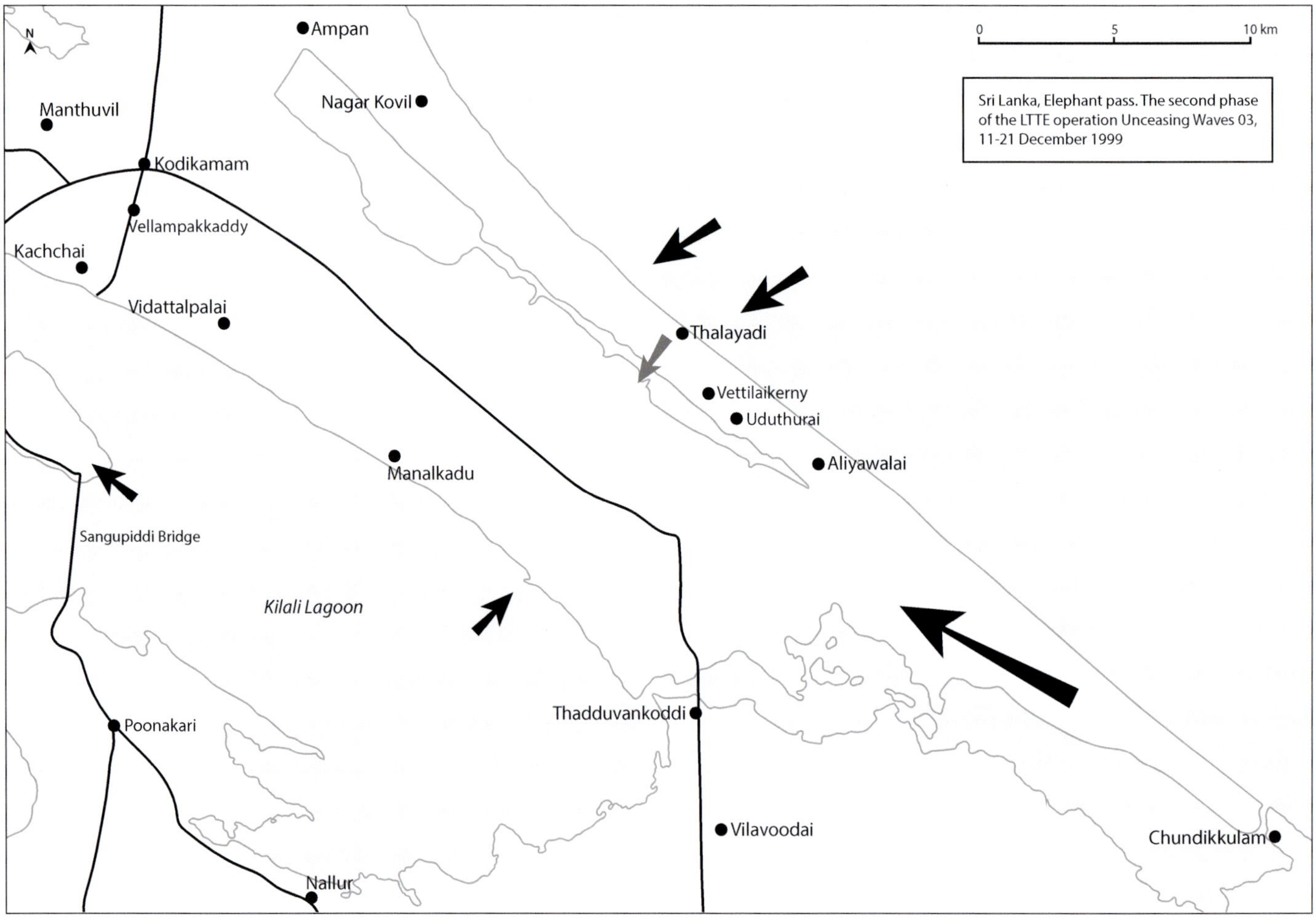

The initial LTTE attacks against the Elephant Pass complex in early December 1995. (Map drawn by George Anderson)

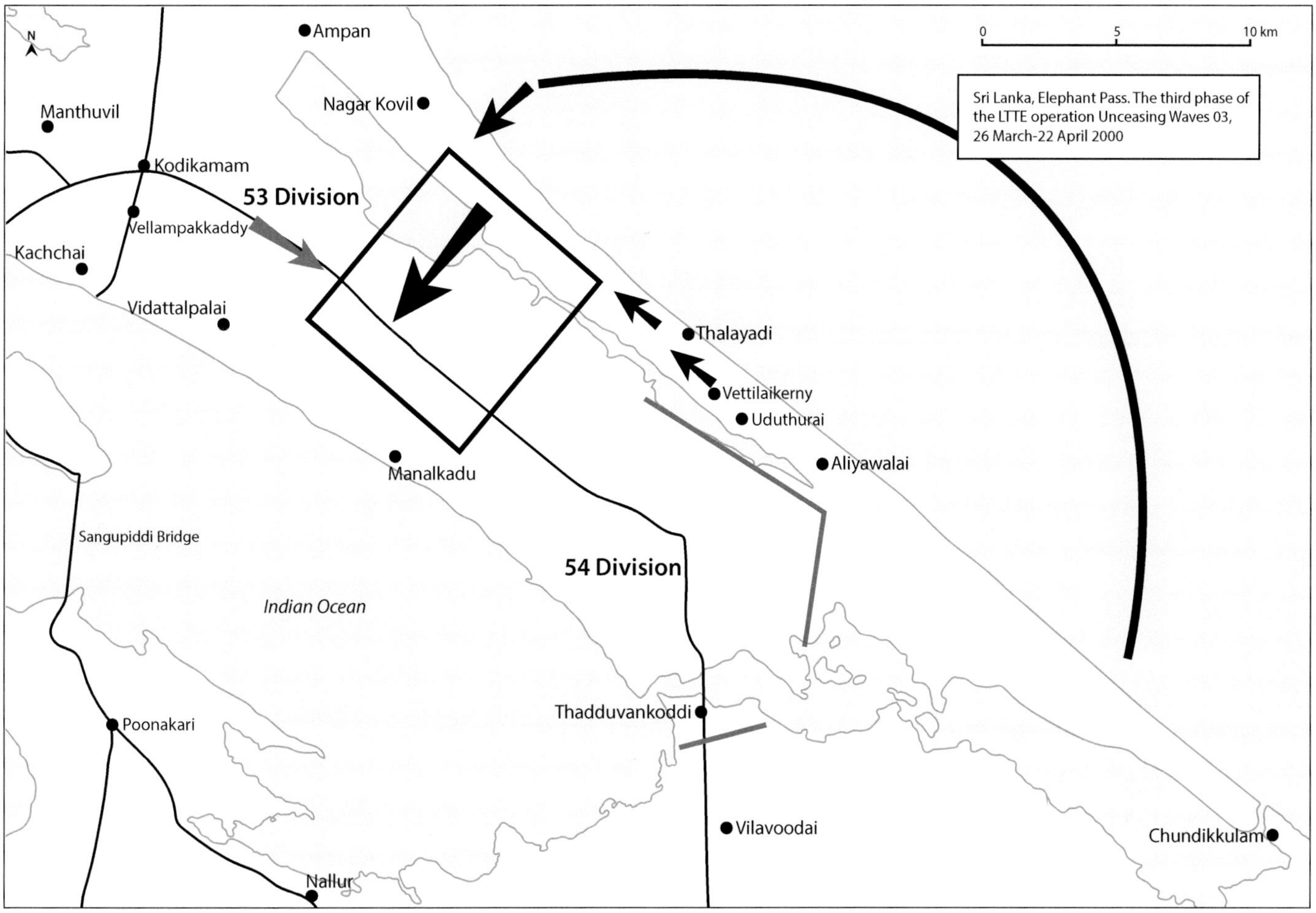

The decisive LTTE onslaught during the last days of March and the first ones of April 2000. (Map drawn by George Anderson)

Killing blow

On 18 April, at around 13:00, Balraj's command launched a new all-out assault, forcing the SLA to withdraw its forward defence line closer to the Kilali Lagoon. As a result, in some areas, LTTE fighters occupied positions within visual range of the sand road. Several other companies also advanced northward, breaking through enemy lines and pushing several kilometres ahead. Meanwhile, additional detachments moved from their long-held beachhead at Thanankilappu—where they had remained since mid-December—and advanced through lagoons and waterways toward the same area from the northwest. However, rather than exploiting the momentum of these early successes, Balraj's detachment dug in, establishing a series of entrenchments and roadblocks, held by a forward screen of fighters. The bulk of the force then turned south and launched an attack towards Pallai, which was still held by the 54 Division. At the same time, Karuna Amman, commanding a strong force including several companies from the Jeyanthan Padai Ani, launched an assault on Iyakachchi from the southeast. By 20 April 2000, the insurgents had succeeded in isolating Iyakachchi from Elephant Pass. That evening, they launched an all-out assault on the camp following hours of artillery and mortar preparation. Iyakachchi—and its vital drinkable water wells—fell the next day. In a desperate attempt to retake the position, two newly arrived battalions—the 1st Sri Lanka Sinha Regiment (1st SLSR) and the 9th Gajaba Regiment (9th GR)—were ordered to counterattack. Though both battalions succeeded in breaching the LTTE's first defensive line at two separate points and continued to push towards the second line, they left only small detachments to secure the breaches. They failed to penetrate the second line, and the LTTE launched a counterattack from the rear, retaking the breaches and encircling both units. Trapped in the open, the two battalions came under sustained crossfire for several hours and suffered heavy casualties. At nightfall, they attempted a desperate breakout towards their original positions west of Iyakachchi, succeeding only due to the support of intense SLA artillery fire. Even so, by morning, the 9th GR had lost more than 70 killed in action and over 600 wounded, leaving barely a hundred men fit for duty. Worse still, the approximately 10,000 soldiers of the 54 Division were now left without any access to drinkable water.

By 20 April 2000, the Sri Lankan command had already concluded that the writing was on the wall and issued orders for a full withdrawal from the Elephant Pass complex before the Tigers could sever its final link to the north. In an effort to avert total disaster, Major General Janaka Perera and Major General Sarath Fonseka were urgently dispatched to Jaffna, assuming the roles of Overall Operations Commander (North) and Security Forces Commander Jaffna, respectively. At this stage, morale had collapsed—not only among many frontline combat units, but also within the senior officer corps. Several officers were reportedly suffering from nervous breakdowns, abandoning their commands and fleeing to Colombo. Under the renewed leadership of Perera and Fonseka, the first elements of the 54 Division began withdrawing along the sandy coastal road at 17:00 on 20 April, with other units following through the night, most advancing on foot across scorched and exposed terrain. For the Sri Lankan soldiers, the retreat turned into an inferno. Large sections of the road were under direct observation by LTTE forward artillery observers (FAOs), snipers, and, in some areas, machine guns—as recalled by Major Lalith Daulagala, who took part in the withdrawal:

> It was the worst experience of my life. I had to walk past the bodies of my men. Mortars were exploding all round, there was nothing to do but to look down and keep walking. If you were lucky you escaped death.[12]

Furthermore, many soldiers suffered from acute dehydration as they marched under the intense heat. For some, the exhaustion was so overwhelming that they failed to take cover even when targeted by enemy machine guns, continuing to advance despite being cut down. The artillery units also suffered; trucks transporting Type 66 howitzers and ammunition were abandoned along the roadside. Hundreds of soldiers died during the withdrawal. On 22 April, once the retreat was completed, the Deputy Defence Minister acknowledged that 758 personnel had been killed, 2,368 wounded, and a further 349 reported missing since the beginning of the battle for Elephant Pass. The Tigers, despite sustaining heavy casualties of their own, captured immense quantities of weapons and ammunition—most notably, three Type 66 152mm and two Type 83 122mm howitzers, along with 12 120mm mortars.[13]

CONCLUSION: BLOODY ENDGAME

On 23 April 2000, the insurgents raised the LTTE flag over Elephant Pass, thus concluding what was the heaviest defeat ever suffered by the Sri Lankan military. Reinforced with a fresh influx of heavy weapons and facing a shattered enemy, the insurgents appeared poised to capture Jaffna within a matter of weeks.

On 30 April, the Tigers seized the isolated town of Palai, located between Ittavil and Iyakachchi, thereby completing their capture not only of Elephant Pass but of the entire southern tip of the Jaffna Peninsula. They encountered little resistance, as the beleaguered SLA had deemed Palai indefensible and instead focused on establishing a new defensive line stretching from Nagarkovil on the Eastern coast to Muhamalai on the A9, and then to Kilali on the western coast, to block further access to the rest of the peninsula. The Army was also in a rush to reorganise itself. Several mauled battalions had to be amalgamated, while the entire 54 Division was disbanded, its subunits reassigned to other divisions. Nevertheless, the SLA still retained significant manpower on the peninsula, with four divisions controlling a total of at least 18 brigades—amounting to over 30,000 troops—well-supported by armour and artillery. For the Army, the proverbial Achilles' heel lay not in manpower or firepower, but in morale, which had been severely shaken by the succession of setbacks and heavy casualties sustained in recent months. The situation was deemed so grave that, on 5 May 2000, Major General Sarath Fonseka issued his key subordinates with a detailed contingency plan for a staged withdrawal from the peninsula, to be activated if necessary.

Table 11 Known SLA units in Jaffna, May 2000

51 Division	511, 512, 513, 514 and 516 Brigades
52 Division	521, 522 and 523 Brigades
53 Division	531 (Airmobile), 532, 533, 534, Special Forces and Commando Brigades
55 Division	551, 552, 553 and 554 Brigades
Armoured Brigade	4 & 5 SLAC

Last Hurrah

Instead of launching a direct assault on the newly established Muhamalai defence line, the LTTE leadership opted for a large-scale outflanking manoeuvre aimed at turning the line and encircling the forces defending it, thereby forcing yet another catastrophic withdrawal. To this end, the Tigers rushed reinforcements—including multiple companies from the Charles Anthony and Malathi Padai Ani—by boat across the Kilali Lagoon and via the half-completed Sanguppidi causeway, to reinforce the small foothold they had held near Thanankilappu since 12 December 1999, which had remained dormant in the months since. Once sufficient forces had been concentrated, the LTTE launched a full-scale assault, well-supported by artillery emplaced in Pooneryn. Simultaneously, a series of diversionary attacks were carried out against the Muhamalai defence line. At last, on 10 May 2000, multiple LTTE detachments attacked the defensive positions guarding access to the Chavakachcheri district. Thanankilappu, Ariyalai, Kovilakandy, and Navatkuli—all held by the 52 Division—came under vicious assault, preceded by heavy artillery and mortar bombardments. This triggered a two-day-long battle, but by the evening of 11 May, the insurgents had broken through. In the northwest, they had captured Ariyalai, and forward elements had advanced as far as the Columbuthurai jetty, in the suburbs of Jaffna city. Further west, LTTE forces overwhelmed the defences at Thanankilappu and Kovilakandy. The troops of the 52 Division withdrew in disarray and struggled to re-establish a defensive line anchored around Chavakachcheri—the second-largest city in the peninsula—to halt further insurgent penetration into the district, and around Navatkuli, in an effort to block another possible axis of advance toward Jaffna town.

The Tigers pressed on across all fronts, denying the Army sufficient time to establish well-organised defensive positions. Fighting continued on the outskirts of Jaffna, while Navatkuli—and its adjacent bridge connecting it to Jaffna town—fell following a large-scale assault during the night of 15 to 16 May. The troops defending the area were forced to retreat eastward along the A9, with the insurgents following in close pursuit. On the evening of 16 May, the LTTE launched another assault, heavily supported by mortar and artillery fire, on the strategically vital Kaithady junction, which housed a major Army base. After twelve hours of fierce combat, the junction fell, leaving the northern flank of Chavakachcheri town dangerously exposed. On the morning of 20 May, the insurgents launched a massive multipronged assault on Chavakachcheri and succeeded in overwhelming its defences. By late afternoon, the town—utterly devastated by artillery fire from both sides—was in LTTE hands. Meanwhile, other LTTE detachments had advanced northward toward Point Pedro, infiltrating through fields and villages, and seized the Sarasalai junction. At this stage, according to Major General Sarath Fonseka—who summarised the situation in Jaffna between 19 April and 20 May 2000—the situation had become extremely worrisome:

> The terrorists however continued their onslaught, broke through the temporary defence line at Palai and forced the troops to withdraw to the Muhamalai area. There too the enemy launched several severe attacks against our troops … the enemy launched disastrous assaults against our troops in Ariyalai and Thanankilappu areas. Subsequentel they occupied not only the

> aforementioned two areas, but also Navatkuli, Kaithadi and Kolumbuuthurei areas. Security forces retaliated to the enemy attacks from the temporary defence line they established at Chavakachcheri. At this juncture, face to face fighting continued between the enemy and the security forces. The distance between the enemey and the security forces was less than 75 metres… The continuous onslaught of the terrorists on the defence line at Chavakachcheri which went on for many hours left our troops with no alternative but to withdraw, abandoning the Chavakachcheri defence line and the town. In this situation, suspicion arose among many personnel as to whether the strength of our troops would suffice to defend strategic areas such as Varani, Kodikamam and Sarasalai and troops were called to defend these strategic points. Further, it was a rather uphill task to defend the Sarasalai area through which there were a number of roads leading to ...the Varani and Kodikamam areas which were always vulnerable to enemy attack…[1]

Firepower to the rescue

However, by 20 May, the 52 Division had halted its withdrawal at Sarasalai, established new defensive positions, and soon received reinforcements from other units, while its commanding officer was replaced. On the other hand, the LTTE units engaged in the campaign had suffered heavy casualties and were beginning to experience significant logistical difficulties. The Sri Lanka Air Force (SLAF) combat squadrons were flying dozens of sorties daily, several of which targeted the Sanguppidi causeway—the Tigers' only land link to their supply base in the Vanni. After several days of concentrated airstrikes, the causeway had sustained such damage that it became impassable for vehicles, leaving only small boats to supply the thousands of fighters deployed around Chavakachcheri. Meanwhile, on 15 May, the first two KRL-122 multiple launch rocket systems (MLRS), ordered from Pakistan, arrived in Kankesanthurai. These were pressed into service a few days later—just in time to support the 52 Division when the LTTE launched an all-out afternoon assault on Sarasalai. Following a night and a day of intense combat, the Tigers were forced to withdraw. From that point onwards, the tide began to turn decisively. The two KRL-122s were soon joined by another four, followed by the arrival of the first RM-70 systems, which provided even greater firepower due to their rapid reloading capability. These, along with several batteries of tube artillery positioned in Palali, were used to relentlessly bombard LTTE positions. The SLAF also escalated its interdiction campaign, which intensified dramatically after 8 August 2000, when the recently delivered MiG-27s of No. 5 Squadron flew their first combat missions. On 29 May, the Army felt confident enough to launch a counterattack from its positions at Sarasalai. Although the assault was swiftly repelled by the insurgents—who had now adopted a largely defensive posture—it had become evident that the momentum built from their series of successful offensives had finally dissipated.[2]

Rivikirana & Kinihira

By the end of August, the Jaffna Security Forces Command had completed its preparations to launch a large-scale offensive aimed at clearing the northern side of the Muhamalai defence line of any LTTE presence. The plan consisted of a series of operations to be executed in quick succession, systematically targeting LTTE-held areas around Chavakachcheri, piece by piece, leaving the insurgents no time to regroup or recover. The offensive began on 1 September with a three-day-long artillery bombardment of LTTE positions. On 3 September, the 51 Division—having concentrated seven battalions under the 512 and 516 Brigades in Jaffna town—initiated Operation Rivikirana I by advancing into the Colombuthurai area. Meanwhile, the elite 53 Division, comprising 12 battalions, advanced from Sarasalai but encountered determined resistance. Both divisions continued with Rivikirana II, pushing along the same axis, during which the 51 Division succeeded in expelling the Tigers from Colombuthurai. The SLAF provided substantial support to the offensive, flying a total of 16 reconnaissance missions—using Beechcraft surveillance aircraft and UAVs—as well as 82 strike missions: 16 by Kfirs, 30 by MiG-27s, and 36 by Mi-24s. The momentum continued with the Kinihira operations, numbered I to IX, beginning on 17 September and concluding on 30 December 2000. These involved the 51, 52, 53, and 55 Divisions, all heavily supported by artillery, armour, and airpower, with firepower concentrated on a relatively narrow front. The LTTE offered fierce resistance and launched several large-scale counterattacks, but was unable to halt the SLA's deliberate advance. By December, the insurgents had been expelled from Maduvil, Kaithady, and Navatkuli. In the weeks that followed, the SLA recaptured the entire Chavakachcheri area, including the town itself. In total, the Army succeeded in reclaiming 139 square kilometres of territory, with limited losses—approximately one hundred soldiers killed in action—and, crucially, eliminated the threat of any future enemy operational-level encirclement.

On 16 January 2001, the 55 Division launched a frontal assault against LTTE positions south of the Muhamalai line. Its troops immediately came under intense machine gun, mortar, and artillery fire, while also having to advance through dense minefields. After two days of heavy fighting—and despite an almost unprecedented effort by the SLAF, which bombed at least 50 targets in a single day—the advance stalled. The 55 Division succeeded in capturing only two small villages and a few square kilometres of territory, at the cost of 55 soldiers killed in action and another 255 wounded.[3]

Exhaustion

The Unceasing Waves 03 onslaught, which lasted from November 1999 to May 2000, left both sides utterly exhausted. While the LTTE secured several major victories and captured significant quantities of weapons and ammunition, these gains came at a steep cost in manpower. In 1999, 1,545 fighters—including 493 female combatants—were killed. In 2000, the toll rose to 1,980 fighters, including 743 women. These were nearly unsustainable levels of casualties, particularly when factoring in the unknown—but undoubtedly large—number of permanently disabled fighters. For a movement with an estimated full-time fighting strength of around 15,000 and reliant on a relatively small demographic pool for recruitment, such losses posed a serious long-term challenge. Moreover, at least some segments of the Tamil population living in LTTE-controlled areas had begun to grow weary of the human cost of the war. Political Wing cadre Thamizhini recalled one such incident during the battles for Chavakachcheri:

> The Liberation Tigers were all so dizzy with victory, we were unable to clearly reflect on the question that arose in the heart, as to why a liberation struggle for the people would cause so much destruction for those very people. Over 25 border patrol fighters had lost their lives in the Chavakachcheri clashes. Since they were all from the same village, and all related to each other, their loss created a lot of anger and frustration among the people. There were incidents where the people got into arguments and fights with the fighters as well.[4]

By the end of the Kinihira series of operations, it had become clear to the LTTE leadership that they lacked the capability to break through the heavily fortified Muhamalai defence line and renew their earlier

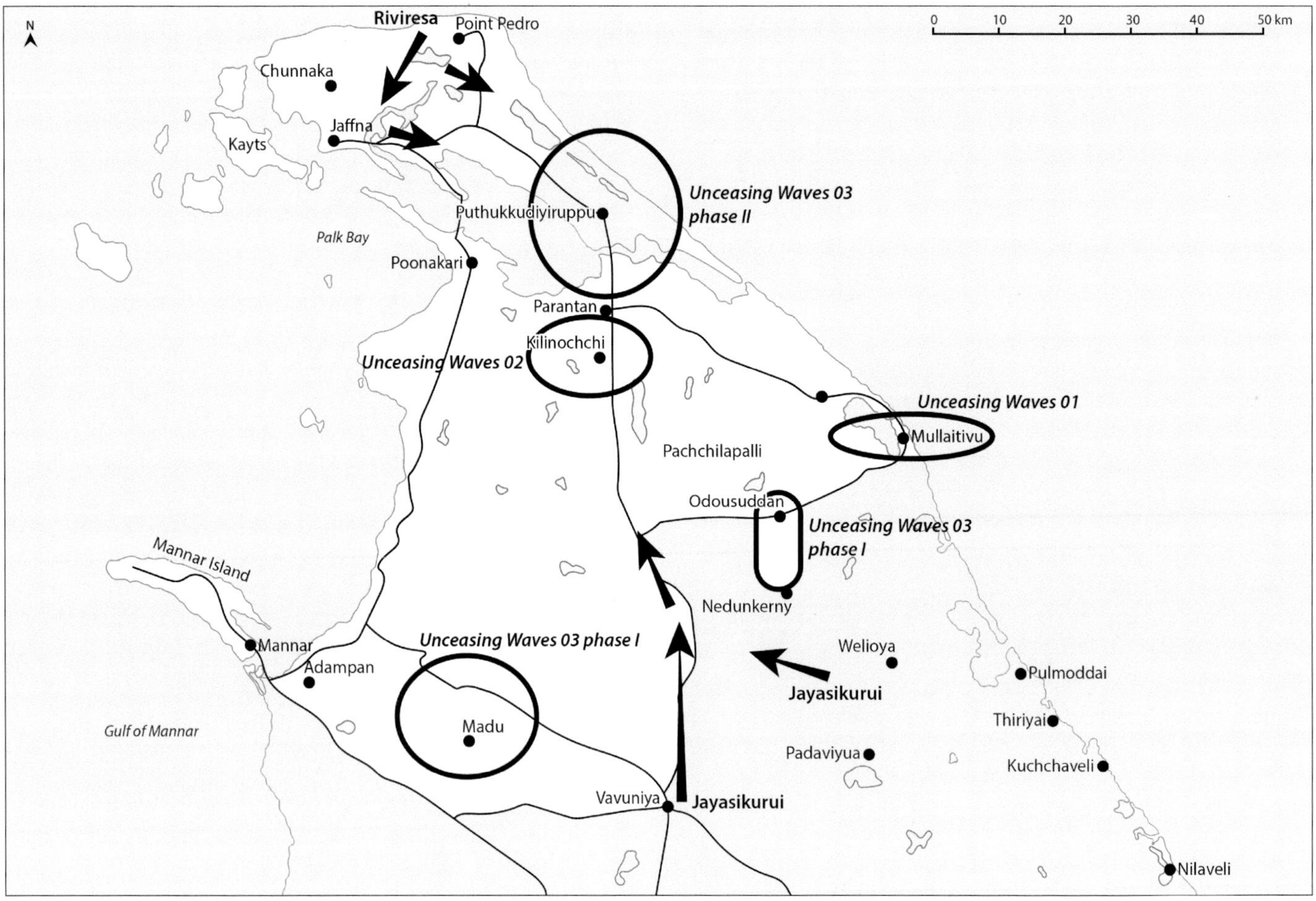

A map presenting major battlefields of the Eelam War III, from 1995 until 2002. (Map by George Anderson)

successes. In early November 2000, the LTTE signalled its willingness to resume negotiations with Colombo through Norwegian mediation, and on 21 December 2000, Velupillai Prabhakaran announced a unilateral, month-long ceasefire. Though the Sri Lankan authorities repeatedly rejected these overtures, the ceasefire was extended several times by the LTTE. However, on 24 April 2001, the insurgents officially called off the unilateral ceasefire—paving the way for a new round of fighting, though this time not one of their own making.

Rods of Iron

In the early hours of 24 April 2001, it was the SLA that launched a full-scale offensive from the Muhamalai defence line, named 'Agni Keela' ('Rods of Iron'). Both the 53 and 55 Divisions—comprising a total of nine infantry brigades and supported by armour, artillery, and the air force—sallied from their positions with the aim of breaking through LTTE lines and capturing Pallai along the A9. However, by that time, the LTTE had had ample opportunity to reinforce its own defensive positions. The advancing troops encountered an even denser concentration of minefields, overlapping machine gun fields of fire, and exceptionally heavy mortar and artillery bombardment. Unsurprisingly, the advance proceeded at a snail's pace and incurred heavy casualties. The operation was called off on 27 April, after four days of intense fighting. A total of 167 soldiers were killed, and another 1,900 wounded. LTTE losses were also significant, due in part to sustained SLAF strikes on their positions and lines of communication. The air force flew 33 Kfir and 45 MiG-27 strike missions, while Mi-24s conducted an additional two. Revenge, however, came on 24 July 2001, when Black Tiger commandos successfully infiltrated Katunayake Air Base and destroyed several combat aircraft on the ground—dealing the SLAF its heaviest blow to date. Still, the failure of Agni Keela made it clear that the battle for the Jaffna Peninsula had reached a stalemate. No new large-scale operations were initiated by either side for the remainder of 2001. Meanwhile, the Sri Lankan Special Forces and Military Intelligence inflicted a series of devastating blows on the LTTE leadership. Operating under a clandestine programme initiated by former SLA Commander Lt. Gen. Lionel Balagalle, several teams of highly trained, Tamil-speaking operatives were inserted deep into LTTE-held territory in the heart of the Vanni. These Long Range Reconnaissance Patrols (LRRPs) carried out a number of successful ambushes, targeting senior LTTE figures. On 15 May 2001, Thamilselvam, head of the LTTE Political Wing, narrowly escaped death when his vehicle was hit by a mine, killing another passenger. On 26 September 2001, Shankar—who had played a key role in the creation of the LTTE's naval and air wings—was killed by a mine while travelling alone near Oddusudan. Several other senior cadres, including Balraj and Karuna Amman, also narrowly survived similar ambushes.[5]

Meanwhile, Sri Lankan political parties had been actively campaigning for the upcoming Parliamentary General Elections, which were held on 5 December 2001. The elections were won by the United National Front, a coalition that had advocated for negotiations with the LTTE as a means of reaching a peaceful resolution to the conflict. As a result, a new government was formed under Prime Minister Ranil Wickremesinghe, significantly accelerating the pace of Norwegian-mediated peace talks. On 19 December 2001, the LTTE announced a new one-month unilateral ceasefire, which was immediately reciprocated by the government—marking a decisive shift in the conflict. This mutual gesture paved the way for a permanent ceasefire agreement, which came into effect on 22 February 2002, thereby officially ending Eelam War III.[6]

Insurgents embarking in their small boats before being shuttled north during one of the several amphibious operations which took place during Eelam War III last battles, such as those which allowed the LTTE to land thousands of fighters in the Tanankilappu area to outflank the Muhumalai defence line. (LTTE)

A MiG-27M in flight, shortly after its induction in SLAF service. These proved extremely potent attack aircraft. (Albert Grandolini collection)

The service entry of the Czech-manufactured RM-70 MRLS, such as this one photographed during a parade in 2012, drastically increased the Arillery Corps' firepower. Such systems proved instrumental in stopping cold the LTTE advance in Sarasalai. (Chamal Pathirana)

BIBLIOGRAPHY

Balasingham, Adele Ann, *The Will to Freedom: An Inside View of Tamil Resistance* (Mitchum: Fairmax Publishing Ltd, 2003).

Balasingham, Anton, *War and Peace: Armed Struggle and Peace Efforts of Liberation Tigers* (Mitcham: Fairmax Publishing, 2004).

Balasuriya, Mahinda, *The Rise and Fall of the LTTE* (Colombo: Asian Network on Conflict Research, 2011).

Blodgett, Brian, *Sri Lanka Military: The Search for a Mission, 1949-2004* (San Diego: Aventine Press, 2004).

Chandraprema, C.A., *Gota's War: the Crushing of Tamil Tiger Terrorism in Sri Lanka* (Colombo: Ranjan Wijeratne Foundation, 2012).

Colombage, JSK, 'Asymmetric warfare at Sea: The Case of Sri Lanka', Thesis, General Sir John Kotelawala Defence University, 2015.

Dissanayake, T.D.S.A., *War or Peace in Sri Lanka* (Colombo: Popular Prakashan, 2005).

Fontanellaz, Adrien, 'Les Tigres des Mers du LTTE', in *LOS* no 37, March-April 2017.

Fontanellaz, Adrien, 'Evolutions organisationnelles et tactiques du LTTE; un exemple d'hybridation', in *DSI* no 126, November-December 2016.

Fontanellaz, Adrien, 'The LTTE's Black Tigers, a military perspective', 2016, unpublished article.

Fontanellaz, Adrien & Cooper, Tom, *Paradise Afire Volume 1: the Sri Lankan War, 1971-1987* (Solihull: Helion & Company, 2018)

Fontanellaz, Adrien, *Paradise Afire Volume 2: The Sri Lankan War, 1987-1990* (Solihull: Helion & Company, 2019)

Fontanellaz, Adrien, *Paradise Afire Volume 3: The Sri Lankan War, 1990-1994* (Solihull: Helion & Company, 2020).

Fontanellaz, Adrien, 'Asymétrie dans la troisième dimension: le cas des Sky Tiger', in *DSI* no 140, March-April 2019.

Gunaratna, Rohan, *International & Regional Security Implications of the Sri Lankan Tamil Insurgency* (Colombo: Alumni Association of the Bandaranaike Centre for International Studies Sri Lanka,1997)

Gunaratne, Kamal, *Road to Nandikadal: True Story of defeating Tamil Tigers* (Colombo: Vijitha Yapa 2016).

Gunaratne, Merril, *Cop in the Crossfire* (Colombo: Merril Gunaratne, 2011).

Hashim, A. S. *When Counterinsurgency Wins: Sri Lanka's Defeat of the Tamil Tigers* (Philadelphia: University of Pennsylvania Press, 2013).

Herath, Tamara, *Women in Terrorism: Case of the LTTE* (London: Sage Publications Ltd, 2012).

Marks, Thomas A., *Maoist People's War in Post-Vietnam Asia* (Bangkok: White Lotus Press, 2007).

Mendis, Nirosha, *The Aerial Tribute: The Role of Air Power in Defeating Terrorism in Sri Lanka* (Colombo, Sri Lanka Air Force, 2014).

Mendis, L.M.H., *Assignment Peace in the Name of the Motherland* (Nugegoda: Self-published, 2009).

Ministry of Defence, *Humanitarian Operation Factual Analysis; July 2006-May 2009* (Ministry of Defence, Democratic Socialist Republic of Sri Lanka, 2011).

Munasinghe, Sarath, *A soldier's version: An account of the ongoing Conflict and the Origin of Terrorism in Sri Lanka* (Colombo: Maj. General Sarath Munasinghe, 2000).

Murari, S., *The Pirabhakaran Saga: The Rise and fall of an Eelam Warrior* (New Delhi, Sage Publications, 2016).

Narayan Swamy, M.R., *Tigers of Lanka: from Boys to Guerrillas* (Delhi: Vijitha Yapa, 1996).

Narayan Swamy, M.R, *Inside an Elusive Mind: Pirabhakaran* (Colombo: Vijitha Yapa, 2003).

Narayan Swamy, M.R, *The Tiger Vanquished: LTTE's Story* (New Delhi: Sage Publications, 2010).

Perera, Sylvester 'The Sri Lankan Civil War: A Personal Reminiscence' in *CTX*, Vol.5, No.4, November 2015.

Pereira, Rienzi, *Wings of Sri Lanka: Fifty Years of Service to the Nation 1951-2001* (Colombo, Sri Lanka Air Force, 2001).

Pratap, Anita, *Island of Blood: Frontline reports from Sri Lanka, Afghanistan and other South Asian Flashpoints* (New Delhi: Viking, 2001).

Povlock, Paul A., *A Guerilla War at Sea: The Sri Lankan Civil War*, (Small War Foundation, 2011).

Ranatunga, Cyril, *Adventurous Journey from Peace to War: Insurgency to Terrorism* (Colombo: Vijitha Yapa, 2009).

Richards, Joanne, 'An Institutional History of the Liberation Tigers of Tamil Eelam (LTTE)', CCDP Working Paper 10 (The Centre on Conflict, Development and Peacebuilding, 2014).

Sakhuja, Vijay, 'The Dynamics of LTTE's Commercial Maritime Infrastructure' (Observer Research Foundation, Occasional Paper, April 2006).

Salter, Mark, *To End a Civil War: Norway's peace engagement in Sri Lanka*, (London: Hurst & Company, 2015).

Senaratne, Jagath. P, *The Sri Lanka Air Force: A Historical Retrospect, 1985-1997* (Colombo, Sri Lanka Air Force, 1998).

Senaratne, Jagath. P, *Sri Lanka Armoured Corps; 60 Years of History, 1995-2015* (Colombo, Sri Lanka Armoured Corps, 2015).

Subramanian, Nirupama, *Sri Lanka: Voices from a War Zone* (New Delhi: Viking, 2005).

Sri Lanka Army, *Sri Lanka Army, 50 Years On 1949-1999* (Colombo, Sri Lanka Army, 1999).

Thamizhini, *In the Shadow of a Sword: The Memoir of a Women Leader in the LTTE* (New Delhi: Sage Publications, 2021).

Wickremesekera, Channa, *The Tamil Separatist War in Sri Lanka* (New Delhi: Routledge India, 2016).

Zaloga, Steven, *Infantry Antiaircraft missiles; Man-Portable Air Defense Systems* (Oxford: Osprey Publishing, 2023).

ENDNOTES

Introduction

1 Quoted from Salter p.27.
2 Quoted from Swamy 2003, p.154.
3 Chandraprema (2012), pp. 219-220; Kamal Gunaratne, p. 340. The four Sea Black Tigers killed in this attack were Rajalakshmi Murugesu, Govindan Sivarajah, Anton Benedict and Vijayathevi Sivasubramaniam. See Sachi Sri Kantha "Homage to the Black Tigers: A Review of Sooriya Puthalvarga 2003 Memorial Souvenir" tamilnation.org, 22 June 2004.
4 Chandraprema (2012), pp. 220-221; Wickremesekera, p.116; Senaratne (1998), p.178; Kamal Gunartane, pp. 341-342; Mendis (2009), pp. 339-340.
5 Wickremesekera, pp. 114-116; Sri Lanka Army (1999), pp. 767, 770-771.
6 Wickremesekera, p. 117; Kamal Gunaratne, pp. 340, 347-349; Mendis (2009), p.343; Munasinghe, pp. 143-144. The SLA claimed to have killed 109 insurgents, the LTTE admitted the loss of 11 KIA.
7 Adele Balasingham (2003), p.310; Munasinghe, pp. 144-145; Senaratne (2015), p. 149; Mendis (2009), pp. 345-348.
8 Munasinghe, pp. 145-146; Thamizhini, p.70; SLA (1999), pp. 523-524; Chandraprema, p. 223; Kamal Gunaratne, p. 352; Mendis (2009), pp. 350-352.
9 Quoted from Thamizhimi, p.70.
10 SLA (1999), pp. 521-523, Wickremesekera, pp. 117-118; Salter, p. 27.

Chapter 1

1 Named after the alias of Sahayaseeli Pedhuruppillai, the first LTTE female fighter killed in action in October 1987, against the IPKF.
2 Named after the alias of Maria Vasanthi Michael, the first commander of the LTTE women military wing, who died from illness in 1990.
3 Named after Anparasi, a female fighter killed in 1995.
4 Named after Kutti Sri, the engineer who developed the first LTTE home-made mortars, and was killed in 1993.
5 Named after the alias of Sathasivam Krishnakumar, killed in 1993.
6 The unit also might have utilised other artillery pieces during Eelam War III, foremost the Type 59-I or M-46 130mm long-range canon, bought by the LTTE and smuggled into the country. By its own admission, the Kittu Padai Ani had five 122mm calibre guns, with at least three captured, in May 1998. See Tamilnet, «A long year on the road,» 13 May 1998, consulted 20 November 2022.
7 Interview by the author under condition of anonymity with two NXO removal experts of a NGO active in Sri Lanka, May 2017.
8 Adel Balasingham (2003), pp. 342-349; Thamizhimi, pp. 5, 9-12, 70, 89, 92; Senaratne (2015), pp. 167-168; Richards, pp. 21-23, Mendis (2009), pp. 501-502; Chandraprema (2012), p. 245. Interview with LTTE veteran 'Johnny' under condition of anonymity, May 2018; Interview with Kagusthan Ariaratnam, April-June 2019. See vol. 3 of this mini-series for detailed overviews of the LTTE training and Intelligence apparatus.
9 Senaratne (2015), pp. 167-168; Gunaratne, pp. 407-410, 425, 437.
10 Quoted from Thamizhimi, p. 9.
11 Quoted in Gunaratne, pp. 407-408.
12 The Type 59-I was the Chinese variant of the Soviet M-46, and the Type 66 of the D-20. The Type 83 was a pure Chinese design with a 15 kilometres range which was produced in small quantities only. These began to be delivered in 1995 whilst the Type 66 followed in 1998.
13 Regiment of Sri Lanka Artillery, https://alt.army.lk/gunner/, consulted 4 November 2022, Stockholm Peace Research Institute, Sri Lanka weapon imports extraction 4 November 2022, Orr's Hill Army Museum's panels, May 2017, author's interview with former Sri Lanka Artillery NCO, May 2017.
14 Quoted from Suren Ratwatte, T-55 in the Tropics, parts 1 to 4, medium.com, consulted 13 November 2022.
15 Quoted from Gunaratne, p. 412
16 Sri Lanka Armoured Corps, https://alt.army.lk/slac/, consulted 10 November 2022; Senaratne (2015), pp. 14-15, 20, 29, 32, 55, 62-68, 80; Stockholm Peace Research Institute, Sri Lanka weapon imports extraction 4 November 2022. The 7 (V) SLAC was the 7th SLNG reassigned to the Armoured Corps, and thus not a new unit.
17 Quoted from SLA 1999, p. 524.
18 The 9th and 11th VIR and the 14th GR.
19 Subchapter drawn from SLA (1999) pp. 526-528, 541-545, 561, 904-907; Gunaratne, pp. 402-404, 412; Munasinghe, p.200; Blodgett, pp. 117,118, 138; Subramanian p.68, 92-93; Wickremesekera, p. 141.

Chapter 2

1 There was, and still are, persistent rumours of the LTTE receiving a small batch of Stinger missiles delivered by the Pakistani infamous Inter-Service Intelligence (ISI) in late 1994 or early 1995 and that these were used to shot down the two HS.748 in April 1995, but no firm evidence ever came to light about such a delivery. Interview with Kagusthan Ariaratnam, May 2019.
2 Fontanellaz, 'Asymétrie dans la troisième dimention: le cas des Sky Tiger', in *DSI* no 140, March-April 2019; Interview with LTTE veteran 'Johnny' under condition of anonymity, May 2018
3 Zaloga, 2023, pp. 22-24.
4 Quoted from Shamindra Ferdinando, 'US-powered Israeli jets enhance SLAF capability', in *War on Terror Revisited*, 30 May 2013.
5 Chandraprema, pp. 221-222, Gunaratne, pp. 342, 344-345; Pereira (2000) pp. 114-115, 177-178, 251; Mendis (2014), pp. 30, 74-75, 124, 158.
6 Quoted from Mendis (2014), p. 125.
7 Pereira 2000, pp. 117, 120, 126-127, 133; Senaratne (1998), pp. 191, 226; Mendis (2014), pp. 124-127, 136.
8 Quoted from Pereira (2000), p. 115.
9 Quoted from Mendis (2014), p. 92.
10 Quoted from Shamindra Ferdinando, 'US powered Israeli jets enhance SLAF capability', in *War on Terror Revisited*, 30 May 2013.
11 Pereira (2000), pp. 116, 118, 120, 127; Senaratne (1998), pp. 191, 204, 226; Mendis (2014), pp. 33, 35, 43, 92-94,98, 102, 106, 138.
12 Quoted from Pereira (2000), p. 108.
13 Pereira (2000), p.108, 113-114, 116, 120, 125, 126-127; Senaratne (1998), pp. 153, 176-177, 191, 235, 240; Mendis (2014), pp. 158, 162.
14 Pereira (2000), pp. 115, 119 120, 126; Senaratne (1998), pp. 190, 224-225.
15 Interview with an SLAF mechanic, May 2017.
16 Quoted from Mendis (2014), p. 106.
17 Pereira 2000, pp. 133, Mendis pp. 34, 35, 106-108, 110, 185, 186.
18 Subchapter drawn from Iqbal Athas, 'Tiger triple jump in the Eastern theatre', *The Sunday Times*, 9 March 1997, *Tamil Guardian*, '20 years since the LTTE assault on Katunayake air force base', *Eelam View*, 'Katunayake Airbase Attack 2001', all consulted on 7 March 2023. Sri Lankan MoD (2011), pp.154-155.

Chapter 3

1 Senaratne (2015) pp.148-150; Sri Lanka Army (1999) pp. 522-531; Gunaratne (2016), pp. 352-355; Chandraprema (2012), p. 224; Munasinghe, p.147.
2 Adele Balasingham (2002), pp. 309, 312; Sri Lanka Army (1999), pp. 527-531; Wickremesekera (2016), p.119.
3 Quoted from Narayan Swamy (1996), p.344.
4 Mendis (2009), pp. 357-358; Adele Balasingham (2002), p. 312; Munasinghe, p. 146; Chandraprema (2012), p. 225; Sri Lanka Army (1999), pp. 526-527.
5 Senaratne (2015), pp. 150-152; Gunaratne (2016), pp. 355-359; Sri Lanka Army (1999), pp. 527-531; Chandraprema (2012), pp.225-226; Munasinghe, p. 148; Hashim, p. 103; Wickremesekera (2016), p. 119; Adele Balasingham, pp. 313-314.
6 Mendis (2009), p. 370; Senaratne (1998), pp. 185-189; Mendis (2014), pp. 124-126.
7 Subramanian, p. 30; Senaratne (2015), pp. 150-152; Gunaratne (2016), pp. 360,362; Sri Lanka Army (1999), pp. 527-531; Chandraprema (2012), pp. 225-226. Losses for the first phase are from Munasinghe, p. 148

8 Quoted in Subramanian, p. 18.
9 Quoted in Subramanian, p. 27.
10 Subramanian, pp. 17-18, 24, 27, 29-33, 35; Wickremesekera (2016), p. 120; Munasinghe, p. 148; Swamy (1996), pp. 344-345. Losses are quoted according to the LTTE's own admission, via eelamweb.com, maveerar, statistics, consulted 24 October 2016.
11 Munasinghe, pp. 149-150; Chandraprema (2012), p. 228; Gunaratne (2016), p. 362; Mendis (2009), pp. 385, 389-390, 392; Senaratne (2015), pp. 152-155; Ministry of Defence (2011), pp. 101, 118; Wickremesekera (2016), p. 122.
12 Quoted from Sri Lanka Army (1999), p. 531.
13 Quoted from Col. Sylvester Perera "The Sri Lankan Civil War: A Personnal Reminescence" in *CTX*, Vol.5, No.4, November 2015, p. 28.
14 Ministry of Defence (2011), pp. 101, 114, 118; Wickremesekera (2016), p. 122; Swamy (2003), p. 257.

Chapter 4

1 Wickremesekera (2016), p. 132; Adele Balasingham, p. 323; Thamizhini, pp. 5,17; Chandraprema (2012), p. 229.
2 Munasinghe, pp. 154-155; Gunaratne (2016), pp. 373-380; Chandraprema (2012), p. 229.
3 ; Senaratne (1998), p. 212; Chandraprema (2012), pp. 230, 232; Munasinghe, p. 156; Gunaratne (2016), pp. 381-382; Mendis (2009), pp. 396-397.
4 Quoted from Senaratne (1998), pp. 215-216.
5 Quoted from Senaratne (1998), pp. 216-217
6 Senaratne (1998), pp. 213-218; Chandraprema (2012), p. 229; Munasinghe, p. 157; Gunaratna (2016), pp. 383-384.
7 Mendis (2009), pp. 369-397; Chandraprema (2012), p. 231
8 Chandraprema (2012), p. 231; Mendis (2009), pp. 404, 407, 410; Gunaratne (2016), p.386; Senaratne (1998), pp. 218-220; 'LTTE's Mulllaitivu Arms Bonanza' in *Tamil Times*, 15 September 1996, maveerar statistics, in eelamweb.com, consulted 24 October 2016.
9 Quoted from Thamizhini, p. 9
10 Wickremesekera (2016), p. 133; Adele Balasingham (2003), p. 324; Thamizhini, p.9; Munasinghe, p. 159; Senaratne (2015), pp. 158-161; Mendis (2009), p. 412-421; Sri Lanka Army (1999), pp. 541-542; "Kilinochchi falls under army control" in *Tamil Times*, 15 October 1996; maveerar statistics, in eelamweb.com, consulted 24 October 2016.

Chapter 5

1 Colombage, p. 73; Human Right Watch, "Funding the final war; LTTE's LTTE Intimidation and Extortion in the Tamil Diaspora", 14 March 2006
2 Sakhuja; Colombage, pp. 50, 65, 69-73, 144, 171-175; Chandraprema (2012), p.222. For further details about the K.P Department inception, see vol. 1 & 3 of this miniseries.
3 Mendis (2009), pp. 379-382, pp. 438-441; Senaratne (1998), pp. 223. Panels, Trincomalee Navy Museum, May 2017.
4 Sakhuja; Colombage, pp. 50, 65, 69-73, 144, 171-175; Chandraprema (2012), pp.222,364.
5 Quoted from Colombage (2015), p. 168.
6 Quoted from Colombage (2015), p. 168
7 Chandraprema (2012), pp. 281, 362-363; Colombage, pp. 66, 157, 167-168, 175-176, 178-179, 195; Povlock, pp. 20-22, Kaghustan Ariaratnam, interviews, May 2019.
8 Quoted from Colombage (2015), p. 169
9 Colombage (2015), pp. 74-75, 164, 169, 179, 196; Chandraprema (2012), pp. 304-305, 362; Povlock, pp. 21-23, 30
10 Kagusthan Ariaratnam, interviews, 10 and 25 May 2019, Mendis 2009, pp. 347-348, 383-384, Chandraprema, p. 222, 372-373, Ministry of Defence (2011), 150
11 Quoted from Colombage (2015), p. 141.
12 Various promotional documents from Colombo Shipyard Ltd, SIPRI, extracted 20 December 2023.
13 Seaforces.org, consulted 28 December 2023; Shamindra Ferdinando "Could GoSL have afforded to lose Israeli help?", in War on Terror Revisited, 20 August 2018, consulted 28 December 2023; Rear Admiral WDEM Sudarshana, "The unnoticed service of Fast Gun Boat Squadron" in *Sri Lanka Navy Journal*, 2018; Adrien Fontanellaz, volumes 1 and 3 of this miniseries.
14 Mendis (2009), p. 355; Blodgett, p. 128; Goldrick, p. 191.
15 Chandraprema, pp. 222, 361, Goldrick, p. 192.
16 Mendis (2009), pp. 421-426; Ministry of Defence (2011), p.151, Iqbal Athas "LTTE attack on Trinco docks foiled" in *Sunday Times*, 27 October 1996, consulted 29 December 2023.
17 Mendis (2009), pp. 433-437; Iqbal Athas, "Navy's moment of glory in Mullaitivu seas" in *Sunday Times*, 30 March 1997, consulted 29 December 2023.
18 Tamilnet, "Eleven Tigers killed in naval battle", 23 February 1998, consulted 30 December 2023; Tamilnet, "Tigers sink Sri Lankan gunboat", 19 October 1997, consulted 30 December 2023 Shamindra Ferdinando, "SLA, SLN wither under Tiger onslaught" in War on Terror Revisited, 11 October 2012, consulted 30 December 2023; Chandraprema (2012), pp. 361, 372-373; Ministry of Defence (2011), p. 151.
19 Tamilnet "Fifteen Tigers killed in sea battle – SLN", 8 February 1999; "Five more casualties from sea battle", 13 February 1999; "Three LTTE boats destroyed – SLN", 18 February 1999; "Sea Tigers attack SLN patrol – VoT", 19 February 1999, all consulted 30 December 2023; Blodgett, p. 129.
20 Tamilnet; "Two Dvoras sunk -LTTE", 7 April 2000; "Dvora survivor swims ashore, helicopter hit", 8 April 2000; "Tigers list weapons taken from Dvoras", 9 April 2000; "SLN, Sea Tigers clash off Katpitty", 12 April 2023, consuted 30 December 2023; Ministry of Defence (2011), p. 151.
21 Tamilnet, "Two super-dvora gun boats sunk", 5 June 2000, consulted 30 December 2023; Ministry of Defence (2011), pp. 115, 151.
22 Tamilnet, "Tigers destroy gunboat in Trincomalee SLN Yard", 23 October 2000; "Mi24 shot down, fighting on Marble Beach", 23 October 2000; "Massive assault on Trincomalee Harbour -LTTE", 23 October 2000; ABC News, "Suicide Attack on Sri Lankan Naval Base", 23 October 2000; consulted 30 December 2023; Ministry of Defence (2011), p.152.
23 Tamilnet, "One Dvora captured, weapons stripped – VOT", 21 March 2023; "Two Dvoras sunk, two damaged in clash", 16 September 2001; consulted 31 December 2023. Mendis (2009), pp. 552-554; Ministry of Defense (2011), p. 152.

Chapter 6

1 Munasinghe, p. 162; Wickremsekera, pp. 133-134; Ministry of Defence (2011), p. 147; Anaiyiravu-Paranthan Battle, Telibrary.com, consulted 25 January 2024.
2 Wickremesekera, pp. 134-135; Sri Lanka Army (1999), p.542; Munasinghe, p. 166.
3 Wickremesekera, pp. 135; Sri Lanka Army (1999), pp. 542, 546; Munasinghe, p.166; Gunaratne, p.395; Adele Balasingham (2003), p. 330; Mendis (2009), pp. 444, 450, 501-502.
4 Wickremesekera, p. 135; Munasinghe, p. 167; Gunaratne, p. 396-400, 412; Senaratne (2015), pp. 169-176; Operation Jayasikuru and the LTTE's counter-attack, in Telibrary.com, consulted 28 January 2024. Interestingly, the latter is an English language translation of the LTTE official narrative of its efforts to counter Jayasikurui.
5 Wickremesekera, p.136; Munasinghe, pp. 167-168; Gunartane, pp. 412, 418; Senaratne (2015), p.177; Chandraprema, p. 234; "Operation Jayasikuru and the LTTE's counter-attack", in Telibrary.com, consulted 28 January 2024; Tamilnet "SLA suffers heavy casualties", 11 October 1997, consulted 29 January 2024.
6 Chandraprema, p. 234; Sri Lanka Army (1999), p. 542; Wickremesekera, p. 136; Munasinghe, p. 169; Gunaratne, pp. 412, 417; Senaratne (2015), pp. 178-185; "Operation Jayasikuru and the LTTE's counter-attack", in Telibrary.com, consulted 28 January 2024.
7 Wickremesekera, p. 136; Munasinghe, p. 169; Gunaratne, pp.424-425; Chandraprema, pp. 234-235; Ministry of Defence (2011), p. 147.
8 Quoted from "Unceasing Waves – 2 – Great Battle of Kilinochchi" in Telibrary.com, consulted 31 January 2024
9 Quoted from Col. Sylvester Perera, "The Sri Lankan Civil War: A Personal Reminiscence", in CTX, Vol. 5, No. 4, November 2015.
10 Quoted from Thamizhini, p. 22.
11 Wickremesekera, p. 137; Munasinghe, pp. 170-171; Gunartane, pp. 424-426; Chandraprema, p. 234; Ministry of Defence (2011), p. 147; Thamizhini, p.22; Adele Balasingham (2003), p.349; Tamilnet "SLA suffers heavy losses in Kilinochchi – VoT", 29 September 1998,

consulted 31 January 2023. The Voice of Tigers radio announced on 29 September 1998 the death of 240 insurgents during the battle, but Karuna Amman, a defector, acknowledged the death of 420 fighters, with another 700 wounded, whilst Thamizhini recalled (p.22) more than 500 KIA on the insurgent side.

12 Wikcremesekera, p. 138; Gunaratne, p.428; Chandraprema, p. 236; Mendis (2009), pp. 473-479, 484, 488, 501-502

Chapter 7

1 Quoted from Gunaratne, pp. 432-433.
2 Quoted from Thamizhini, pp.12-13
3 Wickremesekera, pp. 140-142; Gunaratne, pp. 400-410, 416, 434; Chandraprema, pp. 235, 236; Thamizini, pp. 11-17; eelamweb.com, maveerar, statistics, consulted 24 October 2016.
4 Ministry of Defence (2011), pp. 101-103, 113, 115, 118. See Volume 3 of this mini-series for further details about the LTTE intelligence apparatus and its operations.
5 Quoted from Gunaratne, pp. 430, 438
6 Wickremesekera, pp. 157-159; Munasinghe, pp. 210-212; Thamizhini, p. 23; Chandraprema, p. 237; Gunaratne, pp. 429-439; Mendis (2009), pp. 509, 513; Tamilnet, “Tigers raise flag at Oddusuddan”, 2 November 1999; “Tigers overrun Nedunkerni”, 3 November 1999; “Mankulam said under LTTE control”, 5 November 1999; “Tigers consolidate, press attack”, 9 November 1999; “Years of gains lost in days”, Sundaytimes.lk, 7 November 1999. All consulted on 4 February 2024
7 Sri Lanka Army (1999), p.541; Wickremesekera, p. 160; Munasinghe, pp. 193, 195, 200; Gunaratne, p. 440; Chandraprema, pp. 238-239.
8 Wickremesekera, p. 160; Munasinghe, pp. 212-215; Gunaratne, pp.440-441; Chandraprema, pp. 238-239; LTTE’s “Oyaatha Alaihal 3” (Unceasing Waves 3”) Warfare Study – Article 1, telibrary, consulted 12 February 2024; International Secretariat of LTTE, “Heavy figthing continues in the Peninsula. LTTE consolidates captured positions.”, 15 December 1999.
9 Chandraprema, pp. 238-240; Gunaratne, p.441; Munasinghe, pp. 215-216; LTTE’s “Oyaatha Alaihal 3” (Unceasing Waves 3”) Warfare Study – Article 1, telibrary, consulted 12 February 2024; International Secretariat of LTTE, “Paranthan Military Base Falls to LTTE: Sri Lankan Army suffers further debacle”, 17 December 1999, and “Two more military bases fall to Tigers: Elephant Pass Southern Defences collapse”, 21 December 1999.
10 Quoted from Gopu; “How did LTTE win the historical Second Battle of Elephant Pass in 2000?” Quora.com, consulted 15 February 2024.
11 Quoted from Thamizhini, p.25
12 Quoted from Chandraprema, p. 245.
13 Chandraprema, pp. 241-245; Gunaratne, pp. 443-445; Wickremesekera, pp. 161-162; International Secretariat of LTTE; “Yakachchi Military Complex collapsig: Sri Lankan Army faces serious debacle”, 20 April 2000 and “LTTE capture massive haul of Arms including long range Artillery Pieces”, 24 April 2000. Wickremesekera mentions, p. 162, as many as 800 SLA soldiers KIA during the withdrawal, whilst Chandraprema, p.244, mentions about 300 KIA and 500 WIA.

Conclusion

1 Quoted from Chandraprema, pp. 246-247.
2 Wickremesekera, pp. 166-167; Chandraprema, pp. 249-250; Gunaratne, p. 445.
3 Chandraprema, p.250; Mendis (2009), pp. 536-547; Wickremesekera, pp. 166-167; Senaratne (2015), pp. 188-189; Gunaratne, p. 445.
4 Quoted from Thamizhini, pp. 26-27.
5 Gunaratne, p. 445; Mendis (2009) pp.548-549; Wickremesekera, pp. 167-171; Chandraprema, p. 251; Salter, pp. 62-69; eelamweb.com, maveerar, satistics, consulted 24 October 2016.
6 Salter, pp. 69-84; Gunaratne, pp.447-448; Chandraprema, p.254; Hashim, pp. 114-115. Several authors, such as Hashim, mention that the 11 September 2001 attacks also pressured the LTTE into enter negotiations, as the latter exposed them to international condamnation because of their own use of terrorists attacks, and particularly so of suicide bombers.

ABOUT THE AUTHOR

Adrien Fontanellaz is a Swiss military history researcher and author. He is a member of the Scientific Committee of the Pully-based Centre d'histoire et de prospective militaires (Military History and Prospectives Centre), and has authored and co-authored 20 books published in England, France and Switzerland related to various contemporary conflicts in Africa, Asia, Europe, and the Middle East. He is also a regular contributor to the *Revue Militaire Suisse* and various French military history magazines, foremost *Défense & Sécurité Internationale.*